THE CHILDREN OF LONDON

The Bedford Way Papers Series

THE CHILDREN OF LONDON

Attendance and welfare at school 1870–1990

A. Susan Williams, Patrick Ivin
and Caroline Morse

Bedford Way Papers

INSTITUTE OF
EDUCATION
UNIVERSITY OF LONDON

First published in 2001 by the Institute of Education, University of London,
20 Bedford Way, London WC1H 0AL
www.ioe.ac.uk

Pursuing Excellence in Education

© Institute of Education, University of London 2001

British Library Cataloguing in Publication Data:
A catalogue record for this publication is available from the British Library

ISBN 0 85473 640 9

Back cover photograph © Myfanwy Brade

Page make-up by Cambridge Photosetting Services, Cambridge
Production services by
Book Production Consultants plc, Cambridge

Printed by Henry Ling Ltd, Dorchester

CONTENTS

ILLUSTRATIONS AND TABLES

Plates

Figures

Tables

THE AUTHORS

A. Susan Williams is a Lecturer in History at the Institute of Education University of London. She has published widely in social and cultural history, with a particular focus on the lives of women and children and on social policy. Her most recent books include *Ladies of Influence: Women of the elite in interwar Britain* (Penguin, 2000) and *Women & Childbirth in Twentieth Century Britain* (Sutton, 1997)). She has edited and co-edited many books, including *Mother Courage: Letters from mothers in poverty at the end of the century* (Penguin, 1997) and *The Politics of the Welfare State* (UCL Press, 1995).

Patrick Ivin is an education consultant specialising in social inclusion and he has been involved in the education welfare services of London throughout his life. His family was visited by a Care Committee worker when he was a boy and at the age of 19 he became a School Care Worker. He was later appointed an Education Welfare Officer with the ILEA. In 1988, he became the Director of ILEA Social Work Services (the Education Social Work and School Health Social Work Services combined). During this period he was President of the National Association of Social Workers in Education (NASWE).

Caroline Morse has an MSc in Social Analysis. She has been a researcher at the Institute of Education University of London for a number of years.

FOREWORD

by Baroness Serota, DBE

I HOPE THAT this unique account of the development of education welfare services in London, published by the University of London Institute of Education, and generously funded by the Economic and Social Research Council, will fill the historical gap in this area of education and social policy. I hope, too, that it will assist our thinking about the present and future needs of children and the important policy issues that affect their educational development and social well-being.

The history starts in 1870, when universal schooling became the legal right of all children. For the first time, attendance officers were employed by the newly-elected London School Board to make sure that children went to school. Special groups of voluntary workers, called Care Committees, were organised in 1907 by the Education Committee of the London County Council (LCC) to provide poor children with school dinners, boots, clothing and medical care, so that they could make the best use of their new right to an education. In 1970, these two strands of education welfare care were combined to form London's Education Welfare Service. Some of the needs of children in the metropolis had changed, but they were still pressing.

The themes of the book are several: the suffering of children who are poor or who have trouble in their family; the interface between school and home; the slow change from middle-class charitable work to professional social work; and the uneasy tension between control and care. These themes recur throughout the 120 years of the unified London education service – from the start of the London School Board in 1870 to the demise of the Inner London Education Authority (ILEA) in 1990.

I myself was centrally involved in the services for London's children in the period under review: first, as a voluntary Care Committee worker in East London; and then as an elected member of the LCC and chairman of the Children's Committee. But my most vivid memories of the problems facing London's children and their families flow from my experience as a student volunteer, when I accompanied the children of a Hackney primary school out of London on 1 September 1939 in the great evacuation of the city and lived with them in their unknown destination until the university term began.

All these years after the setting up of London's education welfare services, the same issues are still being debated. What is the right balance between school attendance and social care? What are the needs of children? How will they be met? *The Children of London* draws many important lessons from the past, all of which need urgent attention if policy for the future is to be developed in a way that truly serves the needs of London's children in the twenty-first century. I hope that this book will help all those with these responsibilities to develop and provide progressive and relevant social services for children in London and elsewhere.

Bee Serota

Baroness Serota, DBE. Born in London and educated at LCC primary and secondary schools and at the London School of Economics (BSc Econ.), of which she is an Honorary Fellow. Member of Hampstead Borough Council, 1945–9; member of LCC Education Committee, 1952–65; elected member of LCC for Brixton (Lambeth), 1954–65; chairman of Children's Committee, 1958–65; elected member of Greater London Council and ILEA for Lambeth, 1964–7. Created Life Peer 'for services to children' in 1967. A Deputy Speaker, House of Lords, from 1985.

ACKNOWLEDGEMENTS

THIS STUDY WAS the idea of Miss Mary Maclean, who worked for the School Care Service between 1955 and 1978, when she retired from her post as Deputy Divisional Education Welfare Officer. Miss Maclean believed that it was important for the history of the services to be written down for future generations and she set about contacting other people who had been involved, notably Mrs Peggy Jay and Baroness Serota. This book would not have been written without the inspiration of these women.

The Economic and Social Research Council generously funded the research for the book.

David Watson made a key contribution to the research in its early stages and established the project on a firm footing. Michele Cohen and Elizabeth Murray helped with the research and Nick Bonell compiled the tables. Tendayi Bloom assisted with the numerical data and produced the list of abbreviations.

Muriel Digney was an important source of information and of documentary material. Information was also provided by David Cox, Margaret Currie, Florence Heller, Yvonne Hill, Peggy Jay, Mary Maclean, Berry Mayall, Elizabeth Murray, Methlyn Reid, Penny Lavan, Beatrice Serota, Brenda Stevenson, John Stewart, Estella West and Florence Heller.

For a study like this, we were dependent on the co-operation and good will of archivists and librarians, especially at the London Metropolitan Archives, the Institute of Education, the British Library and the London Library.

A number of people read and commented on drafts of the book – Richard Aldrich, Charlie Chubb, Dennis Dean, Gervase Hood, Beatrice Serota, and Margaret Wynn. Each reader offered invaluable comments and advice, which helped to push the book forward.

Judy Morrison and Anne-Marie Peacock, the administrative staff of the History and Philosophy Group at the Institute of Education, provided administrative help. Myfanwy Brade and her pupils took great trouble to provide photographs of children at school today.

Deborah Spring and Brigid Hamilton-Jones at the Publications Office of the Institute of Education have taken a very real interest in the publication of this book. Liz Dawn, the copy-editor, showed meticulous attention to the text, as well as unfailing patience.

The authors and publishers are grateful to the following organisations for permission to reproduce illustrations: *The Illustrated London News* Picture Library for plate 5; the British Library for plate 6; the London Metropolitan Archives for plates 2, 4, 9, 11, 13, 14, 15, 17 and 19.

A Susan Williams, Patrick Ivin and Caroline Morse

ABBREVIATIONS

CCHF	Children's Country Holidays Fund
CEW	Certificate in Education Welfare
CMO	Chief Medical Officer
CPAG	Child Poverty Action Group
COS	Charity Organisation Society
CQSW	Certificate of Qualification in Social Work
DDEWO	Deputy Divisional Education Welfare Officer
DES	Department of Education and Science
DfE	Department for Education
DfEE	Department for Education and Employment
DHSS	Department of Health and Social Security
DO	Divisional Officer
EO	Education Officer
ESN	Educationally subnormal
ESWO	Education Social Work Officer
ESWS	Education Social Work Service
EWONA	Education Welfare Officers' National Association
EWO	Education Welfare Officer
EWS	Education Welfare Service
FES	Family Endowment Society
GLA	Greater London Authority
GLC	Greater London Council
HMI	Her/His Majesty's Inspectorate
ILEA	Inner London Education Authority
LA	Local Authority

LCC	London County Council
LEA	Local Education Authority
LMA	London Metropolitan Archives
MP	Member of Parliament
NACEWO	National Association of Chief Education Welfare Officers
NASWE	National Association of Social Workers in Education
NHS	National Health Service
NSPCC	National Society for the Prevention of Cruelty to Children
PEWO	Principal Education Welfare Officer
PRO	Public Record Office
ROSLA	Raising of the school-leaving age
SAO	School Attendance Officer
SCW	School Care Worker
SEWO	Senior Education Welfare Officer
SLB	School Board for London
SMO	School Medical Officer
SSD	Social Services Department
STOPP	Society of Teachers Opposed to Physical Punishment
WVS	Women's Voluntary Service
YPA	Young People's Adviser
YPS	Young People's Advisory Service

Chapter 1

INTRODUCTION

'The growing good of the world is partly dependent
on unhistoric acts.'[1]

THIS BOOK TELLS the story of the education welfare services of London. These services have their roots in the period immediately following W.E. Forster's Elementary Education Act of 1870, which established the principle of schooling for every child, poor as well as rich. 'Our purpose in this Bill,' stated Forster to the House of Commons, 'is to bring elementary education within the reach of every English home; aye, and within the reach of those children who have no homes'.[2]

Before 1870, education for working-class children had been provided by private bodies, chiefly religious but also philanthropic, with some financial aid from the government after 1833. Some schools were good but many others, especially 'Dame' schools, were ill-equipped and were staffed by teachers who were barely literate. Numbers of children did not attend school regularly and there were some who did not go to school at all. 'Our poverty has been an insuperable bar to admission into any school, save the so-called charity schools', wrote one working-class

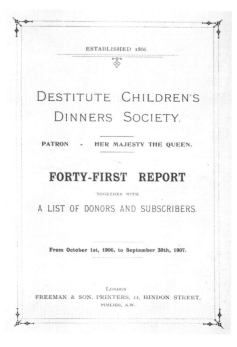

Plate 1 *The cover of a 1907 report by the Destitute Children's Dinners Society, one of many societies set up in London to provide poor and hungry children with school dinners.*

1

man in 1847. Nothing more than 'a mere apology for learning,' he added, had 'been doled out to us – just allowed to learn enough to "get the catechism", some to write their own names, few to learn the simple elements of accounts – then, with such acquirements, early in life, started to the factory or dung-yard, to earn a few pence to assist in producing a family bread loaf.'[3]

London responded swiftly to the Forster Act. It went to the polls in the autumn of 1870 to elect an education authority, the School Board for London (SBL). It was one of only 27 school boards to be set up in England and Wales in the first year of the Forster Act; indeed, only 60 school boards had been established in England and Wales by the end of 1871, although the final number in 1902 reached 2,668. The SBL wasted no time in starting work: between 1871 and 1884, it built 289 new schools to provide places for over 300,000 children.[4] But it was not enough simply to provide a place at school, because many families at this time were desperately poor. Their children were too undernourished and scantily clad to benefit from going to school; without breakfast in their stomachs and boots on their feet, it was difficult for them to concentrate on their lessons. Moreover, there was resistance from many parents to the idea of school: they wanted their children to work and to supplement the family income, or to stay at home to look after younger siblings. 'What a business it was,' observed the preface to *Recollections of a School Attendance Officer* by John Reeves (1913), 'to get the children into the schools.'[5]

To make sure that children went to school, the London School Board employed attendance officers or School Visitors – 'School Board Men'. Meanwhile, numbers of voluntary organisations set up systems to provide poor children with school dinners, clothing and boots, as well as rudimentary medical care. These efforts were supported by the SBL and then formally brought together by the London County Council (LCC) in 1907 to create a School Care Service – a system of Care Committees that was managed by salaried organisers, but used volunteers to care for the welfare needs of London's children at school. Both kinds of service – the enforcement of attendance and welfare provision – relied on visits to a pupil's family and provided a unique bridge between home and school, which was not normally provided in any other way. This dual service was unique to London. Other education authorities in Britain started with a bare attendance service, which gradually took on a limited range of welfare duties.

Despite the common ground between the school welfare and attendance services of London, they worked separately. As groups, they were quite distinct from each other: members of the Care Committees (both volunteers and salaried workers) were almost exclusively women of the affluent classes, while the attendance officers were nearly always working-class men. 'I do not think that any woman of the professional classes would have become an attendance officer ... even if she had not been the victim of sex prejudice,' observed Mary Stocks, an economist and broadcaster, in an account of *The Philanthropist in a Changing World* (1953).[6] Proposals were put forward in 1933 and again between 1948–50 to merge the different strands of care, but they persisted as parallel services. Then, on the recommendations of the pivotal Bedford Report (1967), an independent inquiry commissioned by the Inner London Education Authority (ILEA), the two services were finally brought together in 1970 to form the Education Welfare Service (EWS). This merger produced an attrition in the number of voluntary workers, but great hopes were developed for the future of the EWS as a social work service in which attendance was simply one aspect of a network of concerns about the welfare of children at school. In 1990, the ILEA was dismantled and the responsibility for education in London was devolved to the individual London boroughs. Each borough developed its own education welfare service, which meant that for the first time in history, the system used in London was little different from the rest of England and Wales.

Services to support children at school developed in a different way outside London. In Bradford in the 1890s, a social reformer and socialist called Margaret McMillan described the city as 'a constituency in need of rescue';[7] as a member of the Bradford School Board between 1894 and 1902, she initiated various schemes to provide schoolchildren with breakfasts, dinners, washing facilities and medical care (thereafter she moved to London, where she pioneered nursery school education and was an elected member of the LCC between 1919 and 1922). In other large cities, such as Liverpool, some Care Committees developed;[8] a few also appeared in smaller conurbations like Bedford (where there was one Care Committee to serve the whole population; there appears to have been no committee in Luton, Bedford's poorer neighbour[9]). These Care Committees outside the metropolis were based on the London model, but only at the level of the committee itself: they were not part of any systematic provision for the whole area, which was the unique feature of the London Care Service. 'It may be a matter of some surprise,' said Sir Hubert Llewellyn Smith in 1937, 'that so important and successful a step in social co-operation has not spread from London to the provinces.' The particular achievement of the London situation, he added, was the 'co-ordinating agency' which looked at the child's welfare as a whole.[10] The London service very much regarded itself as a pioneer in this kind of work. Peggy Jay, a volunteer in the 1930s, has recalled that the committees saw themselves as *London School Care Committees*, with a strong sense of loyalty to the LCC.[11]

Although the Care Committee system 'appears to have justified its existence in the London area,' commented M. Penelope Hall, a social scientist, in 1952, 'it has never established itself in the provinces, and over the country generally there is no recognised form of social service reaching out from the school to the family and dealing with family needs and problems as they affect the school child.'[12] The only claimant for this position, she added, was that of the school attendance service. For the most part, the welfare needs of school-children outside the capital were the responsibility of the attendance officer: 'He comes into contact with the homes and parents of children as no other municipal officer does,' commented a *Handbook for School Attendance Officers* (1939), 'and combines with his various duties a considerable amount of welfare work.' The *Handbook* expanded on the nature of this welfare work:

> He is consulted as to what course to pursue respecting treatment for various ailments to which childhood is heir; institutions to which children should be taken for treatment; what homes there are for convalescent treatment; the question of employment for children; on holiday camps; evening school courses; and the adoption of children.[13]

After the 1944 Education Act, attendance officers outside London were officially designated as Education Welfare Officers (EWOs).

Growing up in London

An important influence on the evolution of education welfare work in London was the fact that for 120 years, the metropolis was served by a unified education service (see Figure 1.1). In 1870, the London School Board was set up under the Elementary Education Act. Numbers of distinguished members were elected to the SBL, including Emily Davies, Thomas Huxley and Dr Elizabeth Garrett, the first woman doctor; the Chairman was Lord Lawrence, a former Viceroy of India and an able administrator. By 1890, eight of the 55 members were women.[14] It employed outstanding architects to build new schools and took an innovative approach to the curriculum. It developed higher grade elementary education for older children and inaugurated special schools for the handicapped, as well as truant schools, residential schools and industrial schools.

In 1903, the Education (London) Act abolished the SBL and its responsibilities were transferred in 1904 to the London County Council. The LCC had been established in 1889 and was led at this time by Progressives who were inspired by a vision of making the metropolis into a better and more just society – 'a social mission in the secular metropolis', writes Susan D.

4

Pennybacker in *A Vision for London 1889–1914: labour, everyday life and the LCC experiment* (1995).[15] The immediate educational priorities of the LCC were to integrate the Board Schools and the 'non-provided' schools, which were mostly owned by religious organisations, into a single and united service. It also developed plans for secondary education and after the Second World War promoted comprehensive secondary schools. The political history of the LCC is intricate, comments Roy Porter in his *London: A Social History*, involving complicated wrangles with central government and with the boroughs, as well as struggles between political cliques within the LCC itself. In simple terms, though, its history falls into three periods of dominance: 'by Progressives – that is, by Liberals and others on the left – (1889–1907); by Municipal Reformers – the name the Conservatives used – (1907–34); and by Labour (1934–65).' The Council's apogee, adds Porter, 'lay in the long reign, from 1934, of [Herbert] Morrison and his successors with what may loosely be called a Fabian dream of municipal socialism run by experts for Londoners' good.'[16]

In 1965 the LCC was abolished. It was replaced by the Greater London Council (GLC), which had responsibility not only for the area within LCC boundaries but for the whole of the metropolis. Responsibility for education,

Figure 1.1 *The Greater London Council and some of its predecessors*

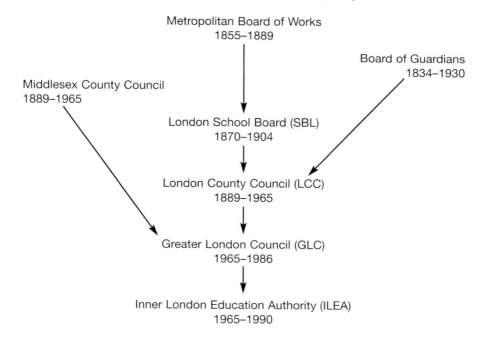

at least for the inner London area that had previously been under the control of the LCC, was transferred to the Inner London Education Authority (ILEA), a committee of the GLC. There were also 32 boroughs. In 1986 the GLC was abolished and the ILEA was reformed as a new *ad hoc* education authority. In 1990, responsibility for education was devolved to the inner London borough councils and the Corporation of London.

These developments in municipal government took place against a backdrop of dramatic social and political change, ranging from world wars to the decline of the British empire and the Education Act of 1944. In the late nineteenth century, children living in the slums of London were underfed and some were homeless beggars; three different books were published with the title of *The Cry of the Children* in the 1870s and 1890s.[17] In 1884, fewer than half of London's households had running water in a city with eight water companies. Most people lived two or more people to a room; many, six to a room.[18] In 1915, a survey in the St Pancras district of north London showed that families with children on the free dinner list eked out a bare and miserable existence:

> Widowed mother scrubs infirmary floor for 3d an hour; works from 9 am to 7 pm. Earnings not sufficient to support the family.
> Father 'odd man', under sized, poor mental capacity. Never earned more than 15s in a week. Wife died of semi-starvation to feed the children.
> Mother dead. Father costermonger and consumptive often ill and losing his capital (now a Hotel Porter) …
> Cabmaster, ruined by motors. Mother dead. Eight children …
> Father a fruit hawker. Consumptive continually in hospitals or infirmaries. Seven children …
> Father in Canada, rarely sends money home. Five children. Mother earns on an average 12s. Two rooms 6s …
> Ex. Omnibus driver. Out of work for two years when motors came.
> Deserted wife. Very respectable and hardworking. Father imprisoned for non-maintenance. Two children in poor-law school.[19]

In the middle of the twentieth century, the creation of the welfare state and the National Health Service (NHS), as well as a period of full employment, produced an enormous improvement in the lives of children and their families. But by the mid-1960s, poverty was starting again to be a widespread problem. By 1990, some one in four of all British children were living in or on the margins of poverty, while one birth in every three was to a family living on means-tested benefits;[20] in 2000, the murder of a school boy called Damilola Taylor, on a council estate in Peckham, south London, apparently carried out by other youths, seemed to exemplify the vulnerability of children in modern London. Many children in the metropolis were living in high-rise flats, vulnerable to drug abuse and gang-related crime. The appearance of poverty had changed – but once again, numbers of girls and boys were beggars with no homes. 'Inner London,' writes Roy Porter, had 'become the nation's capital for poverty, family breakdown, school truancy, delinquency, crime (against the person and against property), alcoholism, vandalism and violence.'[21] Of course, the social and economic picture of London has never been uniform: the needs and experience of its children have always varied from district to district, as well as *within* each district. While the City prospered in late Victorian times, comments Gilda O'Neill in *My East End*,

> people less than a mile away were working as pure finders – collecting buckets full of dog excrement from the streets to sell for use in the leather industry – and desperate girls and women were selling their bodies for pennies in the shadow of the massive blind walls of dock warehouses stuffed with riches from all over the world.[22]

And after the 'Big Bang', which transformed the City in 1986, making its foreign exchange market the most advanced and elaborate in the world, the numbers of poor and homeless people were growing rapidly. 'It is one of the great and continuing paradoxes of London life,' observes Peter Ackroyd in *London. The Biography*, 'that the rich global city contains also the worst examples of poverty and deprivation.'[23]

Baroness Serota, a Care Committee volunteer in Hackney in the late 1940s, who was then elected to the LCC in 1954 and later to the GLC when it was set up in 1964, has said that 'London is special because of its size and diversity – the mixture of its immigrant communities, and the proximity of poor and rich, slums and mansions.'[24] As the capital of Britain, London was the headquarters of the world's largest empire – its port, its administrative centre and its financial hub. Each volume of *The London Education Service*, the LCC's official manual between 1905 and 1939, included the following paragraph:

> London is the home of the world's markets; the centre of international finance; the capital city of a world-wide Empire; the meeting place of nearly every race and people. It is not only, therefore, the needs of the 'locality' which are insistent on their claim on the London Education Authority. The policy of London, including the organisation of its education service, must be largely influenced by Imperial circumstances and the general advance of humanity. For it is on these that its own existence largely depends.[25]

But the empire started to decline quite soon after the start of London's education welfare services. By the end of the Second World War, it had lost its power and wealth and was giving way to the more nebulous framework of the British commonwealth. One of the consequences of the empire was extensive immigration from former colonies, which enriched the cultural diversity that has always been a feature of London. In the earlier years of the twentieth century, this was manifest in the Jewish communities and a large number of Irish families, who were mostly Catholic and had many children. At every moment in its history, London has been changed by the arrival of different immigrant groups, who have created new challenges for its schools and for its education welfare provision.

Care and control

The start of universal schooling has to be understood in the context of a society where ideas about childhood and the treatment of children were very different from those held in Britain at the beginning of the twenty-first century. In 1981, physical punishment of any kind was finally – after a long campaign – abolished in all schools. But in the 1870s, whipping was a common punishment for boys, and girls were caned in schools. Beating had been used as a punishment in Britain from the Middle Ages, although the power to order the whipping of any females was abolished in 1820 (followed by adult male offenders in 1843). Whipping by birch rod or leather tawse of male offenders between the ages of 8 and 17, who had been charged with common law offences, continued until after the Second World War. This punishment was administered, according to strict guidelines, to the bare buttocks of a boy. Corporal punishment left the juvenile justice system in 1948 but did not finally leave the school until 1981. The impact on children of such punishment is described by Charlie Chaplin in his autobiography. Chaplin and his brother Sydney were transferred from the Lambeth Workhouse in the first decade of the twentieth century to the Hanwell School for Orphans and Destitute Children, where punishment was meted out every Friday in the large gymnasium. Two to three hundred boys between 7 and 14 years lined up to watch the punishments:

> For minor offences, a boy was laid across the long desk, face downwards, feet strapped and held by a sergeant, then another sergeant pulled the boy's shirt out of his trousers and over his head, then pulled his trousers tight.
>
> Captain Hindrum, a retired Navy man weighing about two hundred pounds, with one hand behind him, the other holding a cane as thin as a man's thumb and about four feet long, stood poised, measuring it across the

boy's buttocks. Then slowly and dramatically he would lift it high and with a swish bring it down across the boy's bottom … the minimum number of strokes was three and the maximum six. If a culprit received more than three, his cries were appalling. Sometimes he was ominously silent, or had fainted.

Nor was this the most painful punishment. 'The birch was different', adds Chaplin. 'After three strokes, the boy was supported by two sergeants and taken to the surgery for treatment.'[26]

These attitudes were slowly giving way to a more protective and caring approach, which recognised the needs of children, poor as well as rich, and sought to improve their lives. In the early 1880s the Waifs and Strays Society was formed to look after the welfare of orphans and homeless children. In 1884 the Children's Country Holidays Fund (at first called the Country Holidays Fund to Provide Fresh Air for Ailing London Children) was founded, in order to give the poor children of London a holiday in the countryside of not less than two weeks. In 1889 the Prevention of Cruelty to Children Act was passed – a progressive step forward, writes the historian Harry Hendrick, in the 'humane treatment of children and in their protection by the state.'[27] The National Society for the Prevention of Cruelty to Children (NSPCC) was set up in 1884, with a network of 32 provincial aid committees and a further seven in the process of formation. The NSPCC had ten inspectors to deal with its caseload of neglected and abused children. Children could be referred for cruelty or neglect to the NSPCC under section 12 of the Children Act of 1908. Charlie Chaplin was the recipient of NSPCC care on one of many unhappy occasions in his childhood. Shut out from their home by their stepmother, he and his brother were found by the police at three o'clock in the morning, asleep by a watchman's fire. The police took them home and made her let them in, then notified the NSPCC. Chaplin recalled that, 'One day [my stepmother] Louise received a visit from the Society for the Prevention of Cruelty to Children, and she was most indignant about it.'[28]

Running through the story of London's education welfare services is a tension between care and control: care of the needy by the provision of food and clothing; and control through compulsory attendance. However, this is not a straightforward dichotomy, since welfare provision is not necessarily free of coercion and may be used as a means to enforce certain kinds of behaviour. Nor is enforced schooling simply an act of control: even though some historians have tended to regard compulsory education 'as an intensification of the use of schooling as a tool of social control,'[29] the business of

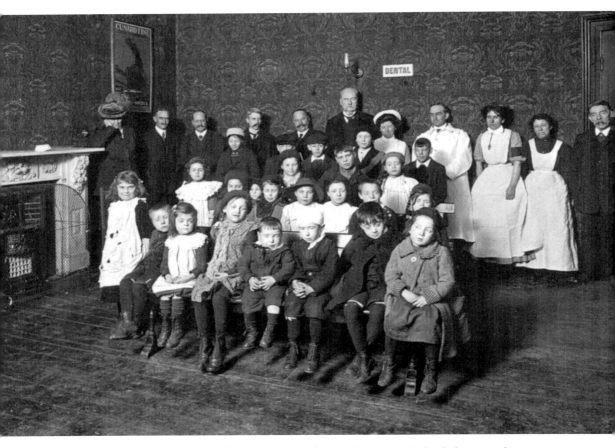

Plate 2 Poor school children in Woolwich, London, 1914. Behind them stand nurses, welfare staff and a School Care Worker. LMA, 26.74, 7092c

making children go to school can also be seen as a liberating and empowering force. It was certainly experienced in this way by many people, including a woman who was taken from school in 1888 at the age of 11 to work in her step-mother's washing business. She had to turn a heavy mangle for hours and to collect and deliver the orders, 'until my arms felt as if they would break, and my back ached so I could not sleep at night'; as a result of this labour, she was partially crippled for life with tubercular hip disease. 'All I ever say when people grumble about the school age being raised,' she said later, 'is, "Oh well, good job for the children, they can't be driven beyond their strength like I was".'[30] The school-leaving age was raised incrementally: from 10 in 1880 to 11 in 1893, 12 in 1899, 14 in 1918, 15 in 1947 and finally 16 in 1972.

At the centre of the story of London's education welfare services are the individual girls and boys themselves, but they are barely visible in documents and reports. Unearthing the story of the children, from *their* point of view, has been a common problem in efforts to write about the history of children and childhood;[31] but it is an even greater problem in the case of *poor* children. From the early years of the London School Board to the start of the twenty-first century, the 'clients' of education welfare care have been the children of poor families, who are least likely to be heard – or even asked – about their experience of school. The Care Committees were described in 1909 by the Principal Organiser of the service as being 'concerned with *all* families containing children of from five to fourteen years of age (emphasis added).'[32] But this was not accurate. Both the Care Service and the attendance officers were only concerned with children going to elementary schools (which were defined as those with fees of up to nine pence a week), which put them at the lower end of the social hierarchy. As a rule, children from the middle and upper classes went to private schools, although some middle-class children went to elementary schools that achieved academic success, such as Fleet Road Board School in Hampstead (which became known as the Eton of the Board schools). The Board of Education operated on the clear basis that elementary education was intended for working-class children. Replying in 1913 to a letter from the office of the Ministère des Sciences et des Arts in Brussels, which asked about school attendance figures in secondary schools and private schools, the Board explained that no figures were kept for these schools. 'Broadly speaking,' it said, 'the parents of Secondary and Private School children are *of a higher social class* than the parents of Elementary School children and the activities of the school attendance officers are mainly, if not wholly, confined to the latter and to the neighbourhoods in which they live (emphasis added).' In most cases, it added,

> a Local Authority and its officials would probably not institute inquiries at all as to the attendance of school children in a better class neighbourhood. If inquiries were instituted, the Authority would, as a rule, accept without further inquiry a statement by the parents that the child was under instruction.[33]

After the 1944 Education Act, the elementary school system was replaced by primary and secondary education. But education welfare services were still not aimed at *all* children. They were limited to those being educated within the state system: the pupils of independent schools were largely exempt from the inquiries of Care Committee workers and the school attendance officer.

In writing this book, it has been difficult to 'find' the children who were the recipients of education welfare care. Nowhere in the records is there any evidence of the reactions of working-class families to home visiting and school meals – because no one appears to have asked them. In any case, they were unlikely to have had the time and resources – and sometimes the literacy – that would be necessary to produce a written account. Stephen Humphries has argued that the absence of information about working people's experience of childhood has meant that conventional histories present a distorted point of view, which is skewed in favour of middle-class perceptions and values. To compensate for this, he collected a range of oral evidence from working-class people about their experience of childhood and youth between 1889 and 1939. This evidence is presented and discussed in *Hooligans or Rebels?* (1981), which has been drawn upon in this book to give some account of working-class memories of school. Another valuable source has been Gilda O'Neill's *My East End* (1999), a collection of memories of life in cockney London derived from archive sources and, especially, from oral testimony. John Burnett's *Destiny Obscure* (1982), a volume of autobiographies of childhood, education and family from the 1820s to the 1920s, provided some useful extracts relating to working-class life in London.

School Visitors and Care Committee workers were powerful. They brought the judgement of the state on those who played truant – and in their hands rested the decision about who should have free school dinners and watertight boots. Those who were given X-ray treatment for ringworm would have lost clumps of hair, while others would have suffered the embarrassment of having their heads shaved and then anointed with purple-coloured gentian violet, as a treatment for impetigo.[34] 'You could tell the kids who had nits,' recalled a former pupil at a school in London's East End. 'The nit nurse would shave all their hair off and paint this red sort of coloured stuff all over their head. We used to really take the mick out of them.'[35] Adolescent children had to suffer the indignity of parading at their medical examination in knickers and vest (which may have been darned and ill-fitting), in front of a Care Committee volunteer and other strangers. Wearing cast-off clothes supplied by charity – especially if they seemed out of place – could be a source of acute embarrassment. In one East End school, clothes and boots were publicly handed out to the worst-dressed children; on one occasion, a complete Eton suit was given to one boy, which caused him great suffering. He remembered later:

> Today, at the age of 84, the sound of a school bell fills me with dread …
> Even in a Board School there were social grades. My feeling of inferiority
> was probably caused by the fact that my boots were of the cheapest kind –

hob-nailed to make them last longer – and that my clothes were made by my mother.'[36]

Between home and school

Some Care Committee workers saw themselves as utilising the power of the state to protect the child from its family – they identified the family, and especially the mother, as the primary cause of a child's problems at school. 'Unwholesome surroundings and overwork out of school hours,' observed Miss Margaret Frere, the pioneer of the School Care Service, 'were *partly* to blame for the condition of the children, but *indolent, incompetent mothers far more so* (emphasis added).'[37] This kind of approach, which was not uncommon in 'respectable' society, tended to shift the responsibility for children's problems away from poverty and social injustice to the individual families affected. It may be contrasted with the campaign of the Family Endowment Society (FES), which was set up by Eleanor Rathbone in 1917 to put public funds into the purses of working-class mothers, to help them in their efforts to care for their families; 'the endowment of motherhood,' argued a FES pamphlet in 1918, is 'the most urgent question of the hour'.[38] A long campaign led finally to the introduction in 1945 of a regular and universal payment of family allowances, which was paid directly to the mother. In Miss Rathbone's model, carefully explained in *The Disinherited Family* (1924), mothers did the best they could, in spite of real material difficulty; but in Miss Frere's model, working-class mothers could be feckless and children needed to be rescued from them by the state, in the form of school dinners and intervention in family life.

Alexander Paterson, a School Visitor who lived and worked among the poor of London, regarded the work of the Care Service simply as a help to the mother, not any kind of rescue by the state:

> her burdened life is made easier by any service done to the children, and the lightening of her duties does not check her love for them. Rather will the work of the school and care committee tend to make her responsibility more sacred to her. For her task becomes more possible, her capacity for worry is no longer overtaxed. The strain of daily duties is relieved, and she has time to look at her children and love them more thoughtfully.[39]

Paterson, like most School Visitors, came from the same social class and community in which he worked, which may explain his more sympathetic attitude towards working-class families. Care Committee volunteers, on the other hand, were women who were comfortably off, who would have had little natural understanding of the lives of the poor. They would have been unfamiliar with the experience of attending an elementary school, since their own children would have gone to private schools.

However, many Care Committee workers were not judgemental and were respectful towards the families they visited. One such volunteer was Eileen Lecky, who was a Care Committee member in Putney from 1907 until 1958 and is one of the few volunteers to have written an account (albeit unpublished) of her work. At first, she said, 'The parents were indignant, feeling it was a slight on the way they brought up their families, and often in those early days the doors were slammed in my face.' She soon learned, though, 'to put my bicycle out of sight further down the road, and when the door opened to put my foot in to prevent it being closed again.' The families started to trust her, once they realised that she wanted to act as their advocate; in the days of the Poor Law, for example, she went to the Poor Law office to 'have good old battle with the officer'. Very soon, 'friendships were made and 'ere long I was accepted as a friend. Great patience was needed, for in those days grannies nearly always lived with the young families and were autocrats, so the chief aim when visiting was to win granny over to your side.' [40] Volunteers like Miss Lecky did not seek any obvious reward; to describe their quiet and anonymous way of working, Miss Frere frequently drew on the final sentence of George Eliot's novel *Middlemarch* (1871–2), which observed that the 'growing good of the world is partly dependent on unhistoric acts.' [41]

Working-class women in the late nineteenth and early twentieth centuries were being visited in their homes by all kinds of outsiders: school attendance officers, inspectors from the NSPCC, parish visitors and, in the case of those applying for charitable relief, visitors from the Charity Organisation Society (COS). 'Most of this activity,' comments the social historian Jane Lewis, 'was confined to the voluntary sector and was conducted by middle-class women, who dealt with working-class wives and mothers.' [42] The Care Committee workers fitted into this pattern, unlike the School Visitors. The vast social gulf between the Care Committee volunteers and School Visitors militated against the development of a fruitful relationship between the two groups – even though they shared the aim of supporting children to make the best use of their education. The fact that Care Committee workers were generally women, while School Visitors were men, would have further divided the two groups; the higher social rank of the women would have been a particular embarrassment, since the men would have claimed a natural superiority if they had all been of the same social class. These complexities emerge from a description by Beatrice Potter (later Webb) of her visit to the home of a school attendance officer in 1887. Miss Potter was middle class and doing voluntary work, much like Care Committee workers. 'What would the conventional

West End acquaintance say to two young women smoking and talking,' she asked, ' in the bed-sitting, smoking, working and bath room of an East End School Board Visitor?'[43]

The purpose and scope of this book

Almost nothing has been written specifically on education welfare work in London. Some books and articles looking at the evolution of education or at the role of London local government have referred in passing to the work of Care Committees and school attendance officers, but not in any systematic way; moreover, some of their accounts are inaccurate. This gap is all the more glaring, given the outstanding historiography on education in London: the definitive *History of Education in London 1870–1990* (1990) by Stuart Maclure, as well as *The London Experience of Secondary Education* (1986) by Margaret Bryant, *Adult Education in Inner London 1870–1980* (1982) by William Devereux, and *The Urban School: Buildings for education in London 1870–1980* (1983) by Ron Ringshall, Dame Margaret Miles and Frank Kelsall. Elementary schooling has also been the subject of high quality historical studies, including *The Lost Elementary Schools of Victorian England* (1984) by Phil Gardner and *Elementary Schooling and the Working Classes 1860–1918* (1979) by John Hurt. Bernard Harris's *The Health of the Schoolchild* (1995), an excellent and comprehensive history of the School Medical Service in England and Wales, does not mention the role of the Care Committees in London.

The Children of London seeks to fill the gap in the particular area of education welfare, offering a historical account which gives some indication of important policy issues and how they have been addressed at different moments in time. It does not, however, aim to be exhaustive. It does not attempt a full account of the practitioners' conditions of service or the activities of their professional association or union. It does not pay a great deal of attention to details about training and qualifications. Nor does it seek to quantify the effectiveness of the services, which in any case would be difficult to measure. Rather, *The Children of London* tells the story of the evolution and development of the education welfare services in London. The story is set against the background of 120 years of a unified education service, which was a unique characteristic of London until the dismantling of the ILEA in 1990.

The structure of the book is chronological. The focus of Chapter 2, which follows this introductory chapter, is the issue of attendance. It starts with the introduction of compulsory schooling in London, following the 1870 Education Act, and the employment of School Visitors. It looks at the difficulties faced in relation to attendance, such as continued child labour. Chapter 3 examines the start of welfare provision set up to enable children to benefit from going to school. It gives an account of voluntary efforts to provide the poor children of London with food and clothing and it charts the creation of the School Care Service by the LCC in 1907, as well as its evolving structure and duties over the next ten or so years.

Chapter 4 looks at both attendance and welfare work between the end of the First World War in 1918 and the start of the Second World War in 1939. At this time the two services functioned in parallel, with some areas of duplication. This was the apogee of the School Care Service; by 1925 there were over 6,000 volunteers and in 1939 there was a Care Committee in every school. In 1933 a proposal was put forward to merge the services, but this was firmly rejected by Miss T.M. Morton, the Principal Organiser of the Care Service.

The years of the Second World War are covered in Chapter 5, with a particular focus on the role of Care Committees in evacuation from the city and on the challenges facing school attendance officers. Chapter 6 looks at

Plate 3 *A map showing the ten divisions of the ILEA, surrounded by greater London. Taken from* Welcome to London Schools 1982–83, *a booklet produced by the ILEA in 1982.*

the postwar period, up to the mid-1960s. It shows that in the postwar period the Care Service became more involved with behavioural problems and also worked more closely with school attendance officers. The Education Officer of the LCC suggested merging the services between 1948 and 1950, but this was fiercely opposed by the Principal Care Organiser, Miss Cram.

The focus of Chapter 7 is the Bedford Report, which was commissioned by the ILEA in the mid-1960s. This was the first thorough investigation of the attendance and welfare services in London and it recommended a merger of the School Care Service and the School Inquiry Service, to form a unified Education Welfare Service. The merger finally took place in 1970. It is discussed in Chapter 8, which chapter covers the EWS between 1970 and 1986, as well as the formation of the Education Social Work Service and its work up to 1990, when the ILEA was abolished. The book ends with Chapter 9, which draws some conclusions and sets out some of the lessons that may be drawn from the story. The appendix looks at the situation that followed the ending of a single education authority for London in 1990 and explores implications for future policy development.

Notes

1. George Eliot: *Middlemarch*, p. 896.
2. *Hansard*, 1869.
3. Statement by Christopher Thomson in 1847, quoted in David Vincent: *Bread, Knowledge and Freedom. A study of nineteenth-century working class autobiography*, p. 97.
4. Alistair Service: *London 1900*, p. 183.
5. Stewart D. Headlam: Preface, in John Reeves: *Recollections of a School Attendance Officer*, p. v.
6. Mary Stocks: *The Philanthropist in a Changing World*, pp. 16–17.
7. Carolyn Steedman: *Childhood, Culture and Class in Britain: Margaret McMillan, 1860–1931*, p. 9.
8. John H. Nicholson: *School Care Committees*, p. 13.
9. Margaret R. Currie, 'Social Policy and Public Health Measures in Bedfordshire within the National Context 1904–38', PhD thesis, pp. 111–13.
10. Sir Hubert Llewellyn Smith: *Borderland between Public and Voluntary Action in the Social Services*, p. 8.
11. Peggy Jay to ASW, 2 November 2000.
12. M.Penelope Hall: *The Social Services of Modern England*, pp. 205-6.
13. John Stevenson and J. Henry Capes: *Handbook for School Attendance Officers*, p. 3.
14. John Hurt: *Elementary Schooling and the Working Classes, 1860–1918*, p. 97.
15. Susan Pennybacker: *A Vision for London*, pp. 2–3.
16. Roy Porter: *London: A social history*, pp. 406–7.
17. Peter Ackroyd: *London. The biography*, p. 654.
18. Susan Pennybacker: *A Vision for London*, p. 20.
19. 'Where War is Blessed. The chronic poverty of London', in *The School Child and Juvenile Worker* VI(1), January 1916, pp. 1–3.
20. Ann Oakley: Introduction, in C. Gowdridge, A.S. Williams and M. Wynn: *Mother Courage*, p. xviii.
21. Roy Porter: *London: A social history*, pp. 453.

22. Gilda O'Neill: *My East End*, p. 33.
23. Peter Ackroyd: *London. The biography*, p. 766.
24. Beatrice Serota to ASW and CM, 16 November 2000.
25. Quoted in Stuart Maclure: *A History of Education in London 1870–1990*, p. 83.
26. Charles Chaplin: *My Autobiography*, p. 23.
27. Harry Hendrick: *Children, Childhood and English Society, 1880–1990*, p. 45.
28. Charles Chaplin: *My Autobiography*, p. 34.
29. W.B. Stephens: *Education in Britain 1750–1914*, p. 81.
30. Quoted in John Burnett (ed.): *Destiny Obscure*, p. 234.
31. Harry Hendrick: *Children, Childhood and English Society, 1880–1990*, pp. 2–3.
32. 'Report of a Lecture on the Duties of Care-Committees given by Miss Morton', 25 June [1909], Patrick Ivin Private Collection.
33. Joseph A. Pease to C. Weemaes, 8 November 1913, PRO, ED 11/77.
34. Charles Webster, 'The Health of the School Child During the Depression', p. 75.
35. Gilda O'Neill: *My East End*, p. 130.
36. Quoted in John Burnett (ed.): *Destiny Obscure*, p. 155.
37. LCC Education Committee – General Purposes Subcommittee, 'Report (22 March 1961). For members' information only – S.O.', 124. Patrick Ivin Private Collection.
38. Quoted in Suzie Fleming: Introduction, in Eleanor Rathbone: *The Disinherited Family*, p. 70.
39. Alexander Paterson: *Across the Bridges*, p. 33.
40. Eileen Lecky: 'Children Then and Now. A survey of Care Committee work in Putney from 1907 to 1958', p. 7, LMA, ILEA S/SB/04/2.
41. George Eliot: *Middlemarch*, p. 896.
42. Jane Lewis, 'Women and late-nineteenth-century social work', in *Regulating Womanhood. Historical essays on marriage, motherhood and sexuality*, (ed.) Carol Smart, p. 79.
43. Beatrice Webb: MS diary, Sunday, May 1887, in *My Apprenticeship*, pp. 302–3.

Chapter 2

SCHOOL BOARD MEN

'There goes that wretched child, not four years old,
tearing along the street shouting "school board, school
board". In a trice the street is empty of children.'[1]

THE LONDON SCHOOL Board led the rest of Britain in its enforcement of
school attendance. From its very start in 1870, it required children to be in
school for five hours every weekday from the age of 5, for a period of five
years, which was later extended to eight years and then nine. Exemption

Plate 4 *Watergate Street, Deptford, in 1911. Photograph provided by LMA*

could be gained by passing a leaving examination or in some other way, perhaps as a 'half-timer', combining education with paid employment. But overwhelmingly, children in London now had to go to school. Elsewhere in Britain, compulsory schooling developed more slowly. The Forster Act had introduced compulsion in the most tentative way and it was not until the 1876 Education (Sandon) Act that a duty was imposed on parents to send their children to school. The 1876 Act also required all school boards to set up school attendance committees but it was not until the Education (Mundella) Act of 1880 that these committees were obliged to introduce by-laws to enforce their aims.

In London, school attendance committees were set up in each of the ten electoral divisions: City, Westminster, Chelsea, Finsbury, Greenwich, Hackney, Lambeth (which was later split into East Lambeth and West Lambeth), Marylebone, Southwark and Tower Hamlets. Each division had a

Table 2.1 *The work of the School Visitors, March 1899–March 1900*

Division	Child now attending school	Child sent to an institution	Family in Workhouse	Family removed	Child ill or illness in house	Child in the country	Family under surveillance	Miscellaneous	Total number of children	Number of visits paid to schools by School Visitor during the year
City and Westminster	58	6	5	—	5	—	1	3	78	253
Chelsea	—	17	7	54	26	13	122	55	294	550
Finsbury	49	—	—	—	194	—	175	1	419	94
Greenwich	62	1	2	31	9	—	1	16	122	88
Hackney	502	5	6	64	20	9	17	6	629	129
East Lambeth	50	2	1	19	—	2	1	11	86	311
West Lambeth	214	—	—	42	—	—	15	—	271	75
Marylebone	355	20	5	52	5	—	20	—	457	120
Southwark	68	2	2	9	17	5	2	3	108	576
Tower Hamlets	239	1	4	30	47	1	37	11	370	392
Total for all children	1,597	54	32	301	323	30	391	106	2,834	2,588

Source: Report on school accommodation and attendance, Appendix to School Board for London Annual Report, 1899–1900. LMA 22.57SBL

superintendent and a team of school attendance officers, known as School Visitors, who carried out the work. These 'School Board Men' had the job of visiting the homes of absentees from school and finding children who were not on the roll of any school. Each visitor was responsible for a particular area of London. They also visited schools to collect lists of truants and to discuss individual cases with the teaching staff. By the end of the nineteenth century, 318 visitors and 65 clerical staff were employed in London overall.[2] Table 2.1, which presents data from the SBL Annual Report for 1899–1900, shows that 2,588 visits were paid to schools in London by Street Visitors (who were School Visitors with the particular task of patrolling the streets) during that year. These visits ranged from 75 in the division of West Lambeth and 88 in Greenwich to 576 in Southwark and 550 in Chelsea.

Charles Booth, who in 1886 started a survey of the *Life and Labour of the People of London*, used visitors to collect many of the data. He observed that they were 'in daily contact with the people, and have a very considerable knowledge of the parents of the school children, especially of the poorest amongst them, and of the conditions under which they live.' Their methods of collecting information, he said, were systematic and thorough:

> The School Board visitors perform amongst them a house-to-house visitation; every house in every street is in their books, and details are given of every family with children of school age. They begin their scheduling two or three years before the children attain school age, and a record remains in their books of children who have left school. The occupation of the head of the family is noted down. Most of the visitors have been working in the same district for several years, and thus have an extensive knowledge of the people.[3]

In 1901 two new categories of visitor were created: 'Special Visitors', who worked in difficult areas; and 'Night Visitors', who patrolled the streets in the evenings in an effort to rescue children from criminal or immoral companionship.[4] The job was hard. One report stressed the importance of recruiting visitors who could run fast, in order to catch the children[5] – hence the nicknames of 'Kidcopper' and 'Kidsnatcher'.

The London School Board first employed visitors in 1872, when it needed reliable people to carry out a child census as a way of estimating the number of buildings required to deliver education to all children of school age. John Reeves, who was a School Visitor for 38 years, recalled later that nobody really knew what he was supposed to do. In his *Recollections of a School Attendance Officer*, he explained that when he was appointed to the position of visitor in 1872, 'three of us were asked to wait for a few weeks until the sphere of our duties could be determined.' His first duty was to take a census of his allocated district, a block on the borders of Shoreditch and Bethnal Green, where he collected the 'names of parent or guardian, with trade and occupation, names and ages of children and date of birth (if possible), which had to be carefully entered into prepared schedules.'[6] It was found that a quarter of a million new school places had to be supplied in London.[7]

Census work by the school attendance officers continued year by year. Their schedules showed the total number of children of the elementary school class between 3 and 14 years of age, as well as the number of children over 14 years of age who were actually on the books of elementary schools. The total number for 1907–8 of children under 14 years of age, on the basis of the Registrar General's figures, was estimated to be 1,346,169, of whom 1,240,192 were children of the elementary school class. The total number of children between 3 and 14 years of age scheduled by the School Visitors for the year 1907–8 was 873,144. There were 740,728 children on the books of the elementary schools, or 84.8 per cent of the number of children (from 3 to 14 years of age) scheduled. Attendance at school was however compulsory only for children over the age of 5 years. The percentage of such children on the books of elementary schools was 97.6. This was higher than the percentage for 1906–7 and 1905–6, which followed increases of 0.1 per cent in 1904–5, 0.1 in 1903–4, 0.2 in 1902–3, 0.2 in 1901–2 and 1.4 per cent in 1900–1.[8]

The children of the poor

The poverty of many working-class children made it difficult for them to attend school. It was not until 1891 that school fees (known as 'school pence') were abolished; although rarely more than a few pence a week, they were a heavy burden on poor families. There was also the problem of finding adequate boots and clothing for school, as well as the weariness of the daily struggle for existence. T. Marchant Williams, a London School Board Inspector, estimated in a letter to *The Times* in 1884 that at least 60,000 families in London lived in one-room homes.[9] Elsewhere he drew attention to three schools in the Finsbury division in which 58, 82 and 85 per cent of the children's families lived in one room. 'To many of the half-starved children of Seven Dials, St. Luke's, Lisson Grove and Saffron Hill,' he said,

> the forty days' fasting in the wilderness and the miraculous feeding of 'five thousand men, besides women and children', with five loaves and two fishes, appear too commonplace, I should say, to excite much comment. It is really most difficult for the Inspectors to know what results to expect

from a year's teaching of these ill-housed, ill-clad, and ill-fed little children.[10]

In the London district of Tower Hamlets, nearly 1500 homeless children of school age were reported in December 1894 to be living in shelters maintained by the Salvation Army or Dr Barnardo's Homes.[11] Even in the more affluent areas of London, there were pockets of extreme deprivation. The School Board for London Annual Report for 1900, shows that 2,656 children were found by Street Visitors to be playing or loitering in the streets or other open places in the City and Westminster. Some 124 children were selling lights (tapers or matches to ignite a fire), 214 were sweeping crossings or picking up wood and rags and 92 were begging or wandering, having no home. In East Lambeth, 2,108 children were found in the streets, of whom 37 were selling lights and 4 were begging or wandering. Out of 28,025 children in the streets of the ten divisions overall, 565 were selling lights, 425 were sweeping crossings or picking up wood or rags and nearly 300 were begging or wandering and had no home.

John Reeves reported that in the area bordering Shoreditch and Bethnal Green, which was his own block, the condition of life was very low. 'Many of the public houses,' he wrote in his *Recollections*, sold spirits at any time and 'had a way right through so that persons could escape at the back and be easily lost in the street behind.' In just one house, 90 people were crowded together: 'The stairways were very dark, the doors broken, the panels often cracked and locks useless, the doors being kept closed by pieces of dirty rag.' The air was thick 'with the most noisome and poisonous stench caused by the practice of the most disgusting habits in the rooms.'[12] The children's lives, he said, were a round of 'sunless drudgery':

> they never played as children play, they never seemed to think as children, they were prematurely old and the victims of awful cruelty. They worked at matchbox-making many hours, and at other times assisted their parents in disposing of their wares in the streets or even worse, stealing. The mortality among the young children was appalling.[13]

These children were seen to be in the greatest need of education. George R. Sims, a drama critic and writer, believed there was a 'seething mass of humanity sunk in the lowest abysses of vice and degradation'. He put great faith in Forster's Act of 1870 and observed in *How the Poor Live* (1883) that:

> The deluge that shall do the work now must come of the opening of the floodgates of knowledge. Already, in tiny rivulets as yet, the waters are trickling even into the darkest corners of our great cities.... It is this river of

knowledge which the modern wanderers in the wilderness must ford to reach the Canaan which the philanthropist sees waiting for them in his dreams.[14]

'Education,' he insisted, 'must be the prime instrument in changing the condition of the poor for the better, whatever results it may have later on upon the condition of the labour market and the political and social

Plate 5 'A London School-Board Capture, 2.40 A.M.', which appeared on the cover of the Illustrated London News on 9 September 1871. The children 'will certainly be much better off when delivered to the tender mercies of a judicious schoolmaster, whether Churchman or Dissenter, than they have ever been while left to enjoy their fatal freedom.'

questions of the future.'[15] This made the matter of school attendance a priority. One visitor who published a *School Attendance Guide* in 1883 commented that working-class children 'should be made to attend school before all others.... Compulsory education cannot be applied to the poor without more or less hardship, but if it's not to be applied to the poor, it has missed its first and most important aim.'[16]

In other parts of England and Wales, the scope of the work of school attendance officers included welfare provision, especially help with school meals, clothing and boots. But in London, this need was largely addressed by the efforts of schools, as well as philanthropic individuals and organisations. These efforts were formalised by the LCC in 1907 as the School Care Service, which comprised a network of Care Committees. The committees were organised by the LCC Education Committee but were staffed by a large number of volunteers, who were nearly always women and were middle or upper middle class. They were quite different, therefore, from School Visitors, who in any case were paid officials. The work of these two groups was closely related, but they operated quite separately from each other (see Chapter 3).

Many School Visitors in London did what they could to help the poor, especially before the formal establishment of the School Care Service. John Reeves recalled that school attendance officers were often moved to pity by the poverty of the families they visited and helped out 'from their own little store'. Charities were approached for help for children who lacked clothes or boots and requests were made for assistance with meals. When an epidemic closed the Stepney Creche in 1880, the school board visitor came daily to ask when it would reopen, 'almost beside himself as the children are staying at home to nurse babies'. Usually, children kept at home for child care were girls and, in recognition of their difficulties, 12 baby rooms were opened in London schools in the late 1880s, where infants could be left during classes.[17]

The scope of School Visitors' work

Until 1902 School Visitors did not regularly check school registers and much of their enforcement work was taken up with apprehending and questioning children who they found at home or in the neighbourhood, when they should have been at school. In 1903, a 'slip system' was instituted in schools, so that the attendance record of individual children could be reviewed on a continuous basis. A slip was made out for each child at the beginning of the scholastic year and a member of the school staff entered on it each week the number of attendances during that week, using the classroom registers. The School Visitor took these slips back to his office and ascertained from them which children had been absent.

The visitors visited the homes of children who had been absent for two or more attendance periods during the week. They were encouraged to take a persuasive approach with parents, rather than threaten them with prosecution. One reason for this was that the London magistrates courts were overwhelmed. Some courts had to hold special sessions to deal with attendance cases. The penalty at that time of a maximum fine of five shillings was not effective, since the numbers appearing in court on a second or subsequent summons were half the attendance cases heard in 1902.[18]

Each day of the week carried a particular challenge for school attendance officers. Washing days were especially bad and at one school, lessons were moved from Wednesday afternoon as it was the local washing day; otherwise, many girls would miss those lessons and might fail their exams. Elsewhere, it was Monday that produced these difficulties. Friday was difficult because child homeworkers (that is, children who did piecework at home for an employer) had to make some money for the weekend. It was also the day when jobs of casual cleaning could be found, so mothers would keep their daughters at home to care for younger children while they went out to work. They also kept girls back to straighten the house for the weekend. By the 1890s, writes Anna Davin in *Growing up Poor*, a special effort was being made in some schools to make Friday afternoons attractive, with extra playtime and talks by visiting speakers.[19]

Many of the School Visitors were retired policemen or ex-non-commissioned officers from the armed forces.[20] No special qualifications were needed. Though consistently low, wages varied: at the turn of the century some officers received about £2 a week, while others earned £1.10 shillings. Women were paid less than men.[21] Beatrice Webb met a visitor who had been a seaman and had taken to school board visiting as a livelihood; he was intensely interested in his fellow-men, she said, with an 'extensive but uncultivated knowledge of science and literature'. His home was just one room: 'The back room of a small working-class dwelling served as dining, sitting, sleeping, working room of this humble individual, with the most ingenious arrangements for all his functions.'[22] The social class of the visitor heavily influenced the way he was seen and treated in education circles. In 1905, Sir Charles Elliott, formerly the chairman of the London School Board's Finance Committee, observed that although the visitor had accumulated experience and knowledge, 'in a good many cases it has not been thought that he was quite of a social standing or official standing to be on a level' with local government officials.[23]

In 1871, the London School Board had recommended that the enforcement of school attendance should be done by 'women who have had experience in similar work, as District Visitors &c.' It also advocated securing the services of women of a higher class, who already had experience of working with the poor.[24] At first, quite a few women were appointed: half of the eight visitors appointed by the Lambeth division were women, while Tower Hamlets employed three women out of ten overall. By March 1873, however, only 17 women were employed by the London School Board as school attendance officers, out of a total of 116. Women – and especially those of a higher class – were more interested in the kind of charitable work that was done by the Care Committees. A view developed, in any case, that this was not appropriate work for women, on the grounds that some neighbourhoods were particularly unsafe for women and they were at risk of assault by parents or older children. The author of *The School Attendance Guide*, himself a former visitor, commented that having observed the employment of women, he could not recommend it:

> The female visitors I have known would, after short experience, have themselves admitted their unfitness and dislike for the work if necessity did not enjoin silence. The witness box in a police court, which they are not more able to avoid than men, is not the proper place for women, and I have always felt much pity for the female visitors whom I have seen in such an uncongenial position. It is cruel, for the sake of a theory, to thrust women into work for which they are unfitted.[25]

For reasons of social class and background, observes David Rubinstein in his 1969 study of *School Attendance in London 1870–1904*, School Visitors have left little written trace of their working lives. Hardly anything remains of their reports to the London School Board and the divisional committees, except for their occasional use as evidence in the writings of other people.[26] However, some visitors did write about their work. One of these was Thomas Wright, who wrote many articles and two books during the course of his career of 35 years as a visitor, under the pseudonym of 'Riverside Visitor'; for the most part, though, his books were more concerned with the poverty of south London than with the matter of school attendance. Another commentator was John Reeves, already mentioned. Many school attendance officers from all over Britain contributed to the *Attendance Officer & School Gazette*, which began in 1893 but was suspended after two years, due to lack of money; it started once more in 1901, this time with the title of *School Attendance Gazette*, but closed down again a few years later. The *Gazette* described the job of visitors as 'pioneer work'.[27]

One of the London contributors to the *Gazette* was Alexander Paterson. In an article entitled 'Reminiscences of a School Attendance Officer', he commented that he 'had no hesitancy in forcing children to school'. For many children, he said, 'school was their happiest and holiest environment, added to the fresh air they got to and fro.' Those who pitied him in his work, he said, 'might keep their pity for themselves, for he was content to work in the gutter, and took pleasure in so doing.'[28] The same enthusiasm emerges from his book, *Across the Bridges. Or life by the south London river-side* (1911). 'Here lies the hope of the nation', he wrote, adding that education was 'the greatest lever of social reform' because for each boy, there was 'a golden chance for every true school … to compensate for the handicaps of the present and prepare him for the future struggle.' The great majority, he added, were 'wonderfully regular in their attendance'.[29]

The work of visitors was not limited to school attendance. In 1873, they prepared a census of wife desertion in London and between 1884 and 1885, 16 of the 110 witnesses before the Royal Commission on the Housing of the Poor were London visitors. When Charles Booth heard about this work, he came up with the idea of using London visitors in his social survey of the capital, especially to find out about the lives of the poor.[30] In the case of east London, just one of the districts of the metropolis, they produced 46 books of notes containing no less than 3,400 streets or places and every house and every family with schoolchildren was noted.

The working conditions of school attendance officers were not good. There was a massive amount of paperwork, which continued even after 1891, when the limit of a 48-hour week was introduced and attempts were made to transfer clerical work to the divisional offices.[31] Officers had no job security or guaranteed pension and their conditions of service were not regulated. Moreover, there was no national pattern of service, even though school attendance officers were employed throughout England and Wales. This was largely the result of the piecemeal development of elementary education across the country. The slow build-up of attendance staff and the lack of uniform procedures, training and recruitment, made it difficult for visitors to form any kind of national group. However, the School Board Officers' Mutual Association was formed in London in 1884. By 1887, when 23 branches had been established with 572 members, it changed its name to the School Attendance Officers National Association.[32]

The conflict between school attendance and employment

Compulsory school attendance was not generally welcomed by employers, especially in the industrial towns and agricultural areas. One farmer complained to the Board of Education that:

formerly we could get a lad of 12 or 13 for a fortnight's harrowing if wanted, a week for mangel harvest, two or three days for stone picking, this I get done on Saturdays when schools are closed, but with frost about mangel pulling must be done at once, a month or generally 6 weeks is absolutely necessary for the Swede thinning … it is a cruel loss to the parents, what I pay to the children has averaged for years from £25 to £35, and it means in most cases, new boots and Sunday Suit.[33]

The Board of Education was not impressed, even though the farmer explained that he had been a school manager for years. It regarded the letter as 'a general grumble that things are much worse than they used to be and that children are not allowed to be taken away from school whenever they are wanted to do anything else.'[34] In August 1914, the National Farmers' Union sent letters to the President of the Board of Education, suggesting that the Board should lower the number of days of school in cases where the harvest was prolonged.[35] The Board replied firmly that the schools should remain open, properly attended, and that the public education service should proceed 'with as little disturbance as possible'.[36]

In London, many of the children who were absent from school were working for pay. A survey of 112 schools carried out by the London School Board in 1899 showed that some 1,143 children put in from 19 to 29 hours a week in employment, while a further 729 worked 30 to 39 hours. Many children's jobs, like milk or newspaper delivery, got the children up very early and kept them up late, so they often fell asleep in class.[37] Some children were half-timers – that is, half-time at school, half-time at work. This loophole in the compulsory attendance system served as a way of placating the demands of employers. It was more common in the industrial areas: in March 1902, for example, the *School Attendance Gazette* reported that while Brighton and Ipswich had no half-timers on their school rolls, in Halifax 18.63 per cent of the numbers on the rolls were half-timers and in Burnley the figure was as high as 20.65 per cent. The half-time arrangement was welcomed by many parents, because they needed the earnings of their children to augment the family income. In recognition of poor parents' difficulties, the social reformer Lord Shaftesbury had moved an amendment to the Education Bill of 1870 to lower the school-leaving age; he explained that 'the extent to which persons in London depended on the labour of their children their Lordships would scarcely be aware of, and it was impossible that a man could maintain wife and family on nine shillings a week, unless he was assisted by such labour.'[38]

As a result of the Factory Acts in the nineteenth century, which made it illegal for young children to work in factories, some manufacturing processes had been redirected into 'home work', which was outside the jurisdiction of the acts. In *The Cry of the Children* (1898), Frank Hird revealed the horrors of child labour in 'homework'. Mothers and children worked all day making paper bags and matches and other products, in constant dread of a knock on the door by the school board man. The mothers justified this work, said Hird, on the grounds that if the children went to school, they did not get tea or dinner. 'These women tell a truth that is painfully obvious,' he added, for 'if the children do not work, the children suffer.'[39] But their work was hard and exhausting. Clementina Black, who argued for a living wage that was sufficient to meet workers' basic needs, wrote a book in 1907 about the sweated industry. Children, she said, were employed in most branches of home work in London.[40] She reported on the ill effects of this practice:

> Sarah W. is thirteen years old and in standard 4. Her father was in prison. Her mother drinks. These parents hid their children for eight months, and the educational authorities had great difficulty in finding them. This child, 'a very bright girl', used to stay up all night making matchboxes, so as to get them taken by 11 the next morning. She now works, between school times, at capping sticks.[41]

In the spring of 1907,

> it was found that in a Hackney school one fourth of the girls were engaged in match box making, steel covering, baby shoe making and fish basket sewing.... Children working with their parents at home are frequently kept at their sewing or pasting until ten or eleven o'clock at night. They are sent to 'shop' before coming to school in the morning, and many of them are never marked for regular attendance.[42]

Lady Dilke was another campaigner against the ills of home work who was a member of the Women's Trade Union League. She reported a conversation that she overheard in 1893 regarding the manufacture of matchboxes in a home in the Shoreditch district of London. 'Of course, we cheat the School Board. It's hard on the little ones,' said one mother, adding, 'but their fingers is so quick – they that has the most of 'em is the best off.'[43]

Attitudes towards school and compulsory attendance

The business of enforcing school attendance was controversial. In 1899, when a debate was held in Parliament over whether or not to limit half-time exemption, many members expressed reluctance to interfere further with parental rights.[44] The member for Birkenhead, Sir E. Lees, argued that the employment of a child of 11 was the lesser evil if the alternative was for a mother to go out to work. Some members of the London School Board complained at a committee meeting in 1900 that the system of awards for regular attendance meant that 'children have been sent to school or insisted on going when their highest duty was to their home.'[45] The enforcement of school attendance was seen by some to interfere in a family's right to run their own affairs.

In this climate of doubt and mistrust, the feelings of the public about School Visitors were mixed. On the one hand, commented John Reeves, 'respect, not to say esteem, of the poor has been given to the officers, who were often regarded as "guide, counsellor and friend".'[46] The fact that the social class of the visitors was largely the same as that of the children's families may have helped to make them welcome; this may also have given them a better understanding of families' problems. But on the other hand, the work of the school board was often regarded as interference. Reeves attributed this to 'the low moral and mental condition of the people, the outcome of neglect for generations.'[47] One remark that he constantly heard was, '"I had to work when I was as old as them, and they will have to do the same".'[48] Certainly there was hostility towards visitors. In *The Pupil's Own Register of School Attendance* (1901), the author (himself a School Visitor, who published this register as a way to help pupils attend school regularly) commented that they were often thought of in the same brutal terms as the beadle who persecuted Oliver in Charles Dickens's *Oliver Twist*. 'Owing to the nature of their duties,' he pointed out, 'Attendance Officers are very frequently looked upon as intruders, and if their calls should be made when one is out of humour, they are likely to be considered a nuisance.'[49] When W.E. Forster attended a public opening of a school a year or so after the London School Board was set up, he complimented the visitors by saying they should have 'MP' after their name – because they were 'moral policemen'.[50] But this was the very aspect of school attendance work to which many parents objected.

It is not easy to find out about the views of working-class children and their parents about compulsory attendance at school. As people who were often poor and illiterate, they were the least powerful members of society and were rarely asked for their opinions. However, some collected memories of growing up in the East End suggest that many parents there supported the work of the School Board Man: 'The truant man was known by everyone in the street. Parents were anxious [regarding] their respectability, even though they were poor. There was no arguing with authority [and] you could be sure of another chastisement from Dad or Mum.'[51] One girl who went to an elementary school in Fulham wrote later that:

School in those days seemed almost uniformly pleasant. Discipline was strict. We stood up and sat down, opened desks and shut them at the teacher's order, and even on occasion blew our noses in unison. Yet classes must have been in spite of their size fairly informal, and we were most of us on quite intimate terms with Teacher. We would bring her bunches of flowers from the back garden and we would burble out our family affairs … and brought along our choicest treasures to show her.[52]

However, other children were less enthusiastic. 'You were scared of the school board man, if he caught you in the street,' recalls another resident of the East End, 'you didn't have to wait for the police to come up to you and say, "What are you doing home from school?" if you saw the school board man, you bolted.' [53] In Manchester, where attendance officers were provided with a blue serge uniform and where each individual officer was known on his district as 'the School Board', a leaflet was published in 1877 with the following rhyme:

Who, forthwith to our lodgings went,
To serve a notice with intent,
Of bringing us to punishment?
'The School Board'.

Who, listened not to Mother's pleading,
That we were clogs and jackets needing,
To get which, she went out a-cleaning?
'The School Board'.

Who, is a terror to each young boy,
And tends to lessen our daily joy,
In tops, whips, kites, and every toy?
'The School Board'.

Who, is there we could do without,
And not feel hurt or put about,
If he were never more seen out?
'The School Board'.[54]

Dissatisfaction with school occasionally erupted in strikes by pupils, often supported by parents. From 1889 onwards, in many parts of Britain, school strikes periodically disrupted the elementary school routine, with children parading the streets to demand shorter school hours and an end to corporal punishment. Stephen Humphries has commented that because such strikes were a source of embarrassment to teachers and education authorities, they were often omitted from committee minutes and official school histories. However, a few of these strikes have been rediscovered, including nationwide strikes in 1889 and 1911, both of which affected many parts of London. The 1911 strike began in Llanelli, Wales, then spread to schools in over 60 major towns and cities.[55]

Teachers had a powerful incentive to support good attendance figures, especially after the Revised Code was changed in 1890. The Code was crucial to the resources of any school, since it was the basis on which government grants were paid. When first established in 1862, payment was largely by results and only a small part of the grant was based on attendance. An elaborate system of examinations were conducted by inspectors to test the 'three Rs' of reading, writing and arithmetic. But in 1890, the Code was changed so that grants were based on attendance, not on results. This gave added value to the work of the school attendance officer: 'The issue of the "New Code" of the Education Department,' observed *The School Attendance Guide*, 'has given a fresh impetus to the interest of the Managers and Teachers of Public Elementary Schools in the subject of regularity of attendance.'[56] Teachers were disappointed at the widespread failure of magistrates to fine parents for poor attendance. In 1906 the National Association of Head Teachers passed a Resolution asking for 'the attention of the Home Secretary [to] be drawn to the smallness of the fines still inflicted by magistrates upon parents for habitually neglecting to send their children to school; and that the Home Secretary be urged to use his influence to ensure that the maximum fine is inflicted in the more serious cases.'[57]

To reward children for regular and punctual attendance, the London School Board started a system of school attendance medals in 1887. The first medal was designated the 'Queen Victoria Medal', with royal sanction; after Queen Victoria's death, it was renamed the 'King Edward VII Medal' and after his death, it became simply 'the King's Medal'. In 1904, the final year of the London School Board, 'white metal' (tin alloy) medals were earned by 38,997 children, bronze medals by 5,192, gilded bronze by 2,218 and silver medals by two.[58] The London County Council continued the awards when it took over as the education authority for London.[59] Up to 1911, the medals had a simple orange ribbon and thereafter, the ribbon was of a special design incorporating red, white and blue.[60] They were very popular with some children, motivating some of them to attend school even when they were seriously ill.

The London County Council was delighted with the increase in funding from the government that followed improved attendance in 1907–8. 'As showing the financial effect of the improvement in attendance which has

Plate 6 'A "B" Meeting', *where parents were warned of prosecution if they did not send their children to school. An illustration from* How the Poor Live *by George Sims (1883).* British Library H276i12

taken place during the present year,' commented the Annual Report, 'it may be mentioned that, if the percentage of average attendance had remained the same as it was for the previous year, viz. 88.7 per cent., instead of 88.9 per cent., the amount payable to the Council in respect of Government grants would have been about £3,000 less than will actually be received.'[61]

Parents were liable to prosecution and a fine if they did not send their children to school. The London School Board was cautious about this, because it recognised that sending a child to school involved the expense of school fees (before 1891), as well as obtaining adequate shoes and clothing. There was also the possible loss of a child's earnings. Enforcement was therefore 'to be carried out especially at first with as much gentleness and consideration for the circumstances and feelings of the parents as is consistent with its effective operation.'[62] Before court proceedings were started, the divisional committees had to issue first an 'A' notice (see Table 2.2), drawing the parents' attention to the by-laws and inviting them to appear before the committee to discuss their child's case. If this failed, a 'B' notice followed, threatening prosecution but again giving the parent an opportunity to explain the background. If a warning at a 'B' meeting proved ineffectual, the school board officers prosecuted the offenders.

In 1903, the *School Attendance Gazette* published an article entitled, 'At a "B" Meeting. A Feast of Excuses at London's Peculiar Court'. It described an assembly at Lant-Street Board School (in Southwark) of between 50 and 60 parents who had been served with a 'Form B':

> They were mostly women who attended the 'B' meeting ... and crowded the corridor of the upper floor of the school – pale, pinched women who looked sad and anxious; more buxom women with florid, blotched faces that told their own tale; silent women who sheepishly edged away from the crowd of garrulous offenders who were 'getting steam up' for the coming interview

Table 2.2 *Issuing of Notice A, Notice B and Summonses by School Visitors, March 1899–March 1900*

| Division | Number of occasions on which various proceedings were taken | | |
	Only notice A necessary	A unsuccessful, so B required	Summonses issued
City and Westminster	1	23	14
Chelsea	124	268	215
Finsbury	15	79	27
Greenwich	9	14	6
Hackney	27	178	93
East Lambeth	13	30	29
West Lambeth	—	—	—
Marylebone	30	—	14
Southwark	13	28	—
Tower Hamlets	228	487	139
Total	460	1,107	537

Source: Report on school accommodation and attendance, Appendix to School Board for London Annual Report, 1899–1900. LMA 22.57SBL

by dilating with more vigour than politeness upon the tyrannical character of the Education Act, and the pertinacity of its officials.

'"No boots"' was a frequent excuse for non-attendance and 'in each deserving case', boots were provided free. '"Helpin' mother, who is ill",' was an explanation given by 'three little defendants'. One little girl came to plead for her mother:

> 'Mrs Slatter!' called the doorkeeper. 'Mrs Slatter' proved to be a child of not more than ten, who laboured into the room under the weight of a puny and discordantly plaintive baby which she carried in her arms, and she had another little child clinging to her skirts.
> 'I come for mother', she explained.
> 'Why does not Mrs Slatter send Florence to school regularly?' asked the interrogator. 'She has missed three Wednesdays in succession.'
> 'I'm Florence, sir,' admitted the child, changing the baby to the other arm. 'I've got to take Winnie – this is Winnie – to Guy's Hospital every Wednesday. She's consumptive, like father died of.'
> 'Could not your mother take her?'
> 'No, sir; she's out charing, and it's all we have.'
> The usual warning.[63]

The final measure was a summons. However, there was no consistent pattern of prosecution in the different divisions. As Table 2.2 shows, in 1900 only 6 summonses were issued in Greenwich, while 215 were issued in Chelsea.

Some magistrates dismissed or adjourned school attendance cases or inflicted minimal penalties. They advocated patience in this matter, on the grounds that enforcing school attendance often deprived parents 'of the means of eking out a scanty subsistence by the labour of their children.'[64] Moreover, the courts were very busy, so dismissals offered one way of reducing the load. A Clerkenwell magistrate complained to the Home Secretary that there were too many attendance cases, which in any case caused misery through fines and imprisonment.[65] In January 1874, a school board visitor for the Finsbury Division objected that the Bow Street magistrate 'will not enforce the penalty, so that the people do not mind being summoned, and compulsion has very little effect in the neighbourhood of St Giles and Drury Lane.'[66] The situation became easier in 1891, when fees were abolished in board schools. There was a drop in the number of summonses, as well as an increase in attendance – from 80 per cent in 1900 to 88 per cent in 1905.[67] 'It may be pointed out,' observed the 1906 LCC Annual Report with some satisfaction, 'that, whilst the percentage of average attendance for the children of all ages has steadily increased, the number of summonses issued under the Education Acts has very greatly decreased.'[68]

In just a few decades, universal schooling had become a fact of British life. Although the children of the poor were 'practically debarred from acquiring for themselves the benefits of the higher branches of instruction,' commented the *School Attendance Gazette* in 1902, 'they have at least the legal birthright to an elementary education.'[69] As one Londoner wrote about his time at school:

> Fifty yards or less from the chimneys of the power station stood the school, elementary in every sense, and dyed by the swirling sulphur smoke to a nice shade of clerical grey just right for a church school. It was not graced with a saint's name, none of them would have owned it; nor hallowed by tradition, nor hampered by reputation.
>
> But we liked it; it was warm and dry and clean.[70]

Notes

1. From Arthur Kellet, 'A Week in the Life of a Pre-War School Attendance Officer,' quoted in Frank Coombes and Dave Beer: *The Long Walk from the Dark*, p. 15.
2. Stuart Maclure: *A History of Education in London*, p. 36.
3. Charles Booth: *Life and Labour of the People in London*. First Series: Poverty, p. 5.
4. LCC Annual Report 1907–8, Education, p. 72.
5. Quoted in the Annual Report of the LCC School Accommodation and Attendance Committee for the year ending 1902, p. iv.
6. John Reeves: *Recollections of a School Attendance Officer*, pp. 118 and 20.
7. Pamela Horn: *Children's Work and Welfare, 1780–1880s*, p. 81.
8. LCC Annual Report 1907–8, Education, p. 71.
9. *The Times*, 1 March 1884.
10. London School Board, Minutes, vol XVIII, 8 March 1883, pp. 505–6, LMA.
11. David Rubinstein: *School Attendance in London, 1870–1904*, p. 58.
12. John Reeves: *Recollections of a School Attendance Officer*, pp. 30–1.
13. Ibid., p. 34.
14. George R. Sims: *How the Poor Live*, p. 30.
15. Ibid., p. 32.
16. J. Hepburn Hume: *The School Attendance Guide*, p. 52.
17. Quoted from F. Green, in Carlen et al.: *Truancy*, p. 16.
18. Bedford Report, p. B.2.
19. Anna Davin: *Growing Up Poor*, p. 102.
20. Bedford Report, p. B.1.
21. Frank Coombes and Dave Beer: *The Long Walk from the Dark*, p. 4.
22. Beatrice Webb: MS diary, Sunday, May 1887, in *My Apprenticeship*, pp. 302–3.
23. Quoted in David Rubinstein: *School Attendance in London, 1870–1904*, p. 19.
24. David Rubinstein: *School Attendance in London, 1870–1904*, p. 43.
25. J. Hepburn Hume: *The School Attendance Guide*, pp. 13–14.
26. David Rubinstein: *School Attendance in London, 1870–1904*, p. 49.
27. *School Attendance Gazette*, January 1903, p. 7.
28. *School Attendance Gazette*, March 1903, p. 47.

29. Alexander Paterson: *Across the Bridges*, p. 61.
30. Beatrice Webb: *My Apprenticeship*, p. 228.
31. David Rubinstein: *School Attendance in London, 1870–1904*, p. 47.
32. Frank Coombes and Dave Beer: *The Long Walk from the Dark*, p. 4.
33. C.F.Priestley to Board of Education, 16 June 1906, PRO, ED 11/77.
34. Minute by Mr Major, Board of Education, 6 July 1905, PRO, ED 11/77.
35. National Farmers' Union to President of the Board of Education, 20 August 1914, PRO, ED 11/77.
36. Minute within Board of Education, 24 May 1914, PRO, ED 11/ 77.
37. Reported in Stuart Maclure: *A History of Education in London*, p. 37.
38. J.L. and B. Hammond: *Lord Shaftesbury*, pp. 257–8.
39. Frank Hird: *The Cry of the Children*, pp. 38–40.
40. Clementina Black: *Sweated Industry and the Minimum Wage*, pp. 104, 108, 141.
41. Ibid., p. 106.
42. Ibid., p. 108.
43. 'The Industrial Position of Women', *Fortnightly Review*, October 1893, p. 501.
44. *Hansard* 1 March 1899, cols 962 and 972.
45. Memo from chairman, School Board for London Subcommittee, Medal System, 1900, quoted in Anna Davin: *Growing Up Poor*, p. 106.
46. John Reeves: *Recollections of a School Attendance Officer*, pp. 10–11.
47. Ibid., p. 13.
48. Ibid., p. 26.
49. Anon: *The Pupil's Own Register of School Attendance*, p. 4.
50. John Reeves: *Recollections of a School Attendance Officer*, p. 13.
51. Gilda O'Neill: *My East End*, p. 129.
52. Quoted in John Burnett (ed.): *Destiny Obscure*, p. 205.
53. Ibid., p. 129.
54. Quoted in A. Dawson: 'The Education Welfare Officer', pp. 145–6.
55. Stephen Humphries: *Hooligans or Rebels?*, chapter 4, pp. 90–120.
56. J. Hepburn Hume: *The School Attendance Guide*, p. iii.
57. Resolution by National Association of Head Teachers, 14 June 1906, PRO, ED 11/37.
58. David Rubinstein: *School Attendance in London, 1870–1904*, p. 42.
59. London Metropolitan Archives, Information Leaflet No 8, 'London School Attendance Medals'.
60. Ibid.
61. LCC Annual Report 1907–8, Education, p. 72.
62. Quoted in Stuart Maclure: *A History of Education in London 1870–1990*, p. 35.
63. *School Attendance Gazette*, April 1903, p. 75.
64. Quoted in Anna Davin: *Growing Up Poor*, p. 86.
65. Quoted in ibid., p. 87.
66. Quoted in ibid., p. 86.
67. Bedford Report, p. B.2.
68. LCC Annual Report 1905–6, Education, p. 61.
69. *School Attendance Gazette*, June 1902, p. 113.
70. Quoted in John Burnett (ed.): *Destiny Obscure*, p. 314.

Chapter 3

CHILDREN'S CARE COMMITTEES

*'I think it is not right that we should insist on the
children coming to school without seeing that they are
fit to come.'*[1]

'IN OUR PLAYGROUND, it was at first a common sight to see children in winter time, either without boots or in broken ones,' wrote Henry Gardner, the headmaster of Hornsey Road Ragged School, in 1887. 'These last were the source of most of our troubles,' he added, because 'broken boots involved sodden stockings. It was far better for the children to sit in school with bare feet than with wet feet.' The children were dressed in ragged clothing and many of them were undernourished. 'To try and teach children in such a state,' said Mr Gardner, 'was a wretched farce.'[2] They were too hungry and too cold to 'profit fully by the teaching given'.[3]

A.J. Mundella, an MP who was vice-president of the Board of Education between 1880 and 1885, appealed to philanthropists for help. 'Benevolent societies in America', he exhorted the House of Commons in 1893, had rescued 'thousands of children from the streets of New York and elsewhere.' He said that 'if the West End would only do a little more in charity for the children of the East End, thousands of these children might be saved from broken health, and induced regularly to attend school.'[4] But in fact, many individuals and groups in London were already doing what they could to help, especially teachers. Mr Gardner, for example, started school dinners for his pupils in the 1880s. With the financial support of a London philanthropist, he

> ordered a large cooker … also a large quantity of tinned basins, plates, spoons, etc. The cooker was planted in the cellar, supplied with gas burners and was fully used for 20 years in the making of soup, or boiling of puddings. … As soon as the cold weather set in the cooker was got to work

and 50 selected children from each department, 150 in all, on four days in the week, were provided with a nourishing dinner. Two days were devoted to soup, one day to boiled suet pudding and one day to large sandwiches.[5]

He was assisted by sympathetic local tradesmen, who 'got to know what was going on and they helped by gifts and by selling their goods at cost price or little more.' A baker brought loaves and sometimes cakes, while two local butchers supplied meat and meat scraps for soups.[6]

In the early 1880s Mrs E.M. Burgwin, the headmistress of Orange Street Board School, Southwark, set up a system of providing her pupils with breakfasts of bread, margarine and cocoa, as well as dinners of soup or stew; her staff of teachers helped with the work and the costs were met out of their own pockets. With the aid of George R. Sims, a reporter for the *Referee* newspaper, this developed into the *Referee* Children's Free Dinner and Breakfast Fund.[7] In the middle of the decade, the number of these voluntary efforts started to expand. Free and penny dinners were provided throughout London's Jewish schools, in a scheme that involved the cooking of 1,400 dinners a week.[8] There were six major organisations in operation in London at the end of the 1880s, as well as a number of minor ones, many of which also provided children with boots and clothes. In the year up to March 1889 they provided school board pupils with 7,943 free breakfasts, 26,585 free dinners and a further 13,900 meals at costs ranging between a farthing and a penny each.[9] Many schoolchildren remained hungry, however: of the estimated 12.8 per cent of pupils in the capital's board schools who were short of food on a regular basis at the end of the 1880s, less than half were fed by these voluntary efforts.[10]

The aim of these schemes was straightforward: to feed hungry children and to make it possible for them to learn. A different kind of approach was taken by a school manager called Miss Margaret Frere (1865–1961), who worked at the elementary school at Great Tower Street in the poor and overcrowded district of Seven Dials. In the winter of 1898, Miss Frere and another woman manager at her school determined to find out why some children continued to be underfed and badly clothed, even though many headteachers had no difficulty in raising money and supplied children with food tickets, boots and clothes. The best way of doing this, they thought, was to visit the children's homes:

> The two managers set out to visit all mothers of underfed children who had appeared year after year on the dinner lists, in order to find out the home conditions and, if possible, help these necessitous children more effectually than by giving them free dinners only. The visiting was carefully done.

Plate 7 *The cover of* Children's Care Committees *(1909), a book by Margaret Frere, the pioneer of the London School Care Service.*

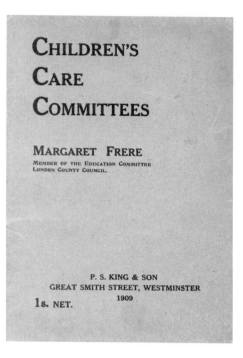

CHILDREN'S CARE COMMITTEES

MARGARET FRERE
MEMBER OF THE EDUCATION COMMITTEE
LONDON COUNTY COUNCIL.

P. S. KING & SON
GREAT SMITH STREET, WESTMINSTER
1909
1s. NET.

The investigation led Miss Frere and her colleague to conclude that the problem lay in the home. 'Only by getting to know and helping the parents,' believed Miss Frere, 'could the sufferings of the children be relieved.'[11] It was then possible, she said, to give them advice and encouragement and to check up on their home conditions. Next month, in January 1899, the managers and teachers of Miss Frere's school set up a 'Charitable Funds Committee', to concern itself with everything affecting the welfare of the children. They visited families in connection with boots and clothing, physical defects, holidays and employment on leaving school.[12] In 1902 the committee's name was changed to 'Children's Relief Committee' and then to 'Children's Care Committee'.[13]

In 1904, when school responsibilities were transferred from the London School Board to the London County Council, the voluntary feeding committees of schools were all brought together under the auspices of a Joint Committee on Underfed Children. Miss Frere's Children's Care Committee was admired as an exemplary scheme: it kept proper records, which were 'sadly lacking' in many schools with relief committees,[14] and the school was known as 'the cleanest and happiest of the poorer schools in London'.[15]

Setting up the School Care Service

Pressure was converging from various quarters – the Tory MP and social reformer John Gorst, the National Union of Teachers, the Women's Labour League and other women's organisations, as well as groups within the labour movement – for central government to do something about the feeding and welfare of schoolchildren. The problem seemed even more urgent following the bad winter of 1904–5. A framework to meet this need was created by the Education (Provision of Meals) Act of 1906, which empowered local education authorities (LEAs) to feed children and to levy a halfpenny rate for the purpose, if they needed to do so. This opened the way for education authorities to take over voluntary efforts to raise funds for feeding children (by 1911–12, a third of all LEAs had adopted the Act; and in 1914 the Act was made compulsory). Section 2 of the Act required local authorities to recover the cost of meals provided for schoolchildren from their parents wherever possible; the parliamentary debates had made it clear, stressed L.A. Selby-Bigge, the permanent secretary to the Board of Education, that the Act was not a measure for supplementing outdoor relief but an educational one.[16]

The LCC responded to the Act by using the model – and the name – of the Care Committee set up by Miss Frere. In 1907 it set up a a network of voluntary Care Committees that was collectively described as the 'School Care Service' or as 'Children's Care Work'; in many cases these Care Committees were the former relief committees of the necessitous schools. Miss Frere, who was now on the Education Committee of the LCC, offered help and guidance throughout the process, supported by Mr Aubrey Hastings Jay, the chairman of the subcommittee. Each committee was staffed by women volunteers, local school managers, teachers, school attendance officers and other interested outsiders, who were co-opted from bodies such as the Country Holiday Fund Visitors.[17] The former Joint Committee for Underfed Children became a subcommittee of the Education Committee; it was renamed the Subcommittee on Underfed Children and was chaired by Mr Jay. It sought to involve the voluntary organisations and one of the district secretaries of the Charity Organisation Society (founded in 1869) was borrowed in 1907 to be an organising inspector.

There were many and vigorous demands for school meals to be supported with money from the rates: 'considerable pressure was continuously put upon the Council by means of resolutions, petitions and deputations from various labour organisations.'[18] However, the LCC, which was taken over by Conservatives in 1907, was anxious to protect the voluntary principle and to put limits on the role of the state; this was related to fears about socialism and the revolutionary ferment that had taken hold of Russia in 1905 and given impetus to socialist teachings throughout Europe. The LCC was determined therefore to implement the Provision of Meals Act with money from charitable sources, apart from the expenditure of £500 for equipment to enable the Care Committees to carry out their duties, which was followed by a further £750.[19] 'This is probably the first instance of the cost of a scheme carried through Parliament being thrown on the offerings of the charitable', observed the Reverend W.H.H. Elliott.[20] Many philanthropic bodies providing school meals handed over to the LCC their equipment, along with the structure they had established: Mr Gardner, for example, handed over his stock of basins and spoons and cooking utensils.[21]

It was estimated that the funds required to provide sufficient meals in 1907–8 would amount roughly to £30,000, although the Education

Committee was hopeful that this figure was too high; against this, a sum of £9,200 was expected from voluntary contributions.[22] To supplement the money furnished by the feeding associations, an appeal for donations was launched in 1907 by Arthur Balfour and the Lords Rosebery, Rothschild and Avebury, under the leadership of the LCC's chairman, H. Percy Harris. They warned of disastrous consequences if insufficient funds were raised – that 'thousands of poor parents, finding that they are themselves rated for the support of their neighbours' children, will be tempted to leave to the State the duty which they have hitherto discharged themselves.' They made 'an earnest appeal'

> to all lovers of children who have comfortable homes to make a voluntary offering towards the sum required, and so avoid the imposition of a rate which will probably entail consequences which those who watch the progress of Socialism cannot contemplate without the gravest misgiving.[23]

In the event, however, the chairman's 'Provision of Meals' Fund[24] raised only £12,000,[25] which left the LCC with the difficulty of finding other ways to pay for the meals.

Despite these financial difficulties, the Care Service became quickly rooted in the life of London's elementary schools. Miss Eileen Lecky, who worked as a volunteer on a Care Committee in Putney from 1907 to 1959, has described the beginning of a Care Committee in her district. 'The managers of All Saints', Lower Common, and St. Mary's Church Schools in Putney,' she said, 'received a letter telling them they were to start a Care Committee to be responsible for the welfare of the children, except in educational matters.' As a response to this letter, added Miss Lecky, 'The vicar (Chairman of Managers) asked me to form a Care Committee and be its first Honorary Secretary.' Although she was young, she had some experience: 'For six years I had worked under the guidance of the Lady Margaret Hall Settlement in Lambeth, and also with Miss Locket, the Lambeth Secretary of the Charity Organisation.' But when she started on the Care Committee work in Putney, she had 'little idea that a lifetime's work lay ahead of me'.[26]

In central London, school dinners were provided mainly by the Alexandra Trust, with headquarters in Finsbury. But in Putney, 'the arrangement was made for our children to go to a small coffee shop in Putney Bridge Road, where they got a good meal for 2½d a dinner.' However, the care workers did not think that a coffee shop was a proper atmosphere for children, so in December 1910 they opened their own dining centre in the Iron Room (built for a boys club) and the cooking was done by Mrs Tovey, the schoolkeeper's wife, in the old soup kitchen in the St Mary's playground. Members of the

Care Committee formed a rota to supervise and serve the meals. This new arrangement flourished, although 'a young clerk at Education Headquarters wrote and told me Mrs Tovey must be dismissed as no school keeper's wife was allowed to work in the same school as her husband'. He was told in no uncertain terms to 'leave us to manage our own jobs'.[27]

Between 1907 and 1908, the number of meals provided to London school-children jumped from 74,423 to 143,962; the number of children who were fed rose from 29,334 to 37,979, while the number of schools involved rose from 290 to 531. While the figures for the period before 1907 are not reliable, owing to the multiplicity of agencies involved, the leap is so great as to be (at the very least) indicative of an increased provision of food.[28]

In January 1908 the LCC appointed Mr Douglas Pepler and Miss T.M. Morton as temporary organisers to manage the Care Committees; they had both gained relevant experience working for the Charity Organisation Society. It was their particular task, with the help of some assistant temporary organisers, to inquire into the whole question of school feeding and welfare – 'with a view to placing the whole work of the Children's Care Committees on as uniform and scientific a basis as possible'.[29] Employing Mr Pepler and Miss Morton for this task reflected a serious commitment from the LCC to the future of Children's Care Work.

Both Mr Pepler and Miss Morton were firm defenders of the voluntary principle and took the view that meals should be provided from charitable sources. In a book called *The Care Committee. The child and the parent* (which was published some years later, in 1914), Mr Pepler argued that aid from the state would erode the voluntary idea and also parental responsibility. Despite 'its philanthropic motive', he warned, the Education (Provision of Meals) Act of 1906 was serving 'to reduce people to poverty through the momentary advantage to their children.' Even the family meal, he said, had ceased to be a necessity.[30]

The reorganisation of the service

This strong commitment to the voluntary principle was not supported by adequate funds, however. Accordingly, some boroughs of London decided to make use of the halfpenny rate, starting in January 1909. Using the rates required a new funding system. This in turn required a new constitution for the Care Service, since teachers and school attendance officers (as public servants) would no longer be able to sit on the committees once their responsibilities included the administration of public money. The need to structure the service was generally seen as a good idea, since Mr Pepler and Miss Morton had identified specific areas in need of improvement. So far, committees had only been formed in schools that were deemed to have necessitous children, and there was no standardised method for the selection of these children. Moreover, the committees comprised managers, teachers and others who had been co-opted, few of whom had enough time for home visiting and making enquiries. In some schools, voluntary workers did the visits, but very often the report of the school attendance officer was the only source of information that was available. This was unsatisfactory, because the criteria used by attendance officers to select children for investigation were not poverty and need, but bad attendance at school. The opportunity to reorganise the Care Service was therefore welcomed as a way of raising standards. In the new structure, each committee now had to consist:

> of two or three managers, two or three social workers of experience, appointed by the managers from a nominated list supplied by the Council, and two or three workers nominated by the Council. In every case … there will be a Committee of six or nine men and women, whose primary business will be to take care of every neglected child in the school, and generally to act as a link between school and home.[31]

The Subcommittee for Underfed Children of the Education Committee was renamed the (Central) Care Subcommittee in January 1909. Overall management of the Care Service was the responsibility of the Principal Organisers – that is, Miss Morton and Mr Pepler, whose temporary jobs as advisers had by now developed into established positions (Mr Pepler left the service shortly afterwards, but Miss Morton remained as Principal Organiser until her retirement in 1930). At the local level, supervision was provided by 12 District Organisers: one for each of the 12 London divisions. The organisers were paid as professional social workers, whose duty was to recruit, train and organise the new body of voluntary workers. In each London division, a Local Association of Care Committees (composed of representatives of the Care Committees, of teachers' consultative committees and of the Children's Care (Central) Subcommittee) was established; the structure of this system is shown in Figure 3.1. Local associations had already been set up in Woolwich, Stepney, Hackney, Bethnal Green, Walworth and other areas, so in effect the LCC was formalising a pre-existing structure.[32] Altogether, 27 local associations of Care Committees were formed to co-ordinate policy and establish standards. The service was also to be enlarged, with a view to having a Care Committee in every school: 'Mentally deficient children have Care-Committees just like the ordinary Elementary Schoolchildren.'[33]

The LCC appealed for more volunteers and recruited about 5,000. Their duties were extended: it was still their first responsibility to select the children in need of free school meals, but they were also to 'deal with all matters which affect the welfare of the child outside the school curriculum … and all be brought into close connection with the feeding problem.'[34] In this way, an emphasis was laid on the need to look broadly at the needs of the child. Clearly underpinning the new system was Miss Frere's philosophy of children's care, which she set out in a book called *Children's Care Committees* (1909). 'School and home,' she insisted, 'must be much more firmly linked together in the new order of things than they were in the old.' The school, she added

> must not be treated as a little world, cut off from all intercourse with the life around it; to be understood it must be studied with, not apart from, the district in which it stands, where are the homes from which the children come, and the workshops and places where their parents are employed.[35]

Figure 3.1 *The relations of Children's School Care Committees to the London County Council*

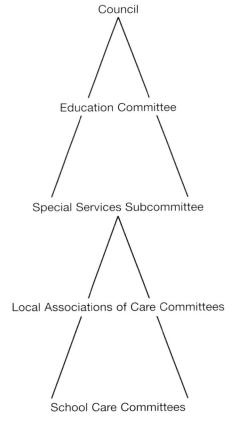

Council

Education Committee

Special Services Subcommittee

Local Associations of Care Committees

School Care Committees

This idea of building a bridge between home and school was echoed by others in the service. 'We must unite the home with the school education,' insisted Miss Morton. 'Education means growth in grace and in the formation of character, and this cannot be if the home and the school are opposed. We must ... build up homes where the virtues taught in schools can flourish.'[36]

Table 3.1 *The 25 LCC schools with the highest percentage of children receiving supplementary food in 1911*

| Electoral Division | School | For week ending 3 February 1911 | | |
		Number of children present	Number of children receiving supplementary food	Percentage of number fed to roll
St Pancras	The Brecknock, M.D.	93	63	67
Greenwich	Randall Place, Deaf	45	22	48
Wandsworth	Mitcham Lane, M.D.	42	20	47
Bermondsey	The Chaucer, M.D.	44	19	43
St Pancras, E.	Aldenham Street, R.C.	182	76	41
Hammersmith	St Hubert's, M.D.	129	52	40
Limehouse	Holy Name, R.C.	455	182	40
Poplar	St Edmund's	256	101	39
Whitechapel	St Anne's, R.C.	533	207	38
Bermondsey	Old Kent Road, Deaf	83	32	38
Woolwich	Powis Street, Blind	42	16	38
Poplar	Culloden Street, M.D.	66	25	37
W. Newington	The John Ruskin, M.D.	69	26	37
S. Hackney	Morning Lane, Blind	24	9	37
E. Finsbury	St Joseph's, R.C.	409	151	36
C. Hackney	Enfield Road, M.D.	74	27	36
N.E. Bethnal Green	Pritchard's Road	883	322	36
N. Camberwell	Boundary Lane, Blind	59	21	35
N. Kensington	Sirdar Road, M.D.	128	45	35
S.W Bethnal Green	Abbey Street, M.D.	108	37	34
St George-in-the-East	St Patrick's, R.C.	569	189	33
N. Kensington	St Francis', R.C.	230	76	33
N. Hackney	Princess May Road, M.D.	73	24	32
Westminster	The Millbank, M.D.	73	24	32
Rotherhithe	All Saints', R.C.	244	80	32

Source: LCC reference paper 1911. Patrick Ivin Private Collection

Children appear to have benefited from the reorganisation of the service. Table 3.1, which presents data about the 25 'worst' schools (that is, the ones with the highest percentage of children in need of supplementary food) in London in 1911, shows that Brecknock School in St Pancras gave meals to 67.7 per cent of the children on its roll per week. After this, the second 'worst' school fed 48.9 per cent of the children on its roll; the fiftieth school in this hierarchy, which was in East Finsbury, fed 28 per cent of its children. In 1912–13, 84,181 children were fed in term time in London. The average number of meals provided per child in term time in this period was 106. This was much higher than the figures for other counties and county boroughs, apart from Northampton, which was 159 per child, and Nottingham, which was 136 (see Table 3.2).

Many elementary schoolchildren were dependent on school dinners by 1914. In the spring of that year, 78,485 children were given supplementary food and 8,439,570 meals were provided (of these, 77.2 per cent were dinners, 11 per cent were breakfasts, 10.2 per cent were milk meals and 1.6 per cent were doses of cod liver oil).[37]

Table 3.2 *Average number of meals provided per child in 1917, excluding school holidays*

Local Education Authority	Average number of meals
Counties	
Lancashire	31
London	106
Yorkshire	7
County Boroughs	
Bath	40
Birmingham	54
Bolton	48
Bristol	–
Coventry	49
Leeds	53
Liverpool	81
Manchester	76
Newcastle	83
Northampton	159
Nottingham	136
Portsmouth	93
Rochdale	64

Source: Annual Report of the Chief Medical Officer to the Board of Education, 1917

The role of the voluntary workers

Care Committee volunteers were always women; indeed, the LCC specified that all appointments in Children's Care Work should be women.[38] They came from affluent families, though rarely from the highest levels of the social elite (apart from some members of the Guinness, Capell and other upper-class families). They were recruited through charity networks, churches and through friends. Clergymen and their wives, as well as prominent members of Catholic parishes and members of the Catholic Women's League, also served as volunteers.[39] Some volunteers worked outside their own neighbourhood (Lady Craik, for example, lived in Westminster but worked in Stepney), but usually they worked in their own neighbourhoods, which meant that the prosperous areas of London were better endowed with committees. Their tasks were those of social workers, but they were untrained amateurs. This was not seen as an obstacle: 'Experience shows that such a visitor is "born, not made"; with true sympathy and insight she ... can enlarge her sphere of interest to include all that pertains to the life of the children.'[40] Their special qualification was their readiness to give 'time, trouble and brainpower'.[41] The salaried Care Organisers, on the other hand, were generally professionals with qualifications in social work, whose job was to support and to facilitate the work of the volunteers. At a meeting of Care Committee representatives held at the LCC Education Department, it was emphasised that 'the appointment of paid workers need not in any way prove detrimental to the voluntary work of the Committees, but should be placed *at their service* to assist them in organizing the work (emphasis added).'[42]

Whenever a suggestion was made of an overlap between the work of the Care Service and that of school attendance officers, Miss Morton was quick to draw a distinction between the two groups. When asked after a lecture in 1909 why volunteers should 'do the work over again, when the attendance officers know as a rule the antecedents of most families whose children are absent from school', Miss Morton replied that if the officer had the necessary information, it should of course be used. But she hastened to add that his work was quite different from that of the Care Committees: '[The school attendance officer] knows the children who attend badly – very little about those who attend well. He does not cover the whole ground, his knowledge is not always sufficient in itself, the statements need verifying.'[43] But in any case, the volunteers were seen as different precisely *because* they were volunteers. Was it possible, asked a contributor to the *School Child*, for paid officials like the School Visitors to bring 'that warm human sympathy and religious devotion which are essential if the work is to be well done?'[44] While the tendency of the official was to work 'primarily from a sense of duty', the voluntary worker, it was claimed, was motivated by 'a sense of altruistic devotion'.[45] The *School Child*, which described itself as 'A Journal for Children's Care Committees and School Managers', was representative of the dominant views held by the Care Service and was started with a view to 'providing a medium of expression for those engaged in such as Care Committees, Medical Inspection and Country Holiday Funds'.[46]

The business of school attendance officers was fairly straightforward – either children did not attend school, or they did. The business of Care Committees was more muddled, with muddled criteria for decision-making. At times, their language and behaviour recalled that of the 1834 New Poor Law, which had drawn a distinction between the 'deserving' and the 'non-deserving' poor. At a meeting at the Education Department in 1908 to discuss the best method of selecting children for meals, a Care Committee representative urged that home visiting should be carried out prior to the commencement of winter feeding, 'so that the *undeserving* cases might be eliminated at the outset (emphasis added).'[47] A study in 1912 found that in the case of one Care Committee, a deliberate strategy of 'least eligibility' was applied, on the model of the New Poor Law. The food provided was so unappetising as to constitute in itself a 'definite test of need': the meals took the form of breakfast between 8.15 and 8.45 on the five school days during the week, consisting of an unvaried diet of porridge and milk, or in a few cases of bread and milk; they were eaten not in a school hall or classroom, but in a parish room in the district. This food 'test' was relied upon 'as a first and last resort to furnish evidence as to the necessity of the family' and had 'restricted the number considerably':

> 'I can give them better at home than what you gives them,' comes from one mother. ... Another applicant declares that 'It ain't worth while to tell lies about a bit of porridge,' and then again emerges the truth, which is reached automatically through the withdrawal of the temptation to lie.[48]

This approach to child nourishment may be contrasted with the more generous approach of some other Care Committees and also that of Bradford Council. 'The food at the Bradford Centre,' said Margaret McMillan in 1911, 'is carefully selected. ... It is varied; not dull or *stupid feeding* [*sic*]. The same dinner is not put before a child twice in 17 days.'[49]

While LCC members publicly praised the work of the Care Committees, privately they were often critical, especially of the volunteers. In a memo of 1911, the Education Officer Robert Blair wrote:

> What I have seen of care committees has led me to think that we must have a very considerable number of useless committees ... [The committees are]

quite incapable of doing investigating work in connection with case papers. Such enquiry work demands qualities of persistency and of sacrifice which the average voluntary worker is hardly prepared to make.

'The average voluntary worker, I am afraid,' he added, 'cares more for actual committee meetings than for enquiry work. Much of the important work of deciding as to cases to be fed and of assessing cost in respect of medical treatment is to a considerable extent left undone … with the resulting possibility of one child in a family being fed and another one being excluded from meals or vice versa.' Blair was keen to curb the power and extent of the Care Committees: 'I can conceive the present system of care committees being reduced to a skeleton and that in the skeleton form each school would have one representative'. He proposed therefore that the first level of organisation should not be the School Care Committee, but an area committee.[50]

But Blair *needed* the voluntary workers – as a way of providing an essential function at low cost. As it was, the allocation of expenditure on medical inspection and meals in 1912–13 was taking up 2.9 per cent of the overall expenditure on elementary education (compared with 3 per cent on books and apparatus and 57.1 per cent on teachers' salaries).[51] Right up to the First World War, the children of many London families were so poor that they were unable to make good use of their education at school without extra feeding and help with clothes and boots. In *Round About a Pound a Week* (1913), a study of working-class life in Lambeth, south London, Maud Pember Reeves wrote that many families, even those with a wage coming in, were undernourished. The 'tiny amounts of tea, dripping, butter, jam, sugar and greens,' she said, 'may be regarded rather in the light of condiments than of food.' Bread was their chief food:

> It is cheap … it comes into the house ready cooked; it is always at hand, and needs no plate or spoon. Spread with a scraping of butter, jam or margarine, according to the length of purse of the mother, they never tire of it as long as they are in their ordinary state of health…. It makes the sole article in the menu for two meals a day.[52]

Numbers of working-class families were unable to cook hot meals because they could not afford basic kitchen equipment or fuel; it was common for families without an oven to send food on Sundays to the neighbouring bakehouse.[53]

Remedy – not relief

'School meals are (by law) an educational measure; not a system of poor relief,' insisted the *School Child*. The success of a Care Committee, it argued, lay in 'removing a child from the feeding list, not by refusing a meal to a

MENU No. 13

Meat Pudding.
Potatoes.
Bread.

INGREDIENTS.					COST.	
					s.	d.
18	lbs. ox-cheek without bone at 3d.			=	4	6
5	qts. water				—	
4	lbs. onions				0	2
6	lbs. haricot beans at 2d. ...			=	1	0
14	lbs. flour at 1½d.			=	1	9
3½	lbs. suet at 6d.			=	1	9
36	lbs. potatoes				1	6
5	loaves at 2½d.			=	1	1½
	Seasoning (pepper, salt)				0	0½
					11	9

METHOD—

Steep the beans in cold water. Stew the meat for two hours on the day before it is required. Turn into an earthenware vessel, and allow it to cool. Remove fat; chop the suet, mix with the flour, add salt and baking powder. Mix to a stiff dough with cold water. Roll out the crust, line a greased pudding tin with it. Put in the meat, chopped onions and seasoning. Cover the meat with the liquor in which the ox-cheek has been stewed. Put on the cover of paste, allow room for pudding to rise. Fix on lid. Plunge into boiling water and cook for two hours, or steam for two and a half hours. The haricot beans should be placed in hot water and boiled for two hours.

Plate 8 One of the menus recommended for school dinners by Margaret Frere. They were intended for 100 children, at an average total cost of 10s. 10d., or 1.3 of a penny per head. Taken from Children's Care Committees (1909).

necessitous child but by removing the causes which make it necessitous,' which could only be done by a thorough knowledge of the family and home circumstances and the dispensing of useful advice and help.[54] This was the very policy that had underpinned Miss Frere's first Care Committee in the late 1890s. Meals were only to be provided when children were actually in attendance at school, not at weekends or during holidays, even though they were 'the worst times at home for the children'. Every case was to be considered at least once a month and enquiries were to be carried out very carefully. Volunteers were told repeatedly that the 'responsibility of feeding or not feeding is on the Care Committee alone. It is their business to discover why the child arrives at school underfed and if possible remove the cause.'[55] For each pupil, the committee was instructed to:

> enter all necessary particulars into a book, such as the total family income, the wages of all earning money in the house, the father, the mother and any older children going out to work; also any relief received from Charitable Societies or [Poor Law] Guardians; the total regular outgoings, rent, fares, insurance, clubs, and the number for whom the income has to provide.[56]

Feeding children at school was only a short-term measure, argued Douglas Pepler. It was far better, he said, to attack poverty at its roots – and in this way to *prevent* destitution.[57] Miss Morton took the view that there were few families for which no remedy at all could be found. In one very bad case, for example:

> The head teacher reported, with regard to a child who came to her school, that she was in despair; the child was eleven years old and was mentally defective, she came to school without food, her clothes were always dirty

and when given more they were found to be pawned. There seemed to be an income, and on enquiry it was found that there was a regular income of 28/- [that is, shillings] a week. There was an older girl of sixteen, who had got into trouble, and four other children. The mother had been twice in prison for neglect, and the home was found to be very dirty.

A Care Committee took up the case and apparently persuaded the woman to take an interest in her children. Within two months, claimed Miss Morton, the child went regularly to school, 'bringing 2d a day for dinner, the general home conditions were changed, and now the whole family, with three mentally deficient children, are much brighter, and the woman seems to have given up drink.'[58]

J.T. Mustard, the chairman of the North and Central Hackney Association of Care Committees, objected to the fact that the number of children being fed was going up, while the number of people who were unemployed was going down. He asked if this was the result of 'lax investigation', or simply that 'we are rearing a class in our cities who do not mean to do anything to provide for their offspring?' A key factor, in his view, was the increase in the number of women in the labour market: 'It would be good for the community, the nation and the married women themselves, if a married woman and women living in the married state were taken off the labour market.' Wherever there were large numbers of necessitous children, he added, there were 'women at work and men loafing around'.[59]

In any case, the Education (Provision of Meals) Act of 1906 had stipulated that parents should be charged for meals if they could possibly afford to pay for them, whether the cost was paid from voluntary contributions or from the rates. On 31 March 1908 the LCC had fixed the amount to be charged to the parent as 1d for each breakfast and 1½d for each dinner. At the same time, it laid down careful regulations to guide Care Committees in determining whether the cost of the food ought to be recovered from the parent, and in what cases proceedings should be taken. These regulations allowed an appeal from the first decision of the Children's Care Committee, so that no proceedings would be taken for payment until the parent had been given at least seven days to pay.[60] This policy was developed in the context of widespread concern that families were becoming dependent on the state (which was the great worry of the Charity Organisation Society). Within the labour movement, only the radical Social Democratic Federation supported the idea of state maintenance for children: the Labour Party was prepared to accept that in the case of feeding schoolchildren, negligent but not impoverished parents should be pursued for the cost of meals. Under socialism, avowed

Ramsay MacDonald, 'the economic and moral unit of government will undoubtedly be the family, and the mother's and children's right to maintenance will be honoured by the family, not by the State.'[61]

The health needs of children at school

It was not long before Care Committees started to take a role in the health care of children in school, to support the operation of the newly-developing school medical service. This area of activity was quickly to become a central feature of their work that was seen to be at least as important as help with school dinners. The undernutrition of schoolchildren was only one of many social concerns in this period: serious problems of ill health and physique, it was feared, were being produced in the working classes by high levels of poverty. In 1885 James Cantlie published *Degeneracy amongst Londoners*, which argued that a progressive deterioration was occurring among town dwellers. By the third generation, he said, the average male could achieve, at maturity, only five feet and one inch: 'His aspect is pale, waxy: he is very narrow between the eyes, and with a decided squint.'[62] These anxieties seemed to be confirmed by the Boer War of 1899–1902, when the Inspector-General of Army Recruiting reported that 37.6 per cent of volunteers had been found unfit for service or had subsequently been invalided out. It was feared that Britain's imperial greatness was under threat from the poor physique of the working class.[63] In 1904, the Report of the Inter-Departmental Committee on Physical Deterioration revealed in its evidence the existence of a marked degree of physical unfitness, if not of deterioration. In relation to the health of schoolchildren, it argued that there was need for a much more complete system of medical inspection in schools than had so far been attempted.[64] In addition, there was the risk of infection, which was seen by many to be increased by universal attendance at school.[65]

The government responded in 1907 by passing the Education (Administrative Provisions) Act, which provided for the medical inspection of children at school. A Medical Department was set up at the Board of Education, with Sir George Newman as the first Chief Medical Officer (CMO). 'It came more and more to be recognized,' wrote Newman in his Annual Report for 1908, 'that a close and vital connection exists between the physical condition of the normal child and the whole process of its education.'[66] However, inspection alone was not enough: parents could not afford medical treatment and hospitals could not take on the extra work. To meet this need, Bradford opened the first school clinics in 1908. In the same year, with financial support from a philanthropist and the 'reluctant sanction'

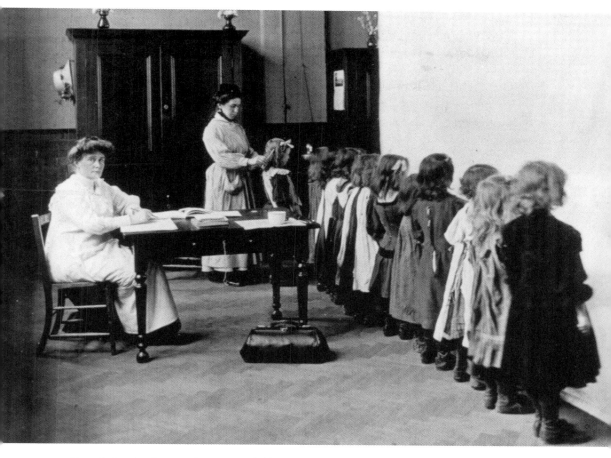

Plate 9 *A school nurse, known to children as 'Nitty Norah', checks heads for lice at a London school in 1911. She is watched by a Care Worker. LMA, 22.51,81/10182*

of the LCC, Margaret McMillan set up the first school clinic in London at the Infants' School at Bow; though supported by the local Children's Care Committee, it was not a success. She then opened a new one, which flourished, to serve a group of schools in Deptford.[67] (By 1910 there were 14 school clinics in Britain and by 1914 most LEAs provided some medical treatment.[68])

The LCC set up a special sub committee in July 1907 to consider the question of developing a system of health care in schools.[69] In fact, though, a basic system had already been in place for some years. In 1890 the London School Board became the first school board to appoint its own medical officer; although he was part time and his primary duty was to examine applicants for teaching posts, he also co-ordinated the efforts of London Medical Officers of Health to combat the spread of infectious disease in schools. He was replaced in 1901 on a full-time basis by Dr James Kerr (who had previously been appointed as the first full-time school medical officer by the School Board of Bradford in 1893). The School Medical Service for the metropolis then expanded rapidly: in 1905 it employed 2 full-time doctors, 23 part-time doctors and 12 nurses.[70]

Nurses had already been employed for a number of years to carry out inspections in LCC schools – their duties were reflected in the nicknames of 'ringworm nurses' and 'nit nurses'. There were regular visits by nurses to inspect for cleanliness and general appearance, recalled a resident of the East End: 'To the children she was known as Nitty Norah, with her steel comb and bowl of disinfectant, to combat lice in the hair.' The battle against lice was determined:

> the parents of children with verminous heads were notified by a white card which also gave directions for cleansing. At the end of a week a further examination was made and, if the head was still unclean, the child was made to sit separately in the class and the school attendance officer served an urgent warning (red card) at the home. If at the end of a further week the unclean condition still persisted, the parent was prosecuted for not sending the children in a fit state to school.

By 1905, this system involved the inspection of over 119,000 children, fewer than half of whom had clean heads when they were first examined. Over 500 cases were taken to the point of prosecution.[71]

Nits were an endless problem for families. One man who grew up as a boy in London recalled his mother's daily efforts to defeat this enemy:

> Bedtime, Mum went through my cropped hair with a toothcomb. 'Siddy, you got nits again,' she said wearily, cracking them with her nails, 'you better get a penn'orth o'soft soap tomorrer, an' I'll 'ave another go at 'em. Otherwise, you'll 'ave to go to the bake, an' I won't 'ave the shame of it.'
>
> 'Dirty little sod', cried [my sister] Flo, whose long dark hair never had nits. I screwed round to poke my tongue at her. I did not care anyway, as long as Mum was combing my hair.[72]

In *A Vision for London*, Susan D. Pennybacker gives an account of 'an unusually violent episode' in 1915 when a 'nit nurse' cut off a girl's hair at school. Her mother was so angry that she struck the nurse and was sent before the magistrate. After appearing in court she came to see the nurse and reproached her, crying,

'What do you mean by cutting her hair ... and why didn't you cut it all off? I know why you didn't; it's because you are wrong, I know what the Magistrate said last week in the Police Court I know. Who do you think we are, Germans that you can do as you like with us, I'll see you don't. I'll have you.'

'Shaking her fist at me,' said the nurse, the mother threatened that 'If I thought you were the one who cut the hair I'd do for you.' As the nurse went to shut the door, the woman's fist came through the glass, and she struck the nurse on the head. The mother was fined, though she denied that she had committed this assault.[73]

The special subcommittee set up by the LCC in 1907 found that additional health provision was necessary for the treatment of such afflictions as ear ailments, ringworm, impetigo and favus. Accordingly, the LCC reorganised and expanded its medical work for schoolchildren. Full-time medical assistants superseded part-time school doctors and school treatment centres were set up. In 1910 some 26,000 children were given medical care; by 1912 treatment was given to 73,058 children at 11 hospitals and 17 centres, at an estimated cost of £20,000. By the end of 1914 there were 42 school treatment centres in London, providing for 99,000 children. Cheap tram fares to the centres were allowed by the LCC from 1914 and it was agreed that attendance at a centre should qualify as school attendance.[74]

Care Committee volunteers were brought in to support this massive expansion of health care in schools. As links between home and school, they were uniquely placed to help prevent leakage between the stages of inspection and treatment.[75] In some cases they visited a child's home in order to persuade parents of the need for treatment. They also acted as advocates for the children, frequently criticising delays in treatment, the long distances which the children had to travel in order to get to hospital, and the treatment itself (which was often inadequate). School doctors paid special attention to the children who had been put on the necessitous registers by the Care Committees, who were given access to the notes made at medical inspections.[76]

Many children were found to need spectacles. A voluntary Association for the Supply of Spectacles in London elementary schools was set up, which supplied the money required for glasses on the recommendation of the head-teacher or the Care Committee.[77]

Developing a total concept of child care

Increasingly, Care Committees were taking a role in child welfare that went far beyond the simple provision of school dinners. They helped with boots and clothing, too, putting children and their families in contact with organisations like the Ragged School Union, which gave grants for obtaining boots at half price. They also encouraged them to pay their pennies to school boot clubs.[78] In urgent cases, Care Committees raised the necessary funds themselves. They worked closely with national organisations like the Invalid Children's Aid Association, the Fresh Air Fund and the Children's Country Holiday Fund (CCHF). They pressed the interests of the children and, in the case of the CCHF, helped to select the children for holidays.

They were also involved in the protection of children from cruelty and neglect, by identifying cases and then referring these to the LCC. The LCC in turn referred these children to the National Society for the Prevention of Cruelty to Children (NSPCC), under section 12 of the Children Act of 1908. The NSPCC carried out the actual work of warning parents and then, where necessary, prosecuting them. The contribution of Care Committees was acknowledged in the LCC's Annual Report for 1911, which attributed an improvement in child protection to the combined efforts of the NSPCC and Children's Care Workers.[79] In difficult or doubtful cases the Special Cases Section of the Children's Care (Central) Subcommittee of the Education Committee assisted the Care Committees with advice and guidance.[80]

The duties of care workers were extended to helping children prepare for life after school; this development resulted from the recognition of adolescence in the late nineteenth century, as well as concern about 'the problem of boy (and girl) labour'.[81] Following the Labour Exchange Act of 1909, they co-operated with the Juvenile Advisory Committees of the Board of Trade to direct school-leavers towards certain types of work or further education. Teachers were expected to submit to the Care Committees lists of the children who would be leaving school in three months' time.[82] The Care Committees then arranged a school-leaving conference at which an official of the Board of Trade, the headteacher and a Care Committee volunteer met the parent and child, to advise on suitable employment and possibly an apprenticeship or further education.[83] This service quickly became known as 'after-care'. Planning for the future in this way was taken very seriously by the Care Service, for two key reasons. One reason was that unemployment was widely regarded as one of the 'most serious and urgent' ills affecting the social body.[84] It was recognised that a chief cause of unemployment was the extent to which children were employed in casual and unskilled work on leaving school, because they had not been properly advised. A second reason was that preparation for a child's future employment emphasised the 'remedy' characteristic of Care Committee work – that it did not offer short-term 'relief', but a positive way to prepare for a secure future.

Joining the Public Health Department

When 'the thunderbolt of war fell upon the nation' in August 1914 (as Sir Robert Blair described the start of the First World War[85]), demands for school dinners and other forms of help for children fell dramatically. This was because many families were made better off by regular separation allowances from the army and navy and by greater opportunities to earn a living.[86] The Care Service itself underwent considerable change during the years of war. In the first decade of their existence, Care Committees were attached to the Education Office of the LCC. But just before the start of war, plans were developed at the LCC to divide the Care Committees between the Education Department and the Public Health Department; this would mean that some committees would be under the control of the School Medical Officer (SMO), while others would remain with the Education Officer (EO). Such a strategy, it was argued, would formalise in an administrative way the growing role of Care Committees in school health and might also improve the delivery of care.

Miss Morton was appointed half time in each department from August 1914[87] and at least one of the Assistant Divisional Organisers in each of the 12 divisions was associated with the Public Health Department rather than the Education Department. By 1915–16, each Divisional Organiser was allocated to one of the two departments; seven organisers were based in the Education Office and the remaining five were based in the Public Health Department.[88] A Principal Assistant Organiser was selected to supervise the organisers in each department, working under the overall supervision of Miss Morton. Miss H.G. Nussey, who was recently appointed but 'stands out as especially able',[89] was selected for education; while Miss Lewis, who 'has always shown a special interest in medical work and ability to manage a large staff of assistants,'[90] was selected for public health. At least half of Miss Lewis's time was taken up with tuberculosis (TB), filling children's beds in the sanatoria and arranging follow-up care.[91] Her staff had a heavy load, because they were responsible for the supervision of medical treatment as well as general work; to help them, five special medical officers were appointed to supervise the work of the treatment centres.

The Principal Organiser, Miss Morton, was fully involved in the discussions leading to this new structure, but with little enthusiasm. She was relieved to see the continued unity of Care Committee work, but believed that the two departments 'had different trends. Education care committee work aims at the self dependence of the family. Medical care committee work drifts towards state dependence.' Between them, she said, there was an 'unbridgeable gulf'.[92] There was also a difficult relationship between the two departments, which sometimes became outright hostility.[93]

None the less, the new association with public health was a step forward for the School Care Service. It broadened its sphere of influence and increased its potential to improve the welfare of children at school. It also led to massive growth: the *London County Council Gazette* on 3 August 1914 (just five days before the outbreak of war) listed a large number of new appointments in the service. These included: 2 new Principal Assistant Organisers, 11 new District Organisers, 64 new Assistant Organisers and 29 Women Clerks. Since only seven other appointments overall were made at this time (including five in the London Fire Brigade), this represented a major investment in the Care Service on the part of the LCC. It also represented a distinct and dramatic growth of professional social workers working with children. The Principal Organiser, Miss Morton, was given an increased salary of £950 per year,[94] which may be contrasted with the much lower annual salary of women teachers in London, which was usually between £80 and £200 (less than men).[95]

London's School Care Service was a pioneering development in the provision of education welfare. It operated on three integrated levels – volunteers, organisers and the LCC – and swiftly evolved into a substantial and citywide structure. The Care Committees delivered a range of services, from school dinners to spectacle clubs, which helped many of the poor children of London to make better use of their right to go to school. When Miss Morton died in 1949, an obituary in *The Times* drew attention to the systematic nature of the service, 'which was for long unique and is still unrivalled'.[96] Another key feature of the service was that it was women-led and women-run. 'The work is not easy, and the apathy of the parents is often disheartening,' wrote Lady Craik, in a letter to *The Times* in November 1915. 'But', she added, '*it is real women's work.*' She pleaded for 'the attention of my sisters':

> The work is pressing, the workers few. Won't the women come forward? It is not as exciting as drilling, or signalling, or motor-driving. It does not involve the wearing of uniform (dear, just now, to the heart of woman). But … its value will reach beyond the generation.[97]

Notes

1. 'Report of a Lecture on the Duties of Care-Committees given by Miss Morton', 25 June [1909], Patrick Ivin Private Collection.
2. Signed statement by Mr Henry Gardner, 25 November 1915, Patrick Ivin Private Collection.
3. 'Report of a Lecture on the Duties of Care-Committees given by Miss Morton', 25 June [1909], Patrick Ivin Private Collection.
4. *Hansard*, Third Series, 282, 26 July 1893, pp. 576–81.

5. Signed statement by Mr Henry Gardner, 25 November 1915, Patrick Ivin Private Collection.

6. Signed statement by P. Wallbank, n.d. [1967?], Patrick Ivin Private Collection.

7. John Hurt: 'Feeding the Hungry Schoolchild in the First Half of the Twentieth Century', p. 179.

8. Patricia Hollis: *Ladies Elect: Women in English local government 1865–1914*, pp. 441–2.

9. Pamela Horn: *Children's Work and Welfare, 1780–1880s*, p. 83

10. Ibid., pp. 83–4

11. LCC Education Committee – General Purposes Subcommittee, 'Report (22 March 1961). For members' information only – S.O.', 124. Patrick Ivin Private Collection.

12. Ibid.

13. Ibid.

14. Ibid.

15. Ibid.

16. Quoted in John Hurt: 'Feeding the Hungry Schoolchild in the First Half of the Twentieth Century', p. 178.

17. LCC, Report of the Education Committee for the year 1908–9, Part II: The Provision of Meals for Necessitous Children and the Work of Children's Care Committees, p. 3.

18. LCC Annual Report 1907–8, Education, p. 73.

19. LCC Annual Report 1907–8, Education, pp. 73–4.

20. Rev. W.H.H. Elliott: 'Children's Care Committees', in J.H. Whitehouse (ed.), *Problems of Boy Life*.

21. Signed statement by Mr Henry Gardner, 25 November 1915, Patrick Ivin Private Collection.

22. LCC Annual Report 1907–8, Education, pp. 73–4.

23. Circularised letter, 1907, 'Underfed School Children. Voluntary Effort'. Signed by Rosebery, Avebury, Rothschild and Arthur James Balfour. LMA, FIND.

24. LCC Annual Report 1907–8, Education, p. 72.

25. H. Jennings: *The Private Citizen in Public Social Work*, p. 77.

26. Eileen Lecky: 'Children Then and Now', p. 4, LMA, ILEA S/SB/04/2.

27. Eileen Lecky: 'Children Then and Now', pp. 5–6, LMA, ILEA S/SB/04/2.

28. LCC Annual Report 1913–14, Education, pp. 7–8.

29. LCC Annual Report 1907–8, Education, p. 72.

30. Douglas Pepler: *The Care Committee*, pp. 26–30.

31. 'Report of a Lecture on the Duties of Care-Committees given by Miss Morton', 25 June [1909], Patrick Ivin Private Collection.

32. *The School Child* I(1), February 1910.

33. 'Report of a Lecture on the Duties of Care-Committees given by Miss Morton', 25 June [1909], Patrick Ivin Private Collection.

34. W.F. Houghton, Education Officer, 'Children's Care Work. History, development and functions', 7/58. Patrick Ivin Private Collection.

35. Margaret Frere: *Children's Care Committees*, p. 2.

36. Ibid.

37. LCC Annual Report 1913–14, Education, p. 7.

38. 'Women Servants of the County Council', *The Times*, 29 July 1914.

39. Mentioned in Susan D. Pennybacker: *A Vision for London*, p. 204.

40. Henry Iselin: 'The Story of a Children's Care Committee', p. 62.

41. London County Council Education Committee – General Purposes Subcommittee, 'Report (22.3.1961). For members' information only – S.O.' 124. Patrick Ivin Private Collection.

42. Minutes of meeting of Representatives of Certain Children's Care Committees, held at Education Department of LCC, 8 July 1908. Patrick Ivin Private Collection.

43. 'Report of a Lecture on the Duties of Care-Committees given by Miss Morton', 25 June [1909], Patrick Ivin Private Collection.

44. *The School Child* I(18), September 1911.

45. *The School Child* II(1), December 1911.

46. *The School Child* I(1), February 1910, p. 3.
47. Minutes of meeting of Representatives of Certain Children's Care Committees, held at Education Department of LCC, 8 July 1908. Patrick Ivin Private Collection.
48. Henry Iselin: 'The Story of a Children's Care Committee', p. 43.
49. Margaret McMillan: *The Child and the State*, pp. 41–2.
50. Document of 7 October 1911 in file entitled 'LCC Education Department, Children's Care Work – Reorganization 1914–1919', LMA, LCC/EO/WEL/1/2.
51. LCC Annual Report 1913–14, Education, Diagram B.
52. Maud Pember Reeves: *Round About a Pound a Week*, pp. 103, 97–8.
53. John Hurt: *Elementary Schooling and the Working Classes 1860–1918*, p. 186.
54. 'Where War is Blessed. The chronic poverty of London', in *The School Child and Juvenile Worker* VI(1), January 1916, p. 8.
55. Ibid., p. 8.
56. 'Report of a Lecture on the Duties of Care-Committees given by Miss Morton', 25 June [1909], Patrick Ivin Private Collection.
57. Douglas Pepler: *The Care Committee*, p. 46.
58. 'Report of a Lecture on the Duties of Care-Committees given by Miss Morton', 25 June [1909], Patrick Ivin Private Collection.
59. *The School Child* II(7), June 1912.
60. LCC Annual Report 1907–8, Education, p. 72.
61. John Stewart: 'Ramsay MacDonald, the Labour Party, and Child Welfare, 1900–1914', pp. 125 and 117.
62. *Degeneracy amongst Londoners*, quoted in Gareth Stedman Jones: *Outcast London*, p. 127.
63. See Bernard Harris: *The Health of the Schoolchild*, p. 15 ff.
64. Annual Report for 1908 of the Chief Medical Officer of the Board of Education, p. 8. For an excellent discussion of the infection issue, see Bernard Harris: *The Health of the Schoolchild*, p. 38 ff.
65. Pamela Horn: *Children's Work and Welfare, 1780–1880s*, p. 84.
66. Annual Report for 1908 of the Chief Medical Officer of the Board of Education, p. 6.
67. Margaret McMillan: *The Camp School*, p. 132.
68. Patricia Hollis: *Ladies Elect: Women in English local government 1865–1914*, p. 442.
69. LCC Annual Report 1913, in chapter 'Medical Treatment of School Children'.
70. Bernard Harris: *The Health of the Schoolchild*, pp. 39–40.
71. 'Cleansing of Persons Act, 1897, miscellaneous reports', quoted in Susan D. Pennybacker: *A Vision for London*, p. 202.
72. Syd Foley's recollections, in John Burnett (ed.): *Destiny Obscure*, p. 315.
73. Quoted in Susan D. Pennybacker: *A Vision for London*, p. 206.
74. H. Jennings: *The Private Citizen in Public Social Work*, pp. 84 and 101.
75. LCC Annual Report 1913, in chapter 'Medical Treatment of School Children'.
76. LCC Annual Report 1913–14, Education, p. 7.
77. Leaflet of the Association for the Supply of Spectacles in London Elementary Schools, 1 December 1909. Patrick Ivin Private Collection.
78. 'Report of a Lecture on the Duties of Care-Committees given by Miss Morton', 25 June [1909], Patrick Ivin Private Collection.
79. LCC Annual Report 1911, Education, p. 38.
80. LCC Annual Report 1913–14, Education, p. 7.
81. D.A. Reeder, 'Predicaments of City Children: Late Victorian and Edwardian perspectives on education and urban society', p. 90.
82. Ibid.
83. LCC Minutes of Care Committee Associations, 1910–14, LMA, LCC EO/WEL/1/2.
84. 'South Holborn Apprenticeship and Skilled Employment Committee', pamphlet by the Committee, February 1910. Patrick Ivin Private Collection.
85. LCC Annual Report 1915–19, Education, p. 4.

86. Ibid., p. 11.
87. LCC Education Service Particulars for the year 1914–15.
88. LCC Education Service Particulars for the year 1915–16.
89. Document of 18 May 1914 in file entitled 'LCC Education Department, Children's Care Work – Reorganization 1914–1919', LMA/LCC/EO/WEL/1/2.
90. Ibid.
91. Undated document, LMA/ILEA/5/SB/04/2.
92. Document of 11 May 1915 in file entitled 'LCC Education Department, Children's Care Work – Reorganization 1914–1919', LMA/LCC/EO/WEL/1/2.
93. Baroness Serota to ASW and CM, 16 November 2000.
94. 'Women Servants of the County Council', *The Times*, 29 July 1914.
95. Dina M. Copelman: *London's Women Teachers: Gender, class and feminism, 1870–1930*, p. 76.
96. *The Times*, 17 March 1949.
97. Letter to *The Times*, 2 November 1915.

Chapter 4

BETWEEN THE WARS

*'We need the voluntary worker to be the eyes and
fingers of the public authority … As the circumference
of public authorities is extended the greater becomes
the periphery.'[1]*

THE FIRST WORLD WAR came to an end in 1918. Its brutality had 'obliged
men to … lay plans for a new future,' wrote Robert Blair, in which 'national
education was the master-key to national reconstruction.'[2] One of the mani-
festations of this spirit was the 1918 Education (Fisher) Act, which raised the
school leaving age to 14. It also abolished the half-time system and extended
provision for meals and medical services. These measures directly affected the
work of School Visitors: on the one hand, it meant that more children had to
be made to attend school; but on the other hand, the obstacles they faced
were reduced, especially by the end of the half-time system. Compulsion to
attend school was reinforced by the Education Act of 1921, which empowered
magistrates to send a child to an industrial or approved school if the parents
could not secure the child's attendance. This was a departure from the
Education Act of 1870, according to which the responsibility for a child's
attendance at school rested entirely upon the parents.

The 1920s saw a spirit of postwar boom in London. The British Empire
Exhibition opened at Wembley in 1924 and palatial department stores and
offices were built in the City and the West End. The Bright Young Things of
the leisured classes behaved as outrageously as they could, making it the
decade of the 'Roaring Twenties'. Meanwhile, the LCC pursued an energetic
housing policy, demolishing slums and building new estates for the poor.
Home life was enhanced by the arrival of the wireless – and the British
Broadcasting Company – in the mid-1920s. There were evident improve-
ments in the life of the poor children of London. The barefoot urchins
virtually disappeared from the streets and were replaced by children wearing
boots, with clothes that were less ragged. Comparing some photographs of

Plate 10 *Photographs showing an improvement in poor children's physique in London between 1894 and 1924. Taken from an appendix to the Education Officer's report in the LCC Annual Report for 1925.*

elementary schoolchildren in Bermondsey, F.N. Kay Menzies, the School Medical Officer, observed in an appendix to the Education Officer's report for 1925 that whereas a photograph from 1894 presented 'great inequality in physical conditions, the types ranging from robust to very ill-nourished,' a later photograph from 1924 showed 'a set of boys of average nutrition without any of the inequalities of the former group.'[3]

However, the growing sense of optimism was diminished by the General Strike of 1926, which brought London to a standstill for nine days. It was followed in October 1929 by the crash of the New York Stock Exchange, which produced a severe economic depression and created massive unemployment in Britain. The Medical Officer of Health for Hammersmith found that a number of working-class families, both employed and unemployed, had a very small margin available for food, fuel, clothing and other necessaries after they had paid their rent. The School Medical Officer for London reported that while the proportion of definitely ill-nourished children was only about one in 6,000, the proportion of children with subnormal nutrition was as high as 4.8 per cent in 1931 and 4.9 in 1932.[4]

In 1934, Labour became dominant on the LCC, which had previously been controlled by Municipal Reformers (Conservatives). This meant a greater commitment to social welfare for the people of London. By 1935 employment started to increase, but many of the ill effects of the Depression lingered on.

The diminishing prestige of School Visitors

Little change took place in methods of maintaining school attendance in the interwar period. School Visitors were responsible to the Divisional Officers and to the local school attendance subcommittees, which met fortnightly.[5] From week to week, 'attendance slips' were recorded by headteachers and then passed on for examination to the attendance officers (as they were becoming known). In 1918 a conference of attendance officers and headteachers considered attaching the system to schools, giving an officer a school roll or rolls, instead of responsibility for all the children of school age in a district. However it was feared that such a change would increase the number of officers required and the time they would spend in travel,[6] so the service remained based on the area rather than on the school. In 1925 each school attendance officer in London was responsible for approximately 3,000 children, a number that stayed more or less constant throughout the interwar period. The average attendance at elementary schools in London in 1927 was 87.7 per cent, which was typical for the period overall.[7]

Attendance officers continued each year to take a census of school-age children in their district, recording the particulars at the Divisional Offices.

They were also involved in the care and protection of children under the Children and Young Persons Act of 1933 and reported to their Divisional Officer any child whose welfare caused concern. They monitored the employment of children and young persons and children taking part in entertainments. Under the Act, the jurisdiction of the juvenile courts was extended to boys and girls up to the age of 17; responsibility for this court work was given to the Special Officers of the school inquiry service. In London, a special officer was selected for this work in each of the 12 divisions of London. However, this sometimes brought attendance officers into conflict with probation officers who also had duties under the Act; it was therefore decided in 1936 that only probation officers should do this work. [8]

Before the First World War, the achievements of School Visitors were regularly discussed in the annual reports of the Education Officer and other LCC education documents. But after the war, they received little more than a summary mention – and they were omitted altogether from Robert Blair's account of the services that had improved 'the physical character and condition of the children in the elementary schools'. These services, he noted in *The Times* in March 1924, included 'the untiring efforts of teachers, doctors, nurses and care committee organisers' – but not, apparently, the efforts of the School Visitor....This omission may have been the result of the Visitor's low social and professional status. It may also have reflected the nature of his job: for while Care Committee volunteers were 'the social agents of the Education Authority',[9] the School Visitors were often perceived as the 'police' agents. Moreover, Care Committees were school-based and had the opportunity for close relationships with teaching staff and officials; attendance officers, on the other hand, were district-based and more firmly rooted in the community.

Elsewhere in Britain, questions were being asked about the value of school attendance officers. In Merionethshire in Wales, the Medical Department set up a subcommittee to consider 'the doing away with School Attendance Officers'.[10] A strong letter was sent to the Board of Education, complaining about a 'waste of money' on the officers; 'we spent over £1000 a year and they are absolutely useless *in my opinion* [sic]', concluded the letter.[11] Following this letter, the Board carried out some investigations and discovered that School Visitors had been dispensed with in Norfolk, one district in Cornwall and one district of Coventry.[12] School attendance officers set about trying to elevate their professional status. Discussions began about the advantage of a national qualification for the service and a motion was put to the 1936 conference that the National Executive should establish an appropriate examination. It was defeated by the argument that qualification was unnecessary and only experience was needed for the job, but the idea of

Figure 4.1 *Officers of the Council connected with Care Committee work in the 1920s*

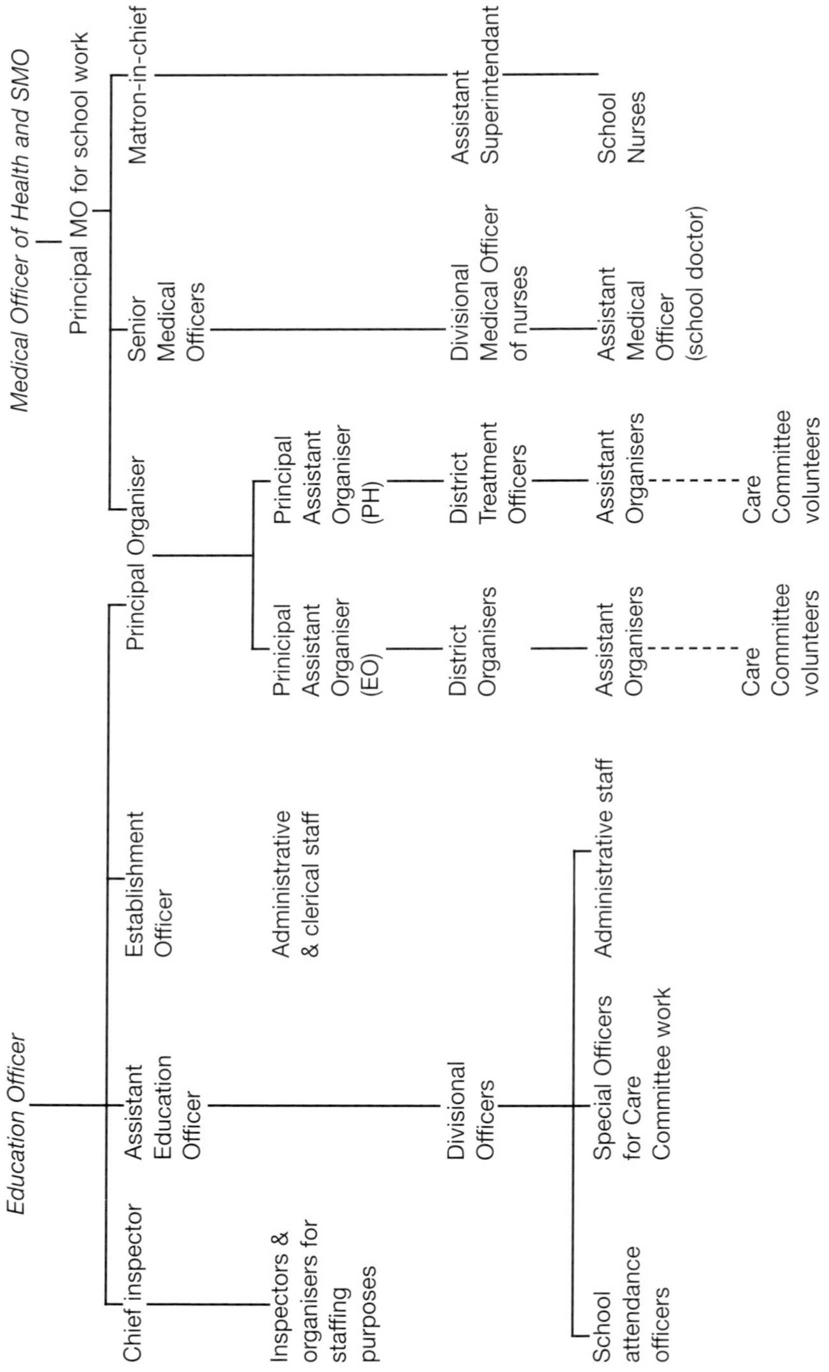

Education Officer

Medical Officer of Health and SMO

Chief inspector

Assistant Education Officer

Establishment Officer

Principal Organiser

Principal MO for school work

Senior Medical Officers

Matron-in-chief

Inspectors & organisers for staffing purposes

Administrative & clerical staff

Principal Assistant Organiser (EO)

Prinicipal Assistant Organiser (PH)

Divisional Officers

District Organisers

District Treatment Officers

Divisional Medical Officer of nurses

Assistant Superintendant

Special Officers for Care Committee work

Administrative staff

Assistant Organisers

Assistant Organisers

Assistant Medical Officer (school doctor)

School attendance officers

Care Committee volunteers

Care Committee volunteers

School Nurses

professionalising the role of the school attendance officer had taken hold. The duties of his role, observed a *Handbook for School Attendance Officers* in 1939,

> call for a different and superior type of officer than were the pioneers of the School Attendance Service. The better educated parent of to-day has a reasonable expectation that the School Attendance Officer who visits his home in regard to the education of children should have received an education of higher merit than the three R's.
>
> It is no reflection upon men who have rendered yeoman service and are nearing the time of retirement to say that something has already been done in seeking to improve the status of men appointed to the position of School Attendance Officer, but finality has not yet been reached.[13]

The growing importance of Care Committees

As school attendance officers moved into the more peripheral corridors of LCC activity, the Care Committees grew in numbers and in strength; Figure 4.1 shows an organisational chart of the education service, in which the role of the Care Service is far more central than that of the attendance officers. In his 1925 Annual Report, the Education Officer G.H. Gater reported that there were 928 Care Committees and that only six out of the 1063 London schools did not have a committee (some committees were shared by more than one school). The number of volunteers had reached 5,588.[14] Given a total of 665,000 pupils in elementary schools,[15] this meant that on average there was one voluntary member to 119 children. But although the number of voluntary workers was high, they were not distributed evenly through London and 'many more voluntary workers are needed, particularly in the poorer districts';[16] this shortage in the poorer districts was hard to avoid, since the volunteers were nearly always well off and lived in the more prosperous parts of London. This picture, regarding numbers and distribution, remained more or less constant over the interwar period. The qualifications of the Care Committee volunteers, said Gater in 1925, were 'knowledge, experience and sympathy'.[17] Their lack of training or even experience in social work care may be contrasted with the professional backgrounds of the organisers. In 1928–9, for example, two out of the 12 District Organisers (Miss A. Corcos and Miss Olive Cram) had BA degrees from the University of London (see Table 4.1); those without specific qualifications had previously obtained social work experience by working for organisations like the Charity Organisation Society, and they all regarded themselves as educated professionals.

There was considerable discussion at this time about the role of the voluntary sector in British society. In *The New Philanthropy. A study in the relations between the statutory and voluntary social services* (1934), Elizabeth Macadam commented that the role of voluntary associations was 'one of the most powerful safeguards which this nation possesses against the interference with freedom and personal liberty that has overtaken other lands.'[18] In other words, it would resist the encroachment of socialism, which was seen by the ruling classes to lurk behind the many strikes and hunger marches of the period. The threat of socialism had been given a new urgency by the Russian Revolution in 1917 and the spread of Bolshevism.

The tradition of voluntary action persisted but was changing its character, said Miss Macadam, as a way of adapting itself 'almost imperceptibly' to changed conditions. An important aspect of this change in character was the newly-developing partnership between the voluntary sector and the state, which took several forms. In one form, individual work supplemented official action, as in the case of 'public assistance, after care, school care, maternity and infant welfare'. In an article published in *Public Administration* in 1934, Miss Macadam quoted Lord Passfield as saying: 'We need the voluntary worker to be the eyes and fingers of the public authority.... As the circumference of public authorities is extended the greater becomes the periphery.'[19]

The business of recruiting 'a sufficient number of suitable volunteers ... has gradually become not more difficult but, if anything, progressively easier,' observed Sir Hubert Llewellyn Smith. 'The voluntary workers themselves,' he added, 'have in fact proved the best recruiting agents.'[20] In 1926, *The Times* published a letter of appeal by Lady Cecilie Goff, which led to increased membership of Care Committees in Shoreditch. Recruitment films were made by the LCC, such as a silent film entitled *The Children of London*, which has been found by the authors of this book; it shows the work of the Care Service in some detail and is a moving account of the deprivation and need suffered by the poor children of London. Recruitment was key to the functioning of the Care Committees, since there was 'considerable annual wastage'[21] from people leaving the service; this was inevitable in a situation where the volunteers were not actually employed – they were not bound by a contract or even the need to earn an income. Peggy Jay was one of the new recruits of the 1930s. Her background was typical of Care Committee members: upper middle class, raised in a world of nannies and servants in 'an enormous redbrick house' in one of the best neighbourhoods of Hampstead, and very well educated. Early in 1934, she went to see Herbert Morrison, the leader of the London County Council (which had been taken over by Labour in the same year), to ask if she could serve on a Public Assistance Committee. He realised at once, she recalled later in her autobiography, 'that my sheltered background in no way qualified me to understand or identify with the problems of family poverty.' He suggested instead that she broaden her experience by joining the LCC School Care Committee organisation (in which her father-in-law, Aubrey Hastings Jay, had taken a great interest as Chairman of the LCC Education Committee). She agreed, starting a routine that took her away from her home in the salubrious district of Sussex Gardens in Paddington, to the rundown district of London's Kings Cross: 'And so, based in an office in the Pentonville Road, I went visiting families, gradually gaining an insight into their needs and problems, which I reported at the children's school medical inspections.' She was appalled by the conditions in which families were forced to live:

> The dreary housing, the institutional prison-like, neglected buildings struck horror into my heart and mind. I remember standing in a public telephone box ringing [my husband] Douglas, the tears pouring down my face as I told him it just wasn't possible for people to live like this and that something would have to be done about it.

'This exposure to the appalling inner city conditions in the mid-Thirties,' she wrote later, 'gave my commitment to the Labour Party a determined swing into practical activity.... I now threw my energies into the battle against poverty.'[22]

Peggy Jay had been brought up to assume that in addition to raising a family she would contribute to society through voluntary work. 'It simply never occurred to me,' she wrote years later, 'that I should do anything but voluntary work. No one during all my childhood had ever made a point of mentioning that someone had to *earn* what was consumed.' Her husband 'continued to pay the bills while I undertook increasing amounts of voluntary work', which put a tremendous strain on her marriage, 'with disastrous results'. These difficulties reflected the tide of social change that was affecting middle-class families in Britain in the 1930s. Servants had become more difficult to find and also more expensive, which made it problematic – and sometimes impossible – for women to do 'good works'. This was a new kind of obstacle to the recruitment of Care Committee volunteers, commented Sir Hubert Llewellyn Smith, who referred to the 'almost total disappearance of a leisured class in some of the industrial areas'. The pool of women available for voluntary service was further eroded, said Sir Hubert, by the 'increasing degree to which women (who have always formed the largest element among voluntary social workers) are now pursuing professional or industrial careers of their own', who consequently 'have less leisure for voluntary service.'[23] In the past, it had been unusual for middle-class women to work for pay. But

Table 4.1 *Children's Care Work: Districts and Offices of District Organisers, 1928–9*

Division		District	District Organiser
1	EO	Chelsea Fulham, E. Fulham, W. Hammersmith, N. Hammersmith, S. Kensington, N. & S.	Miss E.M.S. Paddon
2	SMO	St Marylebone Paddington, N. & S. Abbey, Westminster St Georges's, Westminster	Miss D. Whitmore
3	EO	Hampstead Holborn St Pancras, N. St Pancras, S. E. St Pancras, S. W.	Miss H. Bell
4	EO	Finsbury Islington, E., N., S. & W.	Miss F.A. Rackstraw
5	SMO	Hackney, N., S. & Central Stoke Newington Shoreditch	Miss K. Marriott
6	SMO	City Of London Limehouse Mile End Whitechapel And St George's	Miss C.M. Joseph
7	EO	Bethnal Green, N.E. Bethnal Green, S.W Bow And Bromley Poplar, S.	Miss A. Corcos, BA (Lond.)
8	SMO	Greenwich Lewisham, E. Lewisham, W. Woolwich, E. Woolwich, W.	Miss E.E. Faulkner
9	EO	Camberwell, N. Camberwell, N. W. Deptford Dulwich Peckham	Miss F.G. Burton
10	EO	Bermondsey, W. Rotherhithe Southwark, Central Southwark, N. Southwark, S. E.	Miss E.B.C. Taylor
11	SMO	Brixton Kennington Lambeth, N. Norwood	Miss O.W. Cram BA (Lond.)
12	EO	Balham And Tooting Battersea, N. Battersea, S. Clapham Putney Streatham Wandsworth, Central	Miss E. Thomas

Note: Those marked 'EO.' are under the Education Officer, and those marked 'SMO.' are under the School Medical Officer. Miss T.M. Morton is the principal Organiser supervising all the offices. Miss H.G. Nussey and Miss D.M. Deverell are Prinicipal Assistant Organisers in the Education Officer's and Public Health Departments respectively and are not attached to any particular district.

Source: LMA 22.06, LCC 1928–9

now, women's lives were changing rapidly: the Sex Disqualification Removal Act of 1919 had made women eligible for any profession and for the holding of any civil or judicial post. And by 1928, women had won the right to vote on an equal basis with men.

This increase in working and professional women was reflected in the growth of salaried members of the Care Service. 'The changes which eliminated, or at any rate greatly reduced the ranks of the leisured middle-class women available for public work,' observed Mary Stocks, 'at the same time helped to provide salaried jobs for their great neices.' The salaried service of non-statutory bodies like the Care Service, she added, was starting to grow into a 'vast great army'. This growth, she explained,

> has been compelled by the decline of middle-class leisure, and assisted by the readiness of statutory authorities to integrate their work with that of non-statutory bodies – which almost invariably involves the grant of public money for social work which the statutory authority chooses to contract out as the L.C.C. contracted out the feeding of necessitous schoolchildren to the Care Committees in 1906.[24]

Miss Morton was assisted in her work as Principal Organiser by Miss Helen G. Nussey, the Assistant Organiser in the Education Officer's Department, and by Miss D.M. Deverell, who had by now taken over from Miss Lewis as the Assistant Organiser in the Public Health Department. Seven of the 12 Districts were run by organisers under the Education Officer, while five were under the School Medical Officer (see Table 4.1).[25] When Miss Morton retired in 1930 (after which she continued to be a counsellor to social workers and gave time to other bodies concerned with the training of social workers, such as the Young Women's Christian Association (YWCA) and King's College London),[26] Miss Nussey became the Principal Organiser and remained in this post until retiring herself in 1940. Like Miss Morton, she was unmarried and had obtained considerable experience in voluntary work before joining the Care Service: she was the first almoner at Westminster Hospital and then became involved in slum clearance. She was the last surviving granddaughter of John Nussey, physician to George IV, William IV, Queen Victoria and Prince Albert.

The Local Associations continued to function as before. The role of secretaries and accounting officers was taken by the Divisional Officers, whose responsibilities included the work of school attendance officers. The Divisional Officers were all men[27] – almost the sole male presence in the very female structure of the Care Committees. The 12 District Organisers coordinated the work of the volunteers; Peggy Jay has recalled that meetings with her District Organiser at the Pentonville office were formal and businesslike.[28] The work of volunteers was largely the same as before: they advised families on how to obtain medical treatment and assessed charges to parents for meals, medical care and spectacles. They also assessed charges to parents for the maintenance of children in open-air residential schools, when this was recommended. Where appropriate they referred children to Child Guidance Clinics, which were set up between the wars for children who seemed 'difficult, nervous or anti-social'; treatment was provided by medical psychologists and 'social experts'.[29]

The duties of the Care Service became more difficult once a start had been made in the 1930s on the implementations of the 1926 Hadow Report, which had recommended a reorganisation of schools so that all children were trans-

Plate 11 *A school-leaving conference in the 1930s, which was known as 'After-Care' and organised by the Care Service. Here, a Care Committee volunteer (far right), the head teacher and another teacher, an official of the Board of Trade, and the vicar, meet with a school child and parent to advise on suitable employment or further education. LMA, 22.5, B5718*

ferred to senior schools at the age of 11. This required a new way of doing things for Care Committee workers, who had previously been closely connected with the individual school to which all the members of one family went. They now had to consider how they could retain the ideal of using the same visitor for all the children in each family and yet preserve the link between school and home. Discussions were held about grouping or making special arrangements with the Care Committees of other schools, following all the children of one family through their school career.

Preparing children for life after school

The Care Service became increasingly involved in the work of after-care, helping young people to prepare for life after school. 'Knowing that it would not be long before you were leaving school and working alongside people like your mum and dad,' said one resident of London's East End, 'life took on a new meaning. For months before leaving school you had to be thinking of what job you could get, and childish games began to get less interesting. I was waiting for my first long trousers and stopped playing in the street so much.'[30] From 1914, suitable volunteers were specifically recruited to the Care Committees to deal with the question of juvenile employment. After the young people had been placed in a job, a 'supervisor' was appointed by the Care Committee wherever possible, to keep in touch with them and to encourage their attendance at an evening institute. Supervision was continued until the age of 17 and supervisors were asked to submit reports twice a year for each young person. However, the fact that in many cases, children had found work already (as well, possibly, as a lack of enthusiasm by children's families), led to underuse of the service by nearly half of the eligible children. Of the 17,051 children for whom school-leaving forms were forwarded 'for action', said Miss Nussey in a report in the early 1930s, 8,824 attended an after-care conference.[31]

Miss Nussey pointed out in this report that it was 'not easy for the immature girl or boy of fourteen on the point of leaving school to choose an occupation'; she recommended that the Committees 'steer them widely' and help them to take full advantage of existing facilities for employment, continued education and recreation. She provided some case studies of after-care work, such as the following account of a boy called 'Tom' (not his real name):

When the Care Committee worker had delivered the invitation to Tom's parents, she had found him with his mind made up. He was going to sea, or on the railway. His mother would not agree to the first because she did not want him to go away from home. But she did want him to have a regular job … The Care Committee worker agreed. She knew that Tom's father, a dock labourer, was getting worn out, and so far her efforts to help him find less strenuous work had failed, but she told Tom and his mother that they would have to think about his learning a trade, for Tom had only reached standard V, so that the railway was also a closed door. Tom didn't say much then, but when he came to the conference he had as good as got a job. He might not stand a chance where 'a bright lad was wanted', but 'a willing lad' he certainly was, and he knew it. The Secretary of the Employment Exchange explained that some firms, good firms, needed such boys, and it was a pity sometimes to take the first thing that offered itself. A promise was made to submit him for a vacancy in the transport department of a firm that had its own siding, and where there would be the opportunity to learn to repair lorries.

All this helped to make Tom feel more at ease, so that when it came to being asked what he was going to do in the evenings, he was quite frank. Evening Institute classes were not for the likes of him. The offer of a free admission card for attendance at a Junior Men's Institute, where he could learn to box, was quite a different proposition.

'Celia' was not so promising a subject as 'Tom':

Celia was plain and she was sullen. Celia had a bad school report. She had been in the retarded class and efforts to get her interested in a club, recommended by the Child Guidance Clinic, were only just beginning to show signs of helping her, and preventing her from becoming 'unclubbable'. Celia wanted to leave school; she wanted to be a 'sales lady'. After hearing the recommendation of the Child Guidance Clinic, the Committee advised her to take up dressmaking, holding out the hope that perhaps one day she would be able to sell the gowns she had learned to make. Celia was not responsive; for some time in her day-dreams she had been a 'sales lady'. This long-sighted policy in its realism did not appeal to her. The hope is that, if she must learn from her own experience, this will not be at too dear a price. She was given a letter about an open evening at the Exchange, and someone said that she would look her up in a month's time to see how she was getting on. She was strongly urged to continue at her club. Wasn't it good, someone said, that she was getting keen on folk dancing and stood a good change of getting into the netball team.[32]

'Tom' and 'Celia' did not have a very thrilling future ahead of them. However, they had more options than some other children at this time, especially those leaving a residential school or children's home. Most of the girls were placed in domestic service; on leaving school, they were given a suitable outfit of clothing and other equipment that would help them in their new position. The placing of boys was more difficult, unless they wished to be trained for the sea, in which case they were placed on the training ship 'Exmouth'.[33]

One of the stated objectives of after-care was to integrate the elementary school-leaver into 'civilised' society; this was not a matter simply of acquiring knowledge, but also 'culture'. In an essay called 'The Elementary Schools of London', which was appended to Gater's 1925 Annual Report, an LCC District Inspector called P.B. Ballard described the elementary school as a gateway to culture – 'a sensitiveness to higher and nobler things and the acquisition of some of the graces and refinements of civilised life.' Ballard had been a teacher in crowded East End schools and he looked forward to a time when children were given an education commensurate with their ability, rather than their social origins; he had a great enthusiasm for educational psychology and IQ testing, as a means of identifying children with intelligence. He said that 'in some quarters of London, [it was] part of the teacher's work to turn uncouth boys and girls, grimy and inarticulate, into decent members of society, with some small measure of grace of speech and charm of manner.' The model for this instruction, he said, was the public school: 'The elementary schools are in fact groping their way towards a broader and more human culture. They are trying to secure what the great public schools and the universities have always tried to secure.' [34] This aim was well supported by Care Committee volunteers, who typically sent their own children to public schools and lived in a world that regarded itself as 'civilised'. They hoped to set an example to elementary schoolchildren in their visits to families and by taking a role in the provision of school meals – at which 'proper' manners were taught and expected. A difference was perceived between 'us' (education officials, teachers and care committee workers) and 'them' (working-class families). 'Ordinary habits of health which are so natural to *us* that *we* have ceased to think about them,' observed Robert Blair in 1921, 'are in many working-class homes real virtues, hardly acquired (emphasis added).'[35]

School Visitors also played a role in this process, by making sure that children went to school in the first place. This was acknowledged in 1935 by the Education Officer, E.M. Rich, in a retrospective account of the achievements of the London School Board. 'They found wide areas of London hardly, as yet, touched by a civilising influence,' he said, 'and left them civilised. They encountered widespread hostility to compulsory school attendance, and, often with little enough help from the magistrates, forged a system to enforce it.'[36]

Meals and health care at school

Early in 1922, the LCC instructed the Care Committees not to give school meals in out-relief cases, in accordance with newly-issued national guidelines. A little later, the Board of Education restricted the amount of expenditure on meals which might qualify for grant support, so the LCC issued more stringent feeding regulations. In spite of discontent on the part of some of the voluntary workers, 'who felt that the probable physical benefit to the children outweighed all other considerations', holiday feeding was discontinued and meals were restricted to either breakfasts or dinners. The burden of carrying out these changes and interpreting them to disheartened parents fell onto the Care Committee volunteers, but 'they neither disregarded the new instructions nor gave up their work'. A special meeting of workers was held, where LCC officials explained the reasons for the change in policy. The number of children receiving dinners in London fell from 22,000 at the beginning of the year to little more than 8,000 at the end of it – a drop of 14,000.[37]

Overall, however, people in interwar Britain were eating better than ever before. Comparing the average of the years 1909–13 with 1934, John Boyd Orr and David Lubbock, two nutrition experts, observed in 1940 that, 'the consumption of cheese, eggs, butter, vegetables and fruit increased by 43, 46, 57, 64 and 88 per cent respectively and the consumption of fat by 25 per cent.'[38] The development of the food industry simplified shopping: the family firm of Sainsbury grew from 123 branches in 1919 to 244 in 1939. An increasing variety of foods was available, including prepared foods and a variety of chocolates and sweets wrapped in individual packages. 'Never before in our history,' commented Barbara Drake in a Fabian Tract entitled *Starvation in the Midst of Plenty* (1933), 'have we been better supplied with so rich a variety, or such abundance, of foodstuffs.' Yet, she added, 'in spite of this, thousands of our children are known to be living on diets which do not even provide the minimum conditions of health and growth.'[39] According to Orr in *Food, Health and Income. A Survey of Adequacy of Diet in Relation to Income* (1936), 50 per cent of the nation were underfed. Many undernourished children in London were either not identified as being in need of supplementary nutrition, or were not allocated any extra food. In 1933, a medical examination carried out in West London revealed that no fewer than 33 out of 53 children belonging to 21 unemployed families showed some sign of malnutrition. But of this number, only four were receiving extra nourishment at school.[40]

By 1937–8, school dinners were being supplied wherever possible from central kitchens. Rich, the Education Officer, reported that 6,791 children in London were provided with free dinners, while 2,437 children paid for meals.[41] The LCC was obliged by law to charge parents full or part cost, according to their means: 'Only when a parent, for reasons other than his own default, is unable to pay anything are meals given free.'[42] As well as meals, a daily average of about 27,733 children in elementary schools were supplied with free milk. Milk distribution was started in the holidays, too, and 37 centres were opened in schools; in the Christmas holidays at the end of 1937, the daily average attendance of children for milk was 7,410, of whom 7,297 received it free. [43] Children were also given cod liver oil and malt. One pupil in the East End recalled later that, 'I loved the malt we all got given every day, but I didn't like the cod liver oil so much. Do you know, we all had our spoon of malt off the same spoon!' Another pupil said that, 'The only thing I liked about school, the *only* thing, was the malt. I couldn't get enough of that, but I could get more than enough of school.'[44]

Now that the Care Service was operating under the aegis of both the education officer and the SMO, it was well placed to take a key role in the delivery of health care in schools. Care Committee volunteers were now asked to participate in the school medical examination. By so doing, they were able to explain to parents any instructions by the doctor, on their home visits, and also to bring back to the school and the medical officer any useful information about the child's home background. These school medicals were seen by one volunteer in this period as the chief component of Care Committee work.[45] By 1939, children were given medical examinations on four occasions: on their entrance to school, at the age of 7, at 11 and in the term before the age of 14 was attained. The final examination was carried out to enable the doctor 'to give an opinion as to the type of work to which the child is physically suited'.[46] In 1938, the LCC reported in triumph that 97.7 per cent of its children were free from nits and pediculi.[47]

Less optimism was felt about the progress of dental treatment. The reports of George Newman, the Chief Medical Officer at the Board of Education, described an appalling state of dental health throughout Britain; and for most of the interwar period there was fewer than one dentist to every 10,000 schoolchildren. 'It is admitted on all sides,' observed Newman bleakly in 1920, 'that the incidence of dental defect among school children is wide-spread, almost universal; and one has the uncomfortable impression that in many parts of the country, owing to the social conditions of the time, the matter grows worse instead of better.' Generally speaking, 'the dental problem among school children has scarcely yet been tackled, even if its magnitude has been generally appreciated.' The borough dentist of Cambridge, for example, reported that among schoolchildren in Cambridge between the ages of 4 and 14,

One child in every four examined had unsaveable permanent teeth, and one child in every nine examined had more than eight decayed permanent teeth. As few as 70 children (2.4 per cent) were found with teeth entirely free from decay.... While the toothbrush ... was nearly unknown, it was found that one child in every three examined had free pus in the mouth, some of which would be swallowed every time food was taken, while other portions of it, thrown out in speaking or singing, would tend to pollute the school atmosphere.[48]

By 1920, 46 dental centres had been set up in London and were working at full pressure, but 40 per cent of the children leaving school still had obvious dental caries. There was some slight improvement in the teeth of older children in some areas, such as the capital, and the CMO quoted one London dentist, Dr Hamer, as saying that although little alteration from year to year had been noted in the teeth of children 'on their entrance to school', there was evidence in 1920 of slight ground being gained each year in the condition of the teeth of the older children. 'This must be due entirely,' claimed Dr Hamer, 'to the results of dental inspection and medical inspection of the children, coupled with the increase of facilities for dental treatment.' Dr Hamer took the view that

dental decay is held by all to be preventable disease, and it is clear that in order to cope with this great mass of trouble, all the aid that can be given by education and the practice of hygiene must be pressed into the service. Not by treatment of the worst cases, but by prevention at the outset will success finally be achieved.[49]

When Gibbon and Bell published their survey of London government in 1939, they claimed that since 1902, when the school medical service started,

the death rate of children at school age has fallen by more than half; diseases which were rife in the schools have disappeared ... Green sickness and severe forms of ophthalmia, such as trachoma, have gone. Blindness, deafness and crippling from tuberculosis have greatly diminished. Of ringworm, which kept more than twenty thousand children away from school in 1901, there are now less than two hundred fresh cases a year in the whole of London; in 1908 when children were first stripped for medical examination, a quarter of them in many districts were found to have verminous bodies; many of the younger doctors of today have never seen a body louse upon a school child. In 1910 it was possible to find more seriously ill-nourished children in a single school than are now to be found in the whole of London.[50]

Certainly there was a massive expansion between 1902 and 1938 of a large army of medical officers and auxiliaries working in the school field in London. However, it is not possible to establish to what extent the improvement in the health of London's schoolchildren was due specifically to medical care in school or to the work of the Care Committee workers. Moreover, the emphasis on measurement diminished the resources available for other forms of medical care.

The strength and survival of the Care Service

There was concern at County Hall (where the LCC moved its central offices in 1922) that there was no clear line of demarcation between the duties of Care Committee workers and the school attendance officers – and that on occasion this led to a duplication of work. In 1932, the Education and Public Health Departments appointed an interdepartmental committee to investigate whether economies could be made in the areas of responsibility that overlapped between the two services.[51] The committee's task was to 'consider whether any economy can be affected in the existing administration of children's care work in London consistent with the safeguarding of the voluntary principle.'[52] The Care Committees' work was scrutinised and witnesses examined; the committee heard, for instance, of cases where a Care Committee kept a child away from school for medical treatment, while the school attendance officer tried to enforce the child's attendance.[53] Some LCC officials argued for a reduction in the work of the Care Committees. They declared that 'very little work of great moment was done' at the Local Associations[54] and that the organisers' work was of little value – 'they are turning windmills'.[55] Too many children were being fed altogether, declared one official, adding that they should be fed by the Public Assistance Committee. In his opinion, Care Committees should only have the power to feed children for two weeks and were in any case acting illegally when spending money on feeding: 'He was of the opinion that the Care Committees do not exist as part of the Local Education Authority and could not be entrusted with the Local Education Authority powers.'[56] Since the Care Service spent approximately £25,000 a year of LCC funds, it is understandable that members of the Council wanted control over the work of the Committees.[57]

The interdepartmental committee produced a report in January 1933, which concluded that there was indeed some overlapping between the functions of the local school attendance subcommittees and those of the local School Care Committees. It recommended that District Organisers should become Senior Assistants within the Divisional Offices of the Education Department, which in effect would absorb the School Care Service into the school attendance service.[58] However, the Principal Organiser, Miss Nussey, refused outright: she declared that 'on no account could she agree'.[59]

In the end, the services carried on as before. In theory, the plan for a merger made good sense, as a way of avoiding the duplication of work; but in practice, it would have been difficult to implement. It would certainly have caused utter dismay among the Care Committee volunteers, who do not appear to have had any sense of a relationship with the School Attendance Service; Peggy Jay has since recalled that at the time she was 'oblivious' of even the existence of attendance officers.[60] In this way, the School Care service preserved its autonomy, even during the interwar years of economic crisis. Indeed, the service reached its apogee – never to be repeated – in the years leading up to the start of the Second World War. By 1939, there was a Care Committee in every school and about 5,000 volunteers overall, supported by 158 District and Assistant Organisers, including Treatment Centre staff. There was also a strong spirit of support in society at large for the aims of the Care Committee workers. 'I don't think there's anything in school life today more important that this business of *making children fit to learn*,'[61] observed an article in *The Listener* in January 1939.

Notes

1. Elizabeth Macadam, 'The Relations between the Statutory and Voluntary Social Services', *Public Administration* 12(3), July 1934, pp. 305–10.
2. LCC Annual Report 1915–19, Education, pp. 11–12.
3. Appendix II, Memorandum by School Medical Officer, LCC Annual Report 1925, Vol IV, Education, p. 40.
4. 'Food and Health; The physiological minimum', *The Lancet*, 18 March 1933.
5. Bedford Report, p. B.3.
6. LCC Annual Report 1920, Education, p. 16.
7. LCC Annual Report 1929, Education, p. 5.
8. Report of the Departmental Committee on Social Services in Courts of Summary Jurisdiction, Cmd 5122 para 71. HMSO 1936.
9. Hilda Jennings: *The Private Citizen in Public Social Work*, p. 187.
10. Medical Department, County of Merioneth, to Medical Department, Board of Education, 4 August 1922, PRO ED, 111/265.
11. Mr Haydn Jones, County of Merioneth, to Mr Roberts, Board of Education, 5 October 1922, PRO ED, 111/265.
12. Board of Education report 1922, PRO ED, 111/265.
13. John Stevenson and J. Henry Capes: *Handbook for School Attendance Officers*, p. 3.
14. LCC Annual Report 1925, Education, p. 19.
15. Ibid., p. 3.
16. Ibid., p. 3.
17. Ibid., pp. 14–15.
18. Elizabeth Macadam: *The New Philanthropy*, p. 304.
19. Elizabeth Macadam, 'The Relations between the Statutory and Voluntary Social Services', *Public Administration* 12(3), July 1934, pp. 305–10.
20. Sir Hubert Llewellyn Smith: *The Borderland between Public and Voluntary Action in the Social Services*, p. 7.

21. Ibid., p. 7.
22. Peggy Jay: *Loves and Labours*, pp. 49–50.
23. Sir Hubert Llewellyn Smith: *The Borderland between Public and Voluntary Action in the Social Services*, p. 7.
24. Mary Stocks: *The Philanthropist in a Changing World*, pp. 16–17.
25. Report of LCC Education Service 1927–28, pp. 10–11, LMA, 22.06.
26. *The Times*, 17 March 1949.
27. Report of LCC Education Service 1928–29, LMA, 22.06.
28. Peggy Jay to ASW, 2 November 2000.
29. Report of LCC Education Service 1938–39, LMA, 22.06.
30. Gilda O'Neill: *My East End*, p. 236.
31. Report by Miss Nussey on Children's Care Committee Work under the LCC, n.d.[early 1930s], Patrick Ivin Private Collection.
32. Ibid.
33. Report of LCC Education Service 1938–39, LMA, 22.06.
34. P.B. Ballard, 'The Elementary Schools of London', Appendix I of LCC Annual Report 1925, Education, p. 38.
35. Robert Blair, 'The Work of the LCC Children's Care Committees', LCC, March 1921.
36. LCC Annual Report 1935, Education, p. 3.
37. Hilda Jennings: *The Private Citizen in Public Social Work*, pp. 136–7.
38. John Boyd Orr and David Lubbock: *Feeding the People in War-Time*, pp. 32–3.
39. Barbara Drake: *Starvation in the Midst of Plenty*, p. 4.
40. Reported in ibid., p. 10.
41. LCC Annual Report 1938, Education, p. 20.
42. LCC Education Service 1938–39, LMA, 22.06.
43. LCC Annual Report 1938, Education, p. 20.
44. Gilda O'Neill: *My East End*, pp. 130–1.
45. Peggy Jay to ASW, 2 November 2000.
46. LCC Education Service 1939, LMA, 22.06, p. 60.
47. Charles Webster, 'The Health of the School Child During the Depression', p. 81.
48. Annual Report of the CMO of the Board of Education, 1920, pp. 90-1.
49. Ibid., p. 90.
50. *A History of the L.C.C., 1889–1939*, quoted in Stuart Maclure: *A History of Education in London 1870–1990*, pp. 101–2.
51. Interdepartmental Committee on Children's Care Services, Minutes for 1 December 1932, LMA, LCC/EO/WEL/5/2.
52. Ibid.
53. Report of the Interdepartmental Committee on Children's Care Work, May 1933, LMA, LCC/EO/WEL, 1/3.
54. Interdepartmental Committee on Children's Care Services, Minutes for 18 January 1933, LMA, LCC/WEL/EO, 5/2.
55. Interdepartmental Committee on Children's Care Services, Minutes for 25 January 1933, LMA, LCC/WEL/EO, 5/2.
56. Interdepartmental Committee on Children's Care Services, Minutes for 18 January 1933, LMA, LCC/WEL/EO, 5/2.
57. Peggy Jay to ASW, 2 November 2000.
58. Interdepartmental Committee on Children's Care Services, Minutes for 25 January 1933, LMA, LCC/WEL/EO, 5/2.
59. Interdepartmental Committee on Children's Care Services, Minutes for 11 January 1933, LMA, LCC/WEL/EO, 5/2.
60. Hilda Jennings: *The Private Citizen in Public Social Work*, p. 207.
61. 'Food Health and Games in the School', *The Listener*, 26 January 1939, p. 216.

Chapter 5

WAR AND EVACUATION

*'In place of a relief measure, tainted with the poor law,
[school meals] became a social service, fused into
school life.'*[1]

PEGGY JAY, a Care Committee volunteer in the 1930s, was elected to the
London County Council in 1938 and served on the Education Committee.
'My major concern,' she said, 'was to see a building programme which would
make the great Victorian schools fit for the twentieth century; to bring light,
warmth, colour and comfort into these draughty caverns. I was horrified that
children should often have to use lavatories that were doorless and roofless,
exposed to cold and rain.'[2] But the imminence of war – and then its outbreak
in September 1939 – shattered any plans for the future. 'Increasingly,' wrote
Mrs Jay years later, 'discussion centred on evacuation, sand bags, air raid
precautions and the use of schools as centres for the homeless.'[3] It was
realised that for the first time in history, the civilian population of London
was at risk of extensive air attacks as well as poison gas, which had been used
on the Western Front in the First World War and then by Italy in Abyssinia
in 1936. In this situation, safety and survival became the priority. Peacetime
reforms had to be put aside, both at the local and the national level. The
Board of Education had to shelve the raising of the school leaving age to 15,
which had been planned for 1939 by the 1936 Education Act.

Evacuating children out of London
Two days before war was declared on 3 September, the evacuation of city
children began. The country was divided into three categories: evacuated
areas, which included London and other large cities; neutral areas; and
receiving areas. In the first category, all schools were closed; in the second,
schools remained open as normal; and in the third, schools were expanded to
take extra pupils. Evacuation was never made compulsory and as many as a

quarter of the children stayed behind. Many of those who went returned swiftly: although almost half of the London school population had been dispersed in the first ten days of September,[4] one in seven of the children were back in a matter of weeks. The journey out of London was well planned but exhausting. Baroness Serota, who was a student volunteer in Hackney and accompanied a group of children on the journey out of London to Bishops Stortford, recalls that many of them had not been on a train before; she remembers numbers of little children aged 5 and upwards, with brown bags, singing together the hymn, 'O God Our Help in Ages Past'. The Women's Voluntary Service for Civil Defence (WVS) organised the billeting and wanted to put children and teachers together in some old stables. The teachers refused, but she volunteered to sleep with the children. In the end, she and

Plate 12 *Children evacuated to Reading from a school in Kennington, London, during the Second World War. LMA, LCC/WAR/4/2/279*

her ten young charges were sent to stay in the wing of a large country house.[5] Another Care Committee volunteer gave an eye-witness account of the first assembly at 7.40 a.m., with the division into companies, the calling of rolls, and the fixing of labels to every child. They moved off by 9 o'clock, four abreast, in three blocks, with the infants in the centre:

> We had a peaceful journey as far as Polegate [in Sussex], where we were detrained and marched down the road and fell out for lavatory accommodation behind great screens in a field. Then to a marquee where we drank tea while the children sat on the floor and had their lunch; and it was while we were sitting there that we heard that Germany had invaded Poland. It seemed to make the whole thing come alive, and gave us an uncanny feeling of marching into unknown places and an unknown future. After lunch

Plate 13 *A gathering of the Royal Hill LCC School, Greenwich, which was adopted by Christ Church Schools in St Leonards on Sea, September 1939. LMA, LCC/WAR/4/2/292*

Southdown buses took us into a small village with about 500 inhabitants, with no electricity, and no gas, and no water laid on. We were taken to the village hall and there the billeting began.[6]

In many cases the evacuated school was housed in local halls, with furniture and equipment brought from London; the evacuated schools were kept separate from local schools whenever possible. In some cases, however, it was necessary to merge the London school with a country school. In the case of Putney schools, which was fairly typical, Brandlehow went to Battle, Putney Upper Grade went to Tilehurst, while All Saints', Lower Common, St Mary's and Putney R[oman] C[atholic] were located in various parts of Reading. Many difficulties developed, such as a lack of co-ordination between the different bodies, which led one woman head teacher to comment, 'The whole plan was made by men, apparently without understanding of the fact that taking in children means hard work.... The scheme has put an almost intolerable burden on to some shoulders.'[7]

Many care workers, both volunteers and organisers, accompanied their school to its new site in the country. In East Sussex (Sussex took more London children than any other county), *ad hoc* volunteer committees were made up from members of Rural Community Councils and from Care Committee workers who had left London with their schools or who had a country home in Sussex and were living there for the duration of the war. Eileen Lecky, who was a Care Committee member in Putney from 1907 until 1958, described the distribution of Putney care workers. The recently retired headmistress of the infant school, she explained, went to Reading to carry on the Care Committee work; she and another volunteer went to Reading every three weeks and the LCC gave them a special petrol licence for these journeys. They took school equipment and acted as a go-between for parents and children, carrying parcels and messages. They also visited each school and acted as a kind of trouble-shooter where problems had developed. Many London children were seen as different and strange by the inhabitants of the countryside: 'When I started at the [country] school,' recalled one man who was sent to a village in Devon, 'all the other boys kept looking through my hair. I was upset, because I thought they thought I had nits, but the teacher explained they had never met a Jew before and were looking for my horns.'[8] The foster mothers were not keen on the London children hanging around their overcrowded homes, so the Care Committee workers arranged to rent church halls for two hours every afternoon, five days a week, as a means of keeping the children happy and occupied; the rent was paid by the Children's Health Centre in Putney.[9] Some of the foster parents were annoyed that the children were not, in their view, adequately clothed and shod. They blamed the parents: 'The people here [that is, in the country] are steady hardworking folk who have no patience with people who, instead of sending clothes send dozens of comic papers to their children.'[10]

Miss E. Cosens, a District Organiser, wrote a leaflet about the experience of evacuation just three months after war started. She complained that there were no treatment centres, no one had any experience of such contagious troubles as impetigo, and there was no conception among country foster parents of the need to monitor London children's heads, 'for fear of what may develop from one or two nits'. As for 'Hair Raids', she added,

> they remain the function of any teacher, voluntary helper or foster mother who will undertake them. London sent out what nurses could be spared to the places that asked most urgently for them, but in the main the situation about 'heads', which developed to everyone's horror in a very short space of time, has been dealt with by amateurs.[11]

Coping with war in London

By 1941 the number of Care Committee volunteers working in London had fallen dramatically – from 5,000 in 1939 to 437.[12] This caused concern and Eveline Lowe, the Chairman of the LCC, wrote a letter to *The Times* to attract recruits. Many volunteers, she hoped, would be 'coming forward, *both men and women*, who may be willing to give some of their time regularly each week to a service so important in safeguarding the welfare of the children (emphasis added).'[13] This was the first time that male recruits were sought as well as women and it produced at least one man. 'There is a good band of voluntary workers in this district who do a substantial amount of work,' observed the District Organiser in Islington and Finsbury, adding that 'the honorary secretary, who is most active, is, strange to say, not a woman but a man.'[14] The organising staff now had to take on a larger share of the work than formerly. They stayed strong in numbers, dropping only to 153 from 158, but by the autumn of 1941, only 88 of these organisers were working in London itself. Twelve had been seconded to the Ministry of Health for evacuation work, while 13 were seconded to local authorities in reception areas, and 40 were treatment organisers.[15] Miss Nussey retired from the LCC as Principal Organiser in 1940, when she received the OBE for her work for children in London. She was replaced by Miss Olive Cram, the third Principal Organiser – and like Miss Morton and Miss Nussey before her, formidable and extremely capable. All three woman recall J.B. Priestley's description of Margaret McMillan as 'One of those Terrible Nuisances who are in fact the salt of the earth.'[16]

The remaining care workers in London struggled to keep the service going. Treatment centres were commandeered by the Red Cross, some schools were evacuated while others were damaged by bombs, and staff at the schools were constantly moved around. 'It needed all our resources to hold our care committee work together', remembered Eileen Lecky later.[17] The volunteers tried hard to help mothers left behind in London. They gathered together small groups of women for weekly sewing and cooking meetings, so that they could chat, with a second room where babies and toddlers were taken care of.[18] This reflects the growing commitment of the Care Service to the family and the community as a whole, rather than to individual children at school. Eileen Lecky wrote later that

> There was much help to be given to our mothers who remained in Putney. In 1941 Miss Long returned from Reading and once a week she ran a sing-song, and with a cup of tea and a biscuit it made a happy afternoon, for the women needed a break with husbands and sons on active service and the children evacuated, and constant anxiety about their homes. Heavy raids over London took toll of our families ... More and more were homeless or lost their possessions and we were soon involved in trying to help ... Some of our children were orphaned in the raids, and we had to find permanent homes for them.[19]

Care Committee organisers and volunteers were central to the supply and organisation of clothing schemes for evacuated children. They assessed children and parents for need and ability to pay and then sent vouchers to the reception areas, via the teachers, for clothing and footwear which could be redeemed at the depots of the WVS. This was an essential resource but very intensive and led one LCC official to refer wearily to 'The almost crushing weight of the Clothing Scheme'.[20] Prior to evacuation, the Minister of Health had allocated £3,000 to help children from the poorest London schools obtain clothes, boots and 'materials which have been made up, by voluntary workers, into garments of various kinds'.[21] However, officials emphasised that this was not a handout from the state, but a last resort to be used when parental contribution and voluntary effort were insufficient. On 25 October 1939, E.C.H. Salmon, the Deputy Clerk of the LCC, wrote to the Ministry of Health to say that another £5,000 was needed. But he assured the Minister that 'only when voluntary organisations cannot cope with the demand, and after every effort has been made to ensure that parents will meet their responsibilities, will this sum be drawn upon.'[22] Nothing should be done, he added, 'to detract from the responsibility of parents or to dry up voluntary help in the receiving or evacuating areas.' The Ministry of Health finally agreed to make this money available but insisted that no publicity should be given to the emergency fund, on the grounds that such publicity would defeat 'the object of maintaining parental responsibility and voluntary help'.[23] The School Care Service was described by the Education Officer of the LCC as performing a balancing act: 'the organisers steer between the Scylla of parental irresponsibility,' he commented, 'and the Charybdis of the child's unsatisfied needs.'[24]

A system slowly developed whereby a clothing store was set up in each of the 12 divisions.[25] Care workers were given advances with which to buy articles for the poorest cases and one-quarter to one-fifth of the total value of the clothes provided was recovered from parents. This work was seen as:

> comparable in part to their peacetime duties in assessing parents' contributions towards the costs of spectacles ... Needless to say the stimulation and main- tenance of parental responsibility is an axiom of social welfare and no-one is more qualified to decide this point than those engaged on the work.

It was noted that 'most of the Care Committee offices keep open at the weekends as this is the only time when many mothers or fathers can call to make payments and settle outstanding questions; useful new contacts with the fathers are being made.'[26]

By April 1941 it was acknowledged that although the scheme was 'in theory' based upon voluntary contributions, 'in practice now it is maintained almost entirely, in the case of London and the larger authorities, by confi- dential authorisations from the evacuation account.'[27] In other words, government officials clung to the voluntary idea in principle, but in actual fact they relied on state aid to deliver this essential service.

The supporting role of the state was much in evidence in the area of school nutrition. Whereas school meal provision before 1939 had 'smacked of the Poor Law and public assistance,' school dinners now became an integral part of the education service and of the war economy.[28] Lord Woolton, Minister for Food, stated in 1941 that he wanted:

> to see elementary school children as well fed as children going to Eton and Harrow. I am determined that we shall organize our food front that at the end of the war, unlike the last, we shall have preserved and even improved the health and physique of the nation.[29]

This concern for the nutrition welfare of all people, on an equal basis, has been described by one historian as 'war socialism'.[30] Outlining its plans for the reconstruction of education after the war, the Board of Education stated in June 1942:

The rapid development of provision of meals for schoolchildren that has taken place during the war and the expected widespread institution of communal feeding for the general public may produce a marked change in the social habits of the people. It may well be that the provision of a midday meal will become and will remain a normal element in public education. There is much to be said for the view that midday dinners should be regarded as an integral part of full-time education and, as such, provided free.

Herbert Morrison, the Labour Home Secretary, promised the 'development of ... school meals and that sort of thing which it seems to me under this new order of things will have to be on the basis of universal free service'. The White Paper on Social Insurance, which was issued in September 1944, promised that school meals and school milk would be 'free of cost to the parents and will be available for all the children in a family attending school, including the first.'[31]

By February 1945, more than 1.6 million dinners were being served daily in England and Wales, to 33 per cent of the school population. (Although they were not always appreciated, due to the difficulties of obtaining food in wartime. One former London pupil recalls that 'school dinners, though obviously nourishing, were disgusting, especially Thursday's meatless day which comprised reconstituted dried egg powder, scrambled, swimming in tinned tomatoes.'[32]) Of the meals that were supplied, 14 per cent were free, while the rest were charged at 4d or 5d, the charge being restricted to the cost of ingredients. The school meals service was supported by a subsidy to local authorities varying from 75 to 90 per cent of the cost of the service. School milk was available to 73 per cent of children by February 1945, and about half the children were receiving two-thirds of a pint.[33] According to Richard Titmuss, the official historian of wartime social policy, developments in the provision of meals and milk at school

expressed something very close to a revolution in the attitude of parents, teachers and children to a scheme which only a few years earlier, had not been regarded with much respect or sympathy. In place of a relief measure, tainted with the poor law, *it became a social service*, fused into school life, and making its own contribution to the physical nurture of the children and to their social education (emphasis added).[34]

This was a very different situation from that which prevailed before the war, when determined efforts were made to recover the charge of a school dinner from the parents.

Children return to London

By 6 January 1940, 79,000 of the 241,000 children evacuated from London in the previous September had returned home.[35] 'It represents the strangest, and perhaps most melancholy, instinct,' observes Peter Ackroyd in his *London. The Biography*, 'the need to get back to the city, even if it becomes a city of fire and death.'[36] Emergency schools were set up to provide for them. On 26 January 1940, *The Times* reported that the LCC had opened 97 emergency schools in London and would soon be able to open a further 23. However, the Education Officer, E.M. Rich, warned that children would attend entirely at their parents' risk and that schools would close should serious or frequent air raids occur: 'Each pupil may attend only one session daily, in the morning or afternoon in alternate weeks. The schools are open to all children living in the neighbourhood.'[37] One woman has remembered her experience of life at an emergency school:

> My arrival in Form 1A at the South West London Emergency Secondary School coincided almost to the day with Hitler's Blitzkrieg on London. During the late summer and early autumn of 1940, there were air-raids both during the day and night. The shelter at the school was in the cloakroom and this was too small to accommodate the whole school so we would attend alternate mornings and afternoons until mid September when the daylight raids stopped. However every consecutive night for the next three months the night raids continued and we spent our nights sheltering from the terrifying bombing. During the first week or so we elected unanimously M– S– as our form captain. Sometime in early October our form mistress told us that M– and her entire family had been killed the previous night. We did not cry, we seemed to freeze but we did not talk about it. However from then on, when one of us was away, we were anxious until we knew that all was well. Form 1A did not suffer any more fatalities but from time to time we had walking wounded. The school grounds were dug up and we had little plots of land, 'digging for victory'. We knitted scarves for airmen, adopted a British prisoner of war in Germany and sent him Red Cross parcels and wrote to him. We collected waste paper and scrap metal. No one was fat, we were a lean lot. Every day we had gym or games. ... We were very well taught and cared for.[38]

There was another evacuation in June 1940, although half the children of school-age stayed behind and went to emergency schools. One Care Committee worker referred to the difficulties caused by the continual process of evacuation:

> There were kit inspections, children to be got to the cleansing station before they could go away, and finally getting the children off, then the trickle back

as soon as London seemed quiet, then another surge of evacuation after the next bad bombing, until eventually our children were scattered the length and breadth of England. We tried to keep in touch with them all.[39]

Medical inspections and other school services were not started up again until later in the war.

On 3 December 1940, the LCC announced that school attendance was once again to be enforced in London; a week later, all other education authorities were advised by the Board of Education to do the same. The LCC now employed one school enquiry officer to every 1,500 children. Many of these were temporary staff, who had been employed to replace those on war service. Unlike the officers working before the war, who had prided themselves on their good relations with families, the wartime officers did not know the people of the district in which they worked. They had to spend a great deal of time finding and securing the enrolment of children who had returned from the reception areas. Many visits had to be duplicated if the mother was not at home, which was often the case as many women had to do war work.[40] A strategy of frequent street raids was started, when the officers in every division searched the streets and public places for children who should have been in school.[41]

Many parents withdrew their children from school in the years of war. Some parents were simply taking advantage of the disruption caused by war to send their children to work, even if they were under the school-leaving age of 14.[42] But most others were understandably afraid for the safety of their children in the bombing raids. One of the worst disasters was a daylight raid on Sandhurst School in Lewisham on 20 January 1943, which killed 37 children and six teachers and injured 54 children and two teachers. At one London school, with a highest attendance roll at any stage of 350, nearly 1,000 names were on the admissions register in the course of two years and individual pupils were on and off the roll as many as four or five times.[43] The average attendance for London for the whole of 1942 was about 82 per cent, which was more or less maintained through the rest of the war, though falling at times to the high 70s. It dropped as low as 32 per cent in June 1944, following German flying bomb attacks on London.[44] 'Twice during the war,' remembered one school child living in the East End, 'I was sent to a different junior school because of bomb damage. Classes were doubled up, with teachers having to teach more than 60 children. We sat on the floor, on benches, in the hall, in shelters, we sat three to a desk.'[45]

Miss Cosens, a District Organiser, believed that a new type of society was developing in front of her eyes. Identifying herself and her own class as 'we' (and implicitly, therefore, designating the working-class as 'them'), she wondered whether the 'evacuation experience' would 'be one of the things that will force *us* to accept a levelling up of the income of the insecure section of the community, even though *we* shall inevitably experience a levelling down of *our* comparative middle class ease? (emphasis added).'[46] The extreme conditions created by war helped to break down some of the suspicions and prejudices which had previously divided care workers and attendance officers. When medical inspections were started up once more, for example, attendance officers helped by sending the names of the children.[47] 'The need to improvise,' commented a later report that examined the attendance and welfare services, 'brought the few remaining care committee workers and school inquiry officers closer and helped to break down some of the suspicions and prejudices which had kept them apart in the interwar years.'[48] The chief dividers were sex and class – and in both these areas the Second World War was a great leveller. It forced women and men to mix together in a way that was unprecedented and also brought the different social classes together in a way that was entirely new. Rationing helped to level the classes further, by reducing differences between the expenditure of poor families and those who were prosperous.

Notes

1. R. Titmuss: *Problems of Social Policy*, p. 510.
2. Peggy Jay: *Loves and Labours*, p. 57.
3. Ibid., p. 57.
4. Stuart Maclure: *A History of Education in London 1870–1990*, p. 135.
5. Beatrice Serota to ASW, DW and RA, 15 June 1999.
6. Reported in M. Cosens: *Evacuation*, pp. 4–5.
7. Ibid, p. 13.
8. Gilda O'Neill: *My East End*, p. 267.
9. Eileen Lecky: 'Children Then and Now', p. 21. LMA, ILEA S/SB/04/2.
10. Reported in M. Cosens: *Evacuation*, p. 8.
11. Ibid., pp. 5–6.
12. LCC, Children's Care Work, Report of the Education Committee, 10 May 1950, signed R. McKinnon Wood, Chairman, being Extract from Minutes of the Meeting of the Council held on 23 May 1950.
13. 'Children's Care Committees', *The Times*, 12 February 1940.
14. Middlemass to Leadbetter, 26 February 1942. PRO, HLG 7/224.
15. H.P Wyatt, LCC, to Leadbetter, Ministry of Health, 2 September 1941. PRO, HLG 7/224.
16. Foreword by J.B. Priestley in W. D'A. Cressell: *Margaret McMillan. A Memoir*, p. 9.
17. Eileen Lecky: 'Children Then and Now', p. 25.
18. Reported in M. Cosens: *Evacuation*, p. 18.
19. Eileen Lecky: 'Children Then and Now', pp. 23–4.
20. H.P. Wyatt, LCC, to Leadbetter, Ministry of Health, 2 September 1941. PRO, HLG 7/224.
21. Evacuation. Billeting Equipment. Footwear and clothing. 1939–1944. Letter, E.C.H. Salmon, Deputy Clerk of the Council [LCC] to Secretary, Ministry of Health, 25 October 1939. PRO, HLG 7/223.

22. Ibid.
23. J.C. Wrigley, Ministry of Health to E.C.H. Salmon, LCC, 7 November 1939. PRO, HLG 7/223.
24. 'Government Evacuation Scheme', Report by Education Officer, 12 January 1942. PRO, HLG 7/224.
25. Savage to Secretary, Ministry of Health, 10 February 1941. PRO, HLG 7/223.
26. H.P. Wyatt, LCC, to Leadbetter, Ministry of Health, 7 March 1941. PRO, HLG 7/223.
27. Leadbetter, LCC, to E.D Marris, Board of Education, 7 March 1941. PRO, HLG 7/223.
28. H.C. Dent: *The Education Act 1944*, p. 41.
29. *The Times*, 1 October 1941.
30. John Hurt: 'Feeding the Hungry Schoolchild in the First Half of the Twentieth Century', p. 200.
31. Ibid., p. 193–4.
32. Elizabeth Murray to ASW, 25 February 2001.
33. Charles Webster: 'Government Policy on School Meals and Welfare Foods 1939–1970', p. 192.
34. R. Titmuss: *Problems of Social Policy*, p. 510.
35. 'Children Under 14 Sent to Work', *The Times*, 18 January 1940.
36. Peter Ackroyd: *London. The Biography*, p. 742.
37. 'Education of London Children', *The Times*, 26 January 1940.
38. Elizabeth Murray to ASW, 25 February 2001.
39. Eileen Lecky: 'Children Then and Now', p. 23.
40. Article by Lord Elton in the *Daily Mail*, 3 May 1943.
41. P.H.J.H. Gosden: *Education in the Second World War*, pp. 69–70.
42. 'Children Under 14 Sent to Work', *The Times*, 18 January 1940.
43. P.H.J.H. Gosden: *Education in the Second World War*, p. 58.
44. LCC: 'The Story of Evacuation', n.d. PRO, ED 138/49.
45. Gilda O'Neill: *My East End*, p. 262.
46. M. Cosens: *Evacuation*, p. 3 (emphasis added).
47. Eileen Lecky: 'Children Then and Now', p. 22.
48. Bedford Report, B.5.

Chapter 6

THE WELFARE STATE

'Other dragons to be slain with the sword of love.'[1]

BY THE END of the Second World War in 1945, the centuries-old social hierarchy of Britain was no longer acceptable to its citizens. There was massive support for the Beveridge Report of 1942, which recommended a high level of employment, family allowances, and a unified and universal system of social insurance that was underpinned by a national health service. 'Support for Beveridge spread like forest fire,' observes the historian Charles Webster. More than a quarter of a million copies of the full report were sold and there were many popular versions – 'the Beveridge Plan became known to all sections of the community ... Beveridge became the touchstone for a new social order.'[2] When the Labour Party was elected to implement the Beveridge proposals, many expected to see an end of Want, Disease, Ignorance, Squalor and Idleness, the five Giant Evils identified by Beveridge that divided the nation into rich and poor. The war had produced a set of social services delivered by the state, where milk and school dinners and other kinds of help were distributed to children on the basis of need. 'No longer was it argued (as it often was before the war),' observed Richard Titmuss in 1950, 'that the condition of the people did not warrant such measures ... It was the universal character of these welfare policies which ensured their acceptance and success. They were free of social discrimination and the indignities of the poor law.'[3] When the NHS began in 1948, a leaflet explaining its operation promised that, 'Everyone – rich or poor, man, woman or child – can use it or any part of it ... *it is not a charity* (emphasis added).'[4]

The increased role of the state in daily affairs made old-fashioned voluntary organisations unfashionable and the Charity Organisation Society, which had been founded in 1869, changed its name to the Family Welfare Association in 1946. Some organisations simply disappeared. A new kind of voluntary organisation had appeared with the development of the Women's Voluntary Service (WVS), to which women of every class had belonged during the years of war as a way of helping to defend the nation. Not long before, said Stella Reading, the founder and chairman of the WVS, 'volunteers had come from the leisured class ... the Lady Bountiful sort of thing'; but she added, 'Now that is past'.[5]

This suspicion of the traditional type of volunteer created new challenges for London's School Care Service after the war. So did the provision of welfare and health care by the state, since this removed the very needs for which the Service had been initially created. There were new demands on the school inquiry officer, too, after the school-leaving age was raised in 1947 to 15. The Children's Act of 1948 set up Children's Departments in local authorities that employed professional social workers and took many officers away from the Inquiry Service. This narrowed the work of the inquiry officer and weakened his status in the Education Office.

The 1944 Education (Butler) Act introduced free secondary education in a system where state schooling was divided into three parts: primary, secondary and further education. The all-age elementary school that had catered for children from 5 to 14 was brought to an end, along with its stigma of social inferiority. All children were now to be educated in separate secondary schools after the age of 11 and grammar school fees were to be abolished. The Butler Act swept away many of the restrictions relating to welfare provision by LEAs. Under the 1907 Act, the School Medical Service only had a duty to provide treatment to elementary schoolchildren and the cost of this treatment had to be recovered from parents wherever possible; moreover, only certain kinds of treatment were provided. The 1944 Act, however, made it the duty of the LEA to provide for the medical inspection of all pupils at any school or college and to make arrangements for securing the provision of free medical treatment where necessary. The Act also made the provision of milk and meals a duty of the LEA: 'Regulations made by the Minister shall impose upon local education authorities the duty of providing milk, meals, and other refreshment for pupils in attendance at schools and colleges maintained by them.' School milk was made free when the Family Allowances Act came into operation in August 1946. 'We all took advantage of this [milk], getting a third of a pint at morning break,' said one former pupil. 'Most of the children at school were poorly dressed, clothes being a low priority in a poverty area such as Bethnal Green.'[6] Memories of free school milk are not all positive, however. Many are dominated by the recollection of a bad taste and smell, and the difficulty of swallowing warm milk, which led to a dread of morning break.[7]

School attendance and children's welfare

A new Ministry of Education was set up to replace the Board of Education and one of the chief aims of the Ministry was to provide a firm central direction for education, with a national policy and national standards. This was intended to produce some uniformity in a highly disparate system, where LEAs operated in different ways. It was previously a major defect in English educational administration, comments H.C. Dent, an expert on the workings of the 1944 Act, 'that local authorities could with impunity be laggard or reactionary in their provision'.[8] However, the lack of uniformity continued in some areas, notably that of school attendance and welfare. In London, the dual system of Care Committees and attendance officers was maintained. But outside London, the role of the school attendance officer was formalised into that of the Education Welfare Officer (EWO), with a remit to provide support for pupils in the broader context of school, home and community. The ground for this change in name had been prepared in 1939 by the school attendance officers themselves, by changing the name of their professional association from 'Association of School Visitors' to 'Education Welfare Officers National Association' (EWONA). After the 1944 Act, a number of authorities accepted and used the new title, which reflected the work of the service over the previous half century. The 1944 Act did not itself bring any statutory recognition to the role of the school attendance officer: in the years until the 1950s there were no training courses and no academic support services, unlike the new social work and educational professions which were established in this period. The education welfare services developed on an *ad hoc* basis, without a coherent and statutory framework for the service.[9]

Implicit in the new title adopted by the EWO was the idea that the officer was concerned not simply with the physical presence of children in the classroom, but with ensuring that no problems hindered their progress at school. He therefore had to deal with the provision of welfare facilities such as clothing, school meals, transport and maintenance allowances. Absence from school would still be the main reason for a visit to the home, but not the exclusive reason: 'Where a call is made because of irregular attendance, the object will be to *discover the cause* (emphasis added).'[10] However, the parameters of the EWOs' duties were strictly limited to the sphere of education.[11] They were not seen as a kind of social worker for children in any general sense. In fact, the social work of the EWO was reduced following the 1948 Children's Act, which placed responsibility for children in need of care or protection in local authority departments that were distinct from education. Children's Departments were staffed by Children's Officers, who were mostly women with academic qualifications. Their responsibilities involved the assessment of children's home circumstances, before they were taken into the care of the local authorities. Children's departments were also given partial responsibility for young offenders.[12] Special arrangements were introduced to identify families at risk and EWOs were among the groups of workers with children who were expected to spot 'incipient signs of trouble'.[13] But otherwise, the EWO lost a range of his former duties and was expected to concentrate on attendance. Those attendance officers who were especially interested in the social work side of children's welfare moved to the new Children's Departments, which left the service short-staffed and over-burdened.[14] Because of its potential for making social work with children into a growth area, the Children's Act raised fears in the minds of the predominantly male EWOs. EWONA wrote to 'emphatically protest against the almost total restriction of this field of social work to women holders of a university qualification many of whom will of necessity be young and inexperienced, especially in those matters connected with boys and young men.' The association felt strongly:

> that their Service should be incorporated into the new scheme of Child Care; that there should not be established a 'new intelligentsia' in Child Welfare, but that there should be given the opportunity ... to continue to do the work they have very largely done for the last 60 years, putting at the disposal of Committees and children their unrivalled knowledge of the homes and lives of the people in their respective districts. The Home Office has made it known that men and women with this experience will not be considered for training and appointment in the Child Care service. Is the new service then to consist of those whose theoretical training is great, but has to a great degree divorced them from an understanding of the lives and conditions of ordinary people?[15]

By 1950 there were 154 district and unattached school inquiry officers in London, including 12 women; 15 school inquiry officers were employed for special duties, such as those relating to employment. These officers were organised by nine divisional officers, who were supported by nine assistants. The primary duty of the officers was to verify why a child was absent from school and then to enforce attendance; prosecution was suggested only when all other action had failed.[16] They also dealt with juvenile delinquency and guardian adoption cases, until this work was transferred in 1949 to the LCC Children's Department.

The issue of understaffing was tackled in 1951 with a series of recruitment drives. In response to the first drive there were 1,307 applicants and 31 appointments were made, six of them women; in the second drive 627 people applied and 12 appointments were made, one of them a woman. The applicant had to show evidence of 'an understanding approach to the social aspects of school inquiry work as well as their education and training'. In some cases there was 'a tendency for the very good candidate selected to seek other duties. This happened in the case of one officer who was transferred to child welfare officer duties in the children's department.'[17]

A diminished role for Care Committees

The number of Care Committee volunteers rose slowly from its very low level at the end of the war, reaching 1,600 in 1949.[18] These numbers were not considered sufficient by the Education Committee; only with 2,000 effective voluntary workers, it stated, could the work could be carried on 'with reasonable efficiency'.[19] One of the obstacles to recruitment was the opposition of some Labour Party councils, such as Tower Hamlets, to the idea of involving voluntary organisations in work that ought, they thought, to be done by the state. Herbert Morrison, however, was very supportive of the voluntary principle and was keen to see the continued role of the voluntary sector.[20] A Central Training and Recruitment Committee met once every two weeks and organised publicity through letters and articles in the press, radio talks and appeals to central bodies. A special recruiting campaign in the Church of England was initiated with the help of the wife of the Archbishop of Canterbury, and a meeting at Lambeth Palace was arranged to stimulate interest among Church of England organisations. District Organisers also arranged local meetings and the voluntary workers themselves brought in interested friends. As before, volunteers were not formally trained, on the grounds that few of them had adequate time available:

> Training on a fixed schedule such as is given to social science students, is, therefore, neither possible nor desired, as a rule and in practice training has to be given by the assistant organiser day by day. A new worker, for instance, will have to be taken to a medical inspection several times before she can carry out her duties alone ... In some offices voluntary workers of long standing undertake the training of new workers.[21]

Although Care Committees still had the right to grant free dinners in case of necessity, it was no longer a duty to make assessments for milk, since every schoolchild was now given a third of a pint of free milk every day. Nor was it necessary to assess charges for medical treatment, since this was now freely available under the NHS. However, at least in the first few years following the end of the war, the work of the Care Committees remained the same in its essentials. The start of family allowances in 1947 meant that mothers had more money to spend on their children's clothes, but clothing coupons continued to create difficulties. One new problem was that of school uniform. Grammar schools were allowed to insist on uniform, which caused all sorts of tensions in families. One woman recalls that after she had passed the eleven-plus in 1958,

> the uniform I needed for grammar school was the subject of angry debate. [My father had] been approached for money for the gabardine mac, the tunic, the shoes, and he had handed some over, but not a lot. The uniform must have been a strain on the seven pounds. The issue, this Saturday afternoon, is the blouses that I will have to wear. I'm wearing a new one anyway, one from Marks & Spencer with blue embroidery round the collar, as I approach him at my mother's persuasion and drag his attention away from the form on telly. He asks why I can't wear the one I've got on. I'm profoundly irritated, outraged at his stupidity; they don't allow it, I say: its a *rule*.[22]

Secondary modern schools were not allowed to insist on uniform and they advised parents not to buy anything new until old clothes had worn out. But as one Care Committee volunteer asked, 'Would any child be willing to go to a new school in its old school clothes? Children are cruel to each other and the new child needs the regulation uniform if it is to settle down happily.' She added that parents understood this and did their best to get the uniform, even in the poorest families. The cost of the uniform varied from about £12 to £30. With the help of a Care Committee, parents were able in some cases to obtain from the LCC a grant for a uniform between £2.10 shillings and £8.[23]

School medical inspections still relied on the involvement of the children's care service. It was necessary, stated the 1948 report of the LCC Medical Officer of Health and School Medical Officer, because it formed 'a link between the parents and their homes on the one hand and the school doctors, nurses, teachers and the school on the other.' A care committee representative, added the report, was present at 91.7 per cent of the routine examinations of primary schoolchildren. They also continued follow-up care, especially when parents were not readily convinced of the need for medical attention.[24] Although health care was now provided free to all under the NHS, school medical inspections were still regarded as valuable. One Care Committee worker reported that at one examination a 12-year-old girl was found to have post-scarlet fever heart. Her mother was asked to take her back

Plate 14 *A medical examination at Peckham Park School in London, 1953. A Care Committee worker is seated second from the right and the child's mother is seated next to her. LMA, 22.51, 2097*

to her own doctor who attended her when she was ill and to ask him for a certificate if he considered her fit for school. He was furious and refused, so the Care Committee sent her to a nearby hospital. The girl was in bed for six months but eventually came back and was able to join in all school activities.[25]

In the matter of convalescence the National Health Act affected the work of Care Committees adversely. The LCC lost its hospitals and convalescent homes to the Regional Hospital Boards and the school doctor was no longer empowered to recommend a child directly for convalescence. Meanwhile the Education Committee of the LCC now allocated money for convalescent holidays on the school doctor's recommendation and the children were sent to 'recuperative homes'. This meant the children normally only went for two weeks, that the vacancies were allotted from the Public Health Department at County Hall, and that there was often a query as to whether a child was too ill, or not ill enough, to be sent away.[26] Another change in the area of health was that School Sisters were changed into Health Visitors, whose work was transferred to the Public Health Office. Since the Health Visitors were given a multiplicity of duties, including maternity care and the provision of home helps, their work for schools became the Cinderella of the service.

The school-leaving conference no longer functioned after 1949, when the LCC took over the work of vocational guidance from the Ministry of Labour and National Service. Advisory interviews at schools about choice of employment were now conducted in private, with only the youth employment officer, the young person, the parent and probably the head or class teacher present. However, the Care Committee workers still made a contribution by supplying information about the home circumstances of boys and girls eligible to leave school.[27]

Care Committees had started during the war years to help the community as a whole, rather than simply the children themselves: visits to families were made not simply with a view to finding out about a child's background, but as a way of seeing what could be done to help the family overall. This approach developed further after the war. Eileen Lecky helped her families in Putney to develop strategies for coping with debt and arranged for sympathetic solicitors to help with legal difficulties. She even assisted a childminder whose licence had been revoked as a consequence of LCC bureaucracy – 'They told her they were withdrawing her licence because a new Children's Act had come into force and she had fourteen children to mind and under the new Act she was only entitled to eight.' However, neither Miss Lecky nor the childminder had even known that the Act had come into force. A solicitor agreed to support Mrs Miles against the LCC for a 'Jumble Sale fee' and the licence was restored.[28]

Plans to merge the services

The shortage of Care Committee volunteers prompted Graham Savage, the LCC Education Officer, to consider combining the School Care Service with the School Inquiry Service, making one single and unified education welfare service. Savage had started his work as EO in the middle of the Second World War and was known as a man with energy and vision – 'a breath of fresh air … an innovator … the man whose reaction to a new idea was more likely to be positive.'[29] He made a proposal to the LCC General Purposes Subcommittee in July 1948 that school inquiry officers and assistant organisers, redesignated welfare officers, should be associated together and should undertake school welfare work in its several aspects. At the same time, the services of voluntary children's care workers should be retained and further encouraged. The adoption of such a system, it was suggested, 'might enable homes to be visited by one person where two might now have to go and might permit of a small reduction in the number of staff required.'[30]

Savage sent a memo to Olive Cram, the Principal Organiser of the Care Service, explaining that in his view, 'School attendance and attention to the social and physical needs of children are integral parts of the same problem, and the employment of the work of one group of officers instead of two would *prima facie* appear to be the simplest organisation.' At the very least, he added, this would ensure overall local supervision of both school attendance and child welfare work, to produce:

> a) the greatest economy in effort; b) the elimination of duplication of record and visiting; c) the cutting out of unnecessary work; d) the removal of misunderstanding in the handling of cases; e) the greatest measure of co-ordination.[31]

Miss Cram was 'astounded' by this memo and replied to Savage that 'any planning on these lines would mean the death of the voluntary system'. As long as she was Principal Organiser, she warned him, 'I shall oppose it, unless I am convinced the voluntary system has served its purpose.' London had always led the country, she added, 'in its conception of social work for children and you now appear to propose a retrograde step.'[32] Emotions ran high at this point and Savage replied to Miss Cram that were he to reply to her memo officially, 'it would have to be in terms which I feel you do not deserve and which I should not wish to write. In its present form it is quite unacceptable.'[33]

Savage had attempted unsuccessfully on several occasions to obtain a 'full appreciation of the school care work'. He asked Miss Cram if her workers kept a diary of their activities and said that if so, he would appreciate casting an eye over some samples. Her reply was hostile: that 'voluntary workers do not keep a diary and could not be requested to do so … a varying amount of time is given [for their work] – sometimes only a few hours a week.' She defended her team of voluntary workers against charges of amateurism. 'It has been claimed that the work ought to be done by professional social workers,' she objected, adding, 'We cannot get an even quality, but I consider we gain in the variety of experience brought in.'[34] Savage made some critical observations about the voluntary system, pointing out that there was no measurement of their work and that there were many areas of overlap, duplication of record keeping and 'continuous risks of misunderstanding ... and of a child ... falling between two stools'. [35] Like Robert Blair before him, he was not enthusiastic about the Care Committee system and declared 'it must be frankly admitted that ... a considerable proportion of the care committee members has been made up of persons more fitted for formal committee business than for individual help to the children and the parents'.[36]

At no point in this stage of discussions, as far as can be seen on the basis of the documentary evidence that is available, was any reference made to the role and duties of school attendance officers. However, a letter to Miss Cram from Mr Sharpen, the Divisional Officer of the Education Department, suggests that the inquiry service was not too worried about a possible merger. 'The divisional organisers were sorry and perhaps surprised to learn,' said Mr Sharpen, that 'apprehension was based on the fear the children's care work would be swamped by divisional officers' work.' He added that this fear was 'quite illusory'.[37]

Deadlock was reached between Savage and Cram but the proposal lingered on. It was eventually re-examined in 1949, but in a more rigorous manner. On 12 July, the LCC asked the Education Committee to consider and report on the care committee service generally, looking especially at the co-ordination of the care committee workers with the work of school attendance officers and employment officers. The Education Committee referred the matter to the Children's Care Section of the Education (General Purposes) Subcommittee, which met on four occasions and interviewed a school inquiry officer, a divisional officer and the principal organiser of children's care; it also examined particulars of school attendance and welfare work undertaken by three other local authorities. Meanwhile, the Central Council of Care Committees came out strongly against the proposal to integrate the services.

The Education Committee reached a conclusion in early 1950. It took the view that there were substantial considerations against the proposal. They rejected the idea of placing the school inquiry officers under the direction of the organisers, on the grounds that this would deprive the divisional officer of his main means of contact with the schools. The alternative of absorbing the voluntary workers into the divisional organisation was also rejected. In its Care Committee system, it was argued, London had something of value which other authorities lacked: 'These voluntary workers have each to undertake a responsible piece of work, in which they take a pride, and its seems to us that if their work became absorbed into or more closely attached to the divisional organisation, there would be a grave danger that many of them would before long give up the work.' It would then be necessary to employ further paid staff.[38]

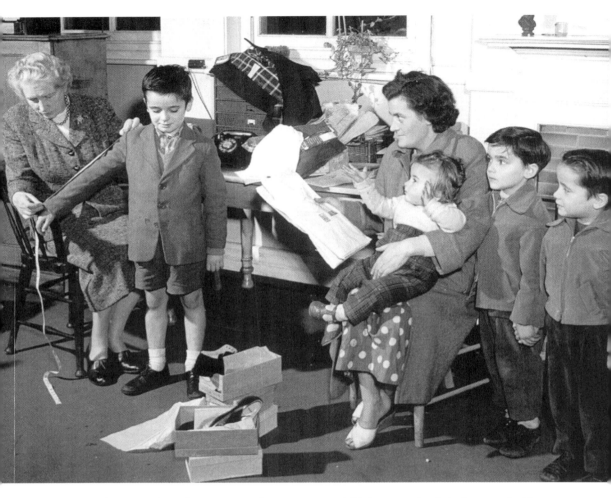

Plate 15 *A Care Committee worker measures a child for new school clothes, watched by the child's mother and siblings, 1961. LMA, 22.55, 90/162*

The Care Committee system managed to survive, but in a somewhat changed form. The LCC introduced a rather more formal structure: it abolished the local associations of care committees and replaced them with district councils. It also recognised officially the Central Council of Care Committees, which had been set up informally in 1943, as the body responsible for co-ordinating care committee work throughout the London area. However, the previous division of the Care Service between the Education Office and the Public Health Department continued as before. In 1959 the staff were distributed as follows:

Education Department	Public Health Department
1 Principal Organiser	1 Principal Organiser
10 District Care Organisers	1 Assistant Principal Organiser
22 Senior assistant organisers	9 Divisional treatment organisers
4 organisers for special duties	15 Senior assistant treatment organisers
38 assistant organisers	58 Senior assistant organisers

For all these posts staff had to be qualified with a certificate, diploma or degree in social work or a similar qualification with recent experience in social work. Posts in the education department were open to both men and women, while those in public health were open to women only.[39]

From children *with* problems, to children who were seen to *be* problems

The welfare state provided a cushion against the desperate living conditions that had led to the birth of the School Care Service in the 1900s. This meant that if the service were to survive, it would need to find a new role for itself. It did this by giving its attention to a new kind of need in children – behavioural problems. In some notes for a speech, the Chairman of the Education Committee observed in 1958 that whereas the pioneer voluntary workers had 'wrestled with problems of poverty and disease and lack of facilities and services', present-day workers dealt with 'problems of anxiety and personal adjustment'.[40] Miss Cram made the same point. In the lead article of the LCC *Education Bulletin* in October 1957, she commented that, 'The "underfed" child has mercifully disappeared but teachers, observing the children day by day, are aware of many factors in their lives which prevent full development. These may be physical needs ... or they may be the more intangible *problems of behaviour and human relationship* (emphasis added).'[41] The number of children with medical health problems decreased; in contrast, there was a sharp rise in the number of children identified as having non-medical health needs, such as speech therapy (see Table 6.1).

'There was a time not so long ago', observed W.F. Houghton, the Education Officer, 'when the greatest need was to relieve actual physical want and poverty in England. Today, thank God, that is no longer true on any great scale. But there are other dragons to be slain with the sword of love.'[42] These 'other dragons' were social problems. Care committee workers continued to give children material help, by for example assessing contributory payments to be made for school meals by parents unable to pay the full charge, or by carrying out duties relating to the provision of clothing. But they also became involved in the care of 'maladjustment' and personal problems. Children's difficulties were less often attributed – as before – to

Table 6.1 *Average number of children per 10,000 on the school roll in London with particular health problems requiring investigation, treatment or special education, 1950–5 and 1960–4*

	Health problem	Average number of cases per 10,000 schoolchildren	
		1950–5	1960–4
New cases, including those treated and those referred for investigation	Speech therapy	22	84
	Rheumatism	23	3
	Minor ailment	3,840	1,617
	Enuresis	20	4
	Ear, nose and throat	164	52
Pupils in day and boarding special schools	Blind and partially sighted	12	11
	Deaf and partially hearing	12	7
	Delicate	42	39
	Educationally subnormal	84	98
	Maladjusted	3	14
	Physically handicapped	37	26
Pupils in ordinary schools	Maladjusted	5	10

Source: LCC statistics, taken from Annual Reports including and between 1950–1 to 1963–4 (the report for 1951–2 was not included). Bedford Report, Table 1, adjacent to p. F.4

their medical or material reality but were explained in the language and terms of psychology and social work. These explanations were consistent with developing theories of social behaviour: the term 'problem family' was first consciously used in 1943 in an attempt to characterise a group of families living in squalor and unable or unwilling to make constructive use of the social services.[43] M. Penelope Hall, a social scientist at the University of Liverpool, commented in her book on *The Social Services of Modern England* (1952), that the Care Committee system had now evolved into 'a form of social case work, centering on the school child, but through him impinging on the life of the family as a whole.... the outlook of the care committee organiser is social rather than medical.'[44]

This was not so much a new phenomenon, however, as a development in the behavioural psychology movement that had grown rapidly between the wars. Cyril Burt's appointment in 1913 to the post of official psychologist to the LCC was the first of its kind anywhere in the world; Burt was influential in the setting up of 'child guidance clinics', which assessed children under the control of psychologists. By 1938, there were 34 LEAs with psychologists in post, half of whom had undergone some training by Burt.[45] Growth in this area was especially rapid in London. By 1958, there were five full-time educational psychologists working for the Public Health Department of the LCC, which was a massive increase from the part-time employment of Cyril Burt before the war. John Bowlby, the Director of Child Guidance at the Tavistock Clinic, popularised current theories of family neurosis in his study, *Maternal Care and Mental Health* (1951), which were disseminated to Care Committee workers through conferences and lectures. At one conference, Dr John Nicholson, the recently retired Vice-Chancellor of the University of Kingston-on-Hull, gave a lecture on the subject of 'The Social Worker and the Modern Approach'. He argued that:

> the role of the social worker was undergoing a progressive transformation from concern with the relief of material distress to the more subtle position of intermediary between the benefits of the Welfare State and the recipient of those benefits.

The problems of the present time, he added, 'were shown to be predominantly those originating out of anxiety in a changing society which is continually having to adjust itself to different ideals, standards and conventions, and is meanwhile beset by uncertainties as to the future.'[46]

Care Committee volunteers were now helping families with personal problems ranging from advice with household budgeting, to frank discussions with husbands about the treatment of their wives. A 'highlight' in one office was 'the visit from a man who had been reconciled to his wife and came to thank the care committee for all that had been done for his wife and children during the period when the poor woman had been desperate about his behaviour.' Assisting parents was seen as essential to the care of their children. 'The broken home is self-perpetuating,' observed a District Council report 'and the maladjusted child almost invariably springs from maladjusted parents.'[47]

New problems, it was thought, had emerged out of the very improvement in living conditions. On the one hand, this improvement was welcomed. School dinners were regarded as essential for children's welfare and in May 1951 in England and Wales, 49 per cent of the school population took school meals, which cost fivepence, while 84 per cent drank free school milk.[48] By the mid-1950s, even though the Treasury was trying hard to charge an economic cost for school meals (that is, above the cost of the raw materials), Sir David Eccles, the Minister of Education, firmly refused: he told Butler that, 'this is an essential Social Service. More children ought to take the meals, not less'.[49] But on the other hand, there was some mistrust of the increased level of affluence. Noting that fewer fathers were out of work and many mothers were working, the Care Committee volunteer Eileen Lecky observed that the absence of parents from the home was leading to an increase in 'problem' families. 'What used to be luxuries have now become necessities,' she observed, adding that, 'The effect of this is not good for the children. Many are locked out from their homes until the parents return from work.' In her view, it was not surprising that more and more children were getting into trouble and coming before the juvenile court.[50]

The Care Organisers were professionally qualified social workers. Voluntary workers, however, were amateurs, whose expertise was based on personal experience and on occasional lectures, refresher courses and day conferences, such as a one day conference on 'The Care Committee in a World of Specialists'[51] (which was by now certainly the case). None the less, they were sent to work with families experiencing serious difficulties. One Care Committee volunteer in Battersea reported that in January 1946 (only four months after joining her Care Committee, which involved working for a minimum of one hour a week and seldom more than four hours), she was sent to care for a family with seven children who were staying away from school. The family's problems were various, some of them stemming apparently from the parents' bad marriage, especially the fact that Mr D. drank too much and physically abused his wife:

> in June 1946 … I had an urgent call for help from Mrs D. She wanted a separation from her husband. His interminable rows and bullying … were causing her much distress. In addition Mr D was denying that he was the father of the expected child. On this occasion she again referred to Mr D's 'peculiarities' and I now gathered that she meant he was obsessed with sex.

Eventually, a serious accident forced him to live in one room of the family house. Several of the children managed to get into grammar school but nearly all of them 'graduated downwards to a secondary modern school', through bullying or low achievement. One of the children had taken 'to leading very much smaller boys into varying forms of mischief' while at primary school; the Care Committee worker blamed his mother for 'rapidly turning him into a potential delinquent' by defending him against all comers and protecting him within the family unit. Most of the children ended up with unhappy lives. The Care Committee worker concluded her report with the comment that, 'With the obvious intelligence of most of these children, one wonders what they might have achieved had their living conditions been different.'[52] Equally, one wonders what might have been achieved if they had been assisted by someone with experience – more than four months – and some training.

On 21 February 1958, the LCC Education Committee held a special Jubilee Reception at London's new Festival Hall to mark the first 50 years of the Care Committee service. By now, the number of volunteers had risen to 2,556 – the service had managed, so far, to adapt to the new reality of postwar. One of the guests was Miss Margaret Frere, now in her nineties, the 'founder' of the Care Committees. Mr Houghton, the Education Officer of the LCC, congratulated the Care Committee service on its achievements. He was confident, he said, that the service 'will prosper, expand, and show the same capacity for adjusting itself to the changing needs of London children and their families in the next fifty years.'[53]

Notes

1. Report by the LCC Education Officer, W.F. Houghton, 20 August 1957, Patrick Ivin Private Collection.
2. Charles Webster, 'Beveridge after 50 years', *British Medical Journal* 305, 17 October 1992, p. 901.
3. Richard M. Titmuss: *Problems of Social Policy*, p. 514.
4. Cover of leaflet, *The New National Health Service*, 1948.
5. A. Susan Williams, *Ladies of Influence*, p. 166.
6. Gilda O'Neill: *My East End*, p. 130.
7. Including those of ASW and CM.
8. H.C. Dent: *The Education Act* 1944, pp. 5–6.
9. Keith MacMillan: *Education Welfare: Strategy and structure*, pp. 31–2.
10. A. Dawson: 'The Education Welfare Officer', p. 148.
11. F.H. Pedley (ed.): *Education and Social Work*, p. 13.
12. Harry Hendrick: *Child Welfare: England 1872–1989*, p. 222.
13. Ibid., p. 237.
14. LCC staff of school inquiry officers, Report by the Education Officer, 6 September 1951, LMA, EO/WEL/1/34.
15. The Children's Bill 1947/48, Incorporation of the School Attendance and Education Welfare Officers' Service in the new scheme, 1948. Letter to John Lewis MP from James Heaton, General Secretary of EWONA, 24 April 1948, PRO, MH 102/16355.
16. LCC, Children's Care Work, Report of the Education Committee, 10 May 1950, signed R. McKinnon Wood, Chairman, being Extract from Minutes of the Meeting of the Council held on 23 May 1950, Patrick Ivin Private Collection.
17. LCC school inquiry officer recruitment report, 29 August 1951, LMA, EO/WEL/1/34.
18. Bedford Report, p. C.5.
19. Ibid.
20. Beatrice Serota to ASW, DW and RA, 15 June 1999.
21. Ibid.
22. Carolyn Steedman: *Landscape for a Good Woman*, p. 57.
23. Eileen Lecky: 'Children Then and Now', p. 28, LMA, ILEA S/SB/04/2.
24. Annual Report of the LCC Medical Officer of Health and School Medical Officer, 1948.
25. Eileen Lecky: 'Children Then and Now', p. 26, LMA, ILEA S/SB/04/2.
26. Ibid., p. 27.
27. LCC, Children's Care Work, Report of the Education Committee, 10 May 1950, signed R. McKinnon Wood, Chairman, being Extract from Minutes of the Meeting of the Council held on 23 May 1950, Patrick Ivin Private Collection.
28. Eileen Lecky: 'Children Then and Now', pp. 29–30.

29. Harry Hendrick: *Child Welfare: England 1872–1989*, p. 147.
30. LCC, Children's Care Work, Report of the Education Committee, 10 May 1950, signed R. McKinnon Wood, Chairman, being Extract from Minutes of the Meeting of the Council held on 23 May 1950, Patrick Ivin Private Collection.
31. Graham Savage, EO, to Olive Cram, 20 June 1947, LMA, EO/WEL/1/34.
32. Olive Cram to Graham Savage, 30 June 1947, LMA, EO/WEL/1/34.
33. Graham Savage to Olive Cram, 4 July 1947, LMA, EO/WEL/1/34.
34. Olive Cram to Graham Savage, 30 June 1947, LMA, EO/WEL/1/34.
35. Graham Savage to Olive Cram, 4 July 1947, LMA, EO/WEL/1/34.
36. Draft report of Graham Savage, Education Officer, to the Education (General Sub-) Committee. Children's Care Work. n.d., 1947, LMA, EO/WEL/1/34.
37. Mr. Sharpen to Miss Cram, 21 July 1948, LMA, EO/WEL/1/34.
38. LCC, Children's Care Work, Report of the Education Committee, 10 May 1950, signed R. McKinnon Wood, Chairman, being Extract from Minutes of the Meeting of the Council held on 23 May 1950, Patrick Ivin Private Collection.
39. 'The Work of the LCC Children's Care Organizers', LCC Leaflet 1959, MA/ILEA/5/SB/4.
40. 'Care Committee Workers' Reception – 21 February 1958, Notes for Chairman of Education Committee', Patrick Ivin Private Collection.
41. Olive W. Cram, 'Jubilee of Care Committees', *London County Council Education Bulletin*, 424, 9 October 1957.
42. Report by the LCC Education Officer, W.F. Houghton, 20 August 1957, Patrick Ivin Private Collection.
43. A.F. Philp and Noel Timms: *The Problem of 'The Problem Family'*, p. vii.
44. M. Penelope Hall: *The Social Services of Modern England*, p. 206.
45. Adrian Wooldridge: *Measuring the Mind: Education and psychology in England, c 1860–1990*, p. 11; see also Deborah Thom: 'Wishes, Anxieties, Play and Gestures: Child guidance in inter-war England', pp. 201–2.
46. LCC, Care Committee Service, Annual Report, 30 September 1957.
47. Ibid.
48. Charles Webster: 'Government Policy on School Meals and Welfare Foods 1939–1970', p. 196.
49. Ibid, p. 200.
50. Eileen Lecky: 'Children Then and Now', p. 28, LMA, ILEA S/SB/04/2.
51. LCC, Care Committee Service, Annual Report, 30 September 1957.
52. The D. family, Battersea. Report by Mrs Lewis, Care Committee worker at a Battersea School, April 1957, Patrick Ivin Private Collection.
53. Report by the LCC Education Officer, W.F. Houghton, 20 August 1957, Patrick Ivin Private Collection.

Chapter 7

THE BEDFORD REPORT

'[Families were] striving honestly to be self-supporting
and to give their children a good start in life against
the odds.'[1]

IN 1965 THE LCC was abolished, under the London Government Act of 1963. It was replaced by the Greater London Council (GLC), which had responsibility not only for the area within LCC boundaries but for the whole of the metropolis. This development was underpinned by political machinations, notably Conservative weariness of Labour rule in County Hall (although Harold Wilson's Labour government was in power by the time the GLC became a reality). However, there was also a sound administrative basis for the change. The LCC had 'long since ceased to be representative of the metropolis', writes Roy Porter. As early as 1900, he adds,

> the actual built-up area (Greater London) stretched well beyond the LCC boundaries. By the 1960s the LCC was resembling a latter-day City Corporation – an isle lapped by a vast metropolitan sea over which it exercised no control. A unified government for the 610 square miles of Greater London made far more economic, fiscal and demographic sense.[2]

The first GLC election was won by Labour; in 1967 the Conservatives were voted into power, staying there solidly until they were routed in 1973.

Responsibility for education, at least within the inner London area that had previously been under the control of the LCC, was transferred to the Inner London Education Authority, which was set up as a 'special committee' of the GLC, but in practice was autonomous.[3] The ILEA was divided into ten education divisions corresponding to the areas covered by the inner London boroughs (Divisions 1 and 2 covered two boroughs each; the other eight Divisions each covered one borough). The Education Committee of the ILEA comprised up to 19 members and its first Education Officer was W.F.

Houghton, who had been Education Officer of the LCC since 1956. Membership of the ILEA consisted of 40 GLC councillors who represented the inner London boroughs and the City of London, as well as 13 members appointed by each of the 12 inner London borough councils and the corporation of London. In changes made to the School Health Service, borough medical officers of health became principal school medical officers for their areas.[4] The ILEA was dominated by Labour for most of its existence and had a clear equal opportunities policy. This was underpinned by the principle that the most socially deprived young people should have proportionately the most support from the ILEA.

The scope of the Bedford inquiry

Very soon after the creation of the ILEA, concern developed about the perceived fragmentation of the numerous services and agencies in London that were involved in the welfare of schoolchildren. The Education Officer of the ILEA commissioned the Social Research Unit of Bedford College in the University of London to produce an independent review of 'services which were concerned with the welfare of schoolchildren in its widest sense' and to suggest any modifications that would achieve a co-ordinated and effective welfare service. At this time, the Seebohm Committee was carrying out a review of 'the organisation and responsibilities of the local authority personal social services in England and Wales' and was considering what changes were desirable 'to secure an effective family service'. The ILEA was aware that the Seebohm Committee was not required from its terms of reference to review the social and welfare services in education; one of its intentions in commissioning the Bedford Report, therefore, was to bring its own services in line with the changes which were likely to result from the Seebohm recommendations.

The inquiry began in January 1966. Margot Jeffries, a sociologist, was appointed director and the rest of the committee were researchers working at the Social Research Unit of Bedford College. The study involved a review of each welfare service for school-aged children: the School Inquiry Service, the School Care Service, the Young People's Advisory Service, the School Psychological service and the School Health Service (including special schools and child guidance facilities). The inquiry was innovative in its multi-disciplinary approach and looked not only at the individual services, but also at the relationships between them. At the centre of the study were the School Inquiry and the School Care services. Although the study collected data for the whole of the London area, it focused in particular upon two of the ten administrative divisions of the ILEA: Division II and Division IX. Division II, which was north of the river Thames, covered the areas of the London boroughs of Westminster and Camden; Division IX was south of the river and covered the London borough of Lambeth. There were approximately 40,000 children in both of the divisions and the sample for the study was made up of 10,000 children from each (approximately 20 per cent). A total of 45 primary schools and 12 secondary schools were selected, with an equal number of boys and girls.

The survey collected data through an examination of records, interviews, group discussions and questionnaires. In the case of the School Inquiry Service, a 'special inquiry' was conducted into the work of school inquiry officers in a single week in June 1966; in the case of the Care Service, an in-depth study of Care Committee workers was carried out in the last two weeks of June 1966. At no time were the views of the children and their parents sought: a mass of information about individual children and their families is presented, but only from the point of view of the professionals working in the service. No attempt was made to discover from the children their own experience of the services or to give them a voice.

The report, entitled 'The Social Welfare Services of the Inner London Education Authority', was completed in 1967. Its most significant recommendation was that there should be a united education welfare service in place of the separate school inquiry service and the School Care Committees, which overlapped in many areas. 'Dealing with attendance problems,' it observed, 'should not, in general, be divorced from dealing with other forms of social difficulty, and for this reason we believe that much will ultimately be gained if the school care service and the school inquiry service are brought together in a single, unified school welfare service.'[5] They should also, recommended the report, be joined by the school psychological service, social workers employed by the school health service in the child guidance clinics, special schools and treatment centres.

This was the first time in their history that the operation of these London services was carefully examined. It had been widely observed that the Care Committee scheme was 'interesting and significant' as an 'experiment in a particular form of child care', as M. Penelope Hall, a social scientist at the University of Liverpool, wrote in *The Social Services of Modern England* (1952).[6] But although questions had been asked about the functioning and use of these services on several occasions in the past, no data had been collected in any systematic way before the Bedford Inquiry. Comprising about 450 pages, with six major sections, several appendices and numerous tables throughout, the Bedford Report provided the first and only comprehensive account of the education welfare services in London, offering a unique snapshot of the functioning of those services in the mid-1960s. For this reason – and also because it had a tremendous impact on the future of the school welfare services of London – its findings and observations deserve close examination in this chapter.

The work of school inquiry officers

In each of the ILEA's ten administrative areas at this time, there was a Divisional Officer (in 1970 there was at least one woman DO, which was a change from the earlier period) and their staff, including school inquiry officers. These inquiry officers were mainly men; recruits were not required to have any social work training and they learned their work 'on the job'. Each officer covered a demarcated district and was responsible for between 2–3,000 children of statutory school-age living within it. He was required to keep an up-to-date record of all children and families in his district (known as a schedule card) and to maintain close and regular contact with the heads of schools. The schedule card was used to record key information about each family, such as the names and ages of all members of the family under the age of 19, the occupations of parents or guardians, and particulars of the schools attended; information concerning individual children such as medical examinations and appearances at juvenile court were also collected. In order to maintain the cards, attendance officers visited families or checked voters' lists and directories. If a family moved, this information was passed to the correct district if within the ILEA, or to another authority if the family moved out of London. On another card, in the form of a street index, details were maintained about the residential area of the district.

Attendance levels for the areas covered by the ILEA had remained relatively constant since before the First World War.[7] It was found that of all visits made by the attendance officer to the family home, over 75 per cent of absenteeism from school was due to a child's ill health or being away on holiday (when the parents had not informed the school). This was an obvious waste of the officers' time and resources and it was suggested that conducting a postal inquiry would be more effective.[8] Apart from these causes, the majority of pupils absent from school spent their time at home with their mother or helping with chores. Missed lesson time was spent at the shops and in the classroom, cloakrooms and toilets.

The monitoring of attendance was carried out by the slip system, which had been used in some form by attendance officers in London since the beginning of compulsory schooling. The officer collected the slips from the school in person during the last session of each week. Back at the divisional office, he extracted information such as on new admissions and medical notes. During the morning of the last day of the school week, the slip was returned to the school, bearing the officer's name, the date and a note of any action taken. Officers sent or handed a warning to parents as soon as there was reason to think there was 'neither unavoidable cause nor reasonable excuse for absence'. When two weeks of broken attendance followed the first warning, a second and final warning was given to parents, explaining that prosecution was likely to follow any continued absences. If attendance was still unsatisfactory the case was referred for prosecution, in which case the inquiry officer submitted a record of proceedings and particulars. There was a difference in prosecution rates depending on the type of school a child attended. Pupils of 'special schools' were more likely to be prosecuted than pupils who attended a mainstream primary or secondary school.[9]

Twelve families involved in legal proceedings between September 1964 and July 1965 were discussed at length in the Bedford Report. Here are two examples of these case studies:

Family 1

Charles: born 1950; *Sylvia*: born 1951.

Living with parents: 9 children in family. Parents prosecuted at Petty Sessions court in *1965* for both children and fined. Sylvia directed to Juvenile Court, but no other order made as attendance improved.

1951: some of the children sent on a recuperative holiday; health visitor reported visiting; help with clothing from care committee from this year onward; housing conditions reported as poor. *1954*: parents prosecuted for eldest boy and fined; fourth boy ascertained as E.S.N. [Educationally Subnormal] *1960*: parents prosecuted twice for second boy and fined. *1963*: parents prosecuted for Sylvia and fined; Sylvia referred for child guidance; Charles brought before Juvenile Court for larceny and fined. *1964*: Charles before Juvenile Court again and conditionally discharged. *1965*: Sylvia sent to open air boarding school but returns later; parents fined second time in the year for her non-attendance; Charles fined in Juvenile Court for larceny and for taking and driving away; second boy in Juvenile Court and placed on probation for one year for possessing drugs.

Family 'well known' to school care service; 'known' to children's department and probation service.

Family 2

Deirdre: born 1951.

Living with mother; 4 children in family. Mother prosecuted in Petty Sessions and fined; Deirdre made the subject of a Fit Person Order in Juvenile Court.

1951: Deirdre born to unmarried mother. *1952*: mother married. *1954*: mother separated and divorced. *1959*: mother remarried; two children of this marriage. *1964*: Deirdre allegedly seduced by step-father; step-father leaves; mother in financial difficulties; children free dinners and help with clothing, shoes, etc.

Family 'known' to school care service and probation service; 'well known' to children's department. [10]

Inquiry officers were also involved in the care and protection of children under the Children and Young Persons Act of 1933 and they reported to the divisional officer any child whom they considered should be brought to the notice of the School Care Committee; to this extent, the inquiry officer was aware of and co-operated with the Care Service. They also monitored the employment of children and the use of young people in entertainments like circuses and the theatre. Any infringements were documented and returned to the divisional office; if possible, the employer was interviewed by the officer at the time of the offence.[11] Officers took the view that most of the children with chronic and intractable attendance problems were from families whose members presented 'a tremendous variety of social pathology'. The ILEA Children's Welfare Officers' Guild, which represented the interests of school inquiry officers, claimed that the service was 'essentially a casework service operating within an authoritative setting'.[12]

The inquiry officer's day was long and hard. Generally, mornings were allocated to visiting in the district, starting at 9 a.m., and afternoons were spent in the divisional office on the clerical work generated by the visits. When it was thought that parents were deliberately avoiding the officer, he varied the order of the streets he visited. His work involved a large amount of administration and paperwork:

> On completion of outdoor work everyday, the officer should deal with his clerical work and indoor duties in the following order:
>
> Enter in the diary … number of visits paid; times and places of first and last outdoor duty; and times of arrival at and departure from the office.
>
> Hand in receipt book and cash collected from the parents.
>
> Clerical work. Every endeavour should be made to clear each day all clerical work in accordance with the instructions in the preceding paragraphs.

The outcome of home visits were few summonses but a number of written warnings; on occasion, families were referred to welfare services or discussed with the school heads.

The Bedford Committee found much overlapping between the School Inquiry Service and the School Care Service: workers frequently visited the same family – to address a child's poor attendance or a welfare issue. It was noted, too, that there was little direct communication between these two closely related services. When a divisional care organiser commented that 'The service and its workers keep a close liaison with other bodies. Contact is kept with the NSPCC, probation officers, the children's department and the health department',[13] it was noticed that the school attendance service was not included in the list of 'other bodies'. This was seen by the Bedford Committee as a major and a problematic missing link. Many school inquiry officers themselves complained of poor communication and clashes of policy with other departments working with children, including the school care service. One officer described the school care organisers as 'playing their hand very close'.[14]

In the 1960s, while the Bedford Committee was carrying out its study, school inquiry officers all over Britain were complaining that their work was undervalued and under rewarded. In response, some important steps were taken to strengthen the service: caseloads were reduced and the salaries and grading of staff at all levels were improved. A senior officer post was created in each division, enabling a person of proven ability to spend more time giving guidance to officers and to refer cases needing further action to other welfare agencies. Provision was made for some training. In 1961, it became possible to sit an examination to gain the Intermediate Diploma in Municipal Administration; in 1963, this was changed to the Certificate in Education Welfare (CEW), which included new subjects such as social services, child development and education welfare. The Plowden Report of 1967 stated that more than 300 officers nationwide were studying for the CEW and 30 had university training. But although the CEW gave attendance officers some level of recognition, the course was described as gruelling[15] and few local authorities made statutory arrangements for officers to be released for the course. Moreover, the CEW did not produce parity of status with social workers or teachers, although merited an increase in salary.

In London, the dissatisfaction of school inquiry officers extended to annoyance with the raincoats they were given to wear when on duty. 'They are at present supplied with a black (shiny) mackintosh,' complained the Honorary Secretary of the ILEA Children's Welfare Officers' Guild in 1965, 'which are absolutely useless when used for long periods on visitation, for the lack of any means of ventilation and become dripping wet with perspiration on the inside.' He added, 'The appearance of the mackintoshes are more in keeping with the clothing of dustmen than that of officers calling on parents and dealing with social problems.'[16] Arrangements for the placing of an order for a better raincoat took over two years, after a long and drawn-out correspondence between the Guild and the ILEA.[17]

The Bedford team uncovered gender-related differences in the way children were treated for non-attendance at school. It found that boys were more likely than girls to be made the subject of a supervision order; where a girl was concerned, it was more likely that her parents would be fined. The reasons for absence that were recorded by the divisional officers reflected different attitudes towards non-attendance by boys to non-attendance by girls. Boys were more likely to be regarded as cases of truancy, where the parents were unable to control the child or supervise his school attendance. Girls were seen as being kept at home to help with housework or to mind younger children in large families and their non-attendance was not viewed as truancy in the same way as boys. In fact, boys had lower rates of non-attendance than girls, although more cases of prosecutions were brought against them.[18] Table 7.1 shows the difference between boys and girls in relation to the causes of non-attendance.

Data collected on the School Care Service

The Care Service had maintained the unique but complex combination of voluntary and paid organisers that had developed in the first two decades of the twentieth century. Each school had a Care Committee attached to it,

Table 7.1 *Percentage of boys and girls in Bedford Inquiry sample whose non-attendance was attributed to various causes, 1965–6*

Reason given for non-attendance	Boys	Girls
Illness, accompanied by some medical certificates	19	30
Illness, unaccompanied by medical certificates	16	22
Illness of mother or other relative	10	11
Child doing housework or minding other children	6	14
No clothes, uniform or shoes	5	7
Child truanting	37	18
Child dislikes specific school, teacher or activity	17	9
Frightened by other children	2	–
Child refuses to get up in the morning	2	1
Parent withholding over-age child	7	3
Child allegedly at school elsewhere	2	–
No reason recorded	16	19
Total (adding to more than 100%, as 2 or more reasons possible)	139	134

Source: Adapted from the Bedford Report, Table 13, adjacent to p. B.24

formed of voluntary workers. There was also a paid staff of organisers in each ILEA division, whose primary function was to recruit, train and guide the Care Committee workers. In addition to the School Committees there were one or more District Councils in each administrative division, formed of representatives from each School Care Committee. Their main duties were to co-ordinate generally the activities of the Care Committees and to report to the central council.

There was one divisional organiser in charge of the work in each Division. Below her were three grades: the assistant divisional school care organiser; the senior school care organiser; and the school care organiser. In most divisions there was at least one sub-office in addition to the head office. The ratio of paid organiser to voluntary staff was about 1 to nearly 20. Officially the organisers were supposed to be an experienced body of trained social workers, with a social science qualification. However, the Bedford Committee were informed that these social work qualifications were not always insisted upon. All but three of the organisers in the sample that was studied by the Bedford team were women, and over half were married. Generally, divisional organisers were in their late 50s; the intermediate grades

Plate 16 *The cover of a leaflet to recruit new School Care Organizers, which was produced by the ILEA in 1968.*

were occupied by women in their 50s; and the most junior grade, the school care organisers, were for the most part in their 20s and 30s.

The membership of Care Committees had to consist, at the least, of an honorary secretary who was normally an active voluntary worker, a chairman who was often a local clergyman, and other members. Representatives of local branches of voluntary organisations and other local people, such as retired headteachers, were co-opted into the service to serve as committee members. Headteachers and organisers attended meetings in an advisory capacity. The statutory duties of the committee included the approval of free school meals and clothes and the consideration of the problems of certain children and their families. They visited pupils' homes mainly to investigate the need for free school dinners (see Table 7.2). The honorary secretary was the committee member who usually attended the medicals, checked financial statements of free dinner applicants, dealt with requests for clothing and shoes, and visited the families where necessary.

Table 7.2 *Reason for visit or action by Care Committee workers in a Bedford Inquiry sample, 1965–6*

Reason	Number of times recorded
Free school dinners	104
Medical follow-up	51
Clothing and footwear	49
School journey, holiday	38
Parental illness	17
Neglect, maltreatment, moral danger	17
Special schooling, tutorial class	10
Child guidance	9
Non-attendance	9
Housing	6
Other	56
Total number of reasons	**366**

Source: Bedford Report, Table 22, adjacent to p. C.48

The volunteers were given no official training but learnt 'on the job', just like the inquiry officers. Volunteers were usually women (only 9 per cent were men), married or formerly married, and over 50 years of age. Nearly all volunteers were from affluent backgrounds and sent their children to independent schools, which provided a very different experience of education to the state schools assisted by volunteers. Recruitment mainly took place through friends and word of mouth:

Miss Knox who was the head of the welfare service in London was very, very good at recruiting people and she really was, she had been at the same Oxford College as me, each year she used to go through the list of old girls and see if anyone was near. I can remember distinctly she rang me up and told me all about it. Would I like to come for an interview? When I got there she took it for granted that I was going to join. She was a very forceful lady.[19]

An advertisement placed in the *Guardian* in 1963 to recruit volunteers gives a flavour of the volunteers' work. It reproduced an article written by a Care Committee member, in which she described the start of her school care work:

My first visit was to a very dirty house to ask the mother of three boys why one of them had not gone to have his eyes tested as the doctor had recommended. She had 'clean forgotten', she said. And anyway he hadn't liked the doctor when he went earlier. A little persuasion was needed here but she agreed. I had to report back to my office her willingness and from then on all the arrangements were made by the professionals ... [There] is a real link between school, home, and doctor and a friend to mothers who need one.

Plate 17 *A Care Committee volunteer pays a visit to a mother and her children in their home in 1961. LMA, 22.5, 9332*

This volunteer derived tremendous job satisfaction from her work: 'But the job has done much more for me. On my care committee days I am completely absorbed in other people. A whole new life is opened up and the gain is all mine.'[20] Her only reservation was that, 'Sometimes one feels that there is a little too much record keeping,' but the general view was that volunteers did very little of this. Indeed, the Education Officer observed in a report in 1966, when explaining why it was impossible to give an accurate statistical return on the work of the Care Committees in 1965–66, that 'voluntary workers always prefer to do the work rather than to write detailed reports about it.'[21]

The volunteers believed they were welcome in families' homes: 'someone to talk to ... neither the authorities or the next door neighbour.'[22] A man whose family were visited by a Care Committee volunteer when he was a boy has since recalled his mother's pleasure at the arrival:

> While at secondary school, the School's Care Committee Worker visited my mother and myself on more than one occasion, to see if any material or general help was needed. There was no stigma attached to this, from my mother's point of view. She regarded the visits as well-meaning and supportive. I was too busy playing football to be bothered about them, either way. The School Care Committee Worker, who was a volunteer, was a very well presented and professional person.[23]

However, the Bedford team suggested it would be better to recruit young working-class women instead of older middle-class women. Women from a similar social background to the families visited, it was argued, 'may find it easier to transcend the economical, social, cultural barriers which undoubtedly separate well to do upper middle class women from the majority of London mothers.'[24] It was also hoped that younger women would be able to give up more of their time in the evening as well as during the day, whereas older women were understandably reluctant to make evening visits. Another suggestion was that families presenting complex difficulties ought to be helped by a trained professional, not a volunteer with no training. Certainly some volunteers felt uncomfortable about their lack of training. One has observed that:

> You felt very, very inadequate and you felt so tremendously conscious of the problems of poverty that they were dealing with, because they were really dealing with the impossible. I fancy now how strange it must seem that people should take on totally untrained people to do this kind of work.[25]

The Bedford Report recommended that volunteers should be restricted to practical tasks like helping parents to complete forms for free dinners, clothing, or assistance with school holidays and journeys. But volunteers should be carefully selected, it added, and should receive training for these tasks.

The rediscovery of poverty

The general improvement in living conditions that followed the Second World War started to give way in the early 1960s to an increasing social inequality. On the one hand, the American weekly *Time* proclaimed on its cover 'LONDON – THE SWINGING CITY', and real earnings had risen in the 1960s by approximately 70 per cent in the 20 years since the war.[26] But on the other hand, this was also the age of tower blocks, increased crime and the movement of industry out of the city; trade with the Commonwealth was rapidly decreasing and one by one, the docks – starting with the East India Dock in 1967 – ceased activity.[27] In 1965, social reformers met in the middle of London to set up a campaigning organisation called the Child Poverty Action Group (CPAG), as a way of starting to address the problem; it has been said that the poverty of Britain was rediscovered at the meeting where CPAG was founded. Studies carried out by campaigners like Peter Townsend and Dorothy Wedderburn, among others, argued that many clients of the social services were suffering real economic hardship and that many others in similar circumstances were not receiving any help from welfare agencies.[28] In 1966 the School Care volunteers and their organisers collected some information about cases of acute poverty and financial hardship and made suggestions to the ILEA's School Subcommittee about ways in which material distress might be diminished.[29]

A typical family visited by a Care Committee worker at this time was large, with one parent; when a father was present, he was often unemployed. In the majority of these families at least one child received free school dinners and help was given with clothing, footwear, school journeys or holidays. In a smaller group of families, children had been recommended for child guidance or special schooling. Miss Adeline Wimble, who was now the Principal Care Organiser, wrote later about the kind of work done by the Care Committees at this time. She gave the following example of a family that was helped by the care service:

At the beginning of 1963 a family of parents and three children was about to be evicted once more on account of rent arrears. On investigating, the care committee worker discovered that their total debts, including rent arrears, amounted to just under £200. These had been accrued partly through the parents' illness and partly for maintenance of the children in care following a previous eviction. The family was again in danger of breaking up and completely losing heart.

A small grant from a voluntary fund staved off the immediate danger and avoided the expense of court action. Free meals, clothing for the mother and children and a recuperative holiday for the children all helped, but for the next 18 months the Care Committee visited regularly and through their support and practical help the family cleared all but one small debt. One child was referred to a child guidance clinic owing to a lack of progress at school and the psychiatrist was reported as saying that, 'this is a worthwhile family, not very expert at accounts, that has responded well to the supportive action of the Care Committee Service'.[30]

In another case, an Irish family with six children under the age of 12, the father was 'indolent' and the mother – though devoted and hardworking – was a 'poor manager'; they all lived in two small rooms. The Care Committee was in close touch with the family, but the mother did not reveal the fact that debts were mounting until eviction was threatened. The father then took a labouring job and the mother asked for help. With a grant from the Children's department, the Care Committee provided the father (who was slightly crippled) with suitable working boots and cleared the electricity and grocer's bills, so that the family was able to reduce the rent arrears. Most importantly, the committee recommended the family for priority rehousing.[31] However, care workers were by no means the only people who were now in a position to identify children in need: there were also school medical officers, school nurses, the children's worker and the inquiry officer. This led to a lack of uniformity, observed the Bedford Report, especially since there was no working definition of 'need':

> there is no general agreement on what constitutes need, that is on the range of characteristics which children have to display before they can be said to need help over and beyond that provided by the normal facilities of the schools. Nor is there any general agreement on the level of need which services should seek at present to be meeting, nor on what measures should be used to judge how successful they are in meeting need.[32]

Possibly as a consequence of the lack of criteria by which to judge need, the minutes of some Care Committees reveal difficulties in deciding which children needed assistance. Often, children were discussed in terms of whether they were 'deserving' or 'undeserving':

> Free dinners for Susan B was discussed. 'Mr. Barnes thought there was no hardship – she smoked a lot.' 'Jane Y appears to have everything that she

wants and also has a telephone in her house.' 'Enquiries were made as to how much money John B was sent when he was away at Sayers Croft as he seemed to be buying a lot of sweets.' (The children's names have been changed.)[33]

But overall, the volunteers did not bother about the *meaning* of need – most of them seemed to think they were able to recognise it when they saw it. In Division 3 (Islington), for example, they gave help in 1965–6 to 1,567 families suffering from poverty, 650 families that were fatherless (including 23 with fathers in prison), 17 motherless (with one mother in prison), 371 with more children than their income could support, 129 with the main breadwinner incapacitated, 110 with unstable parents, 192 with low wages and 144 where high rents were considered the main cause (many of the others also had high rents).[34] In support of their work, the Education Officer Houghton commented that most families were 'striving honestly to be self-supporting and to give their children a good start in life against the odds.' There were many families, he added,

> who never complain and whose difficulties would not be known were it not for the visits of the school care workers, and many a lone woman has a very hard struggle to keep her family adequately fed and clothed, and cannot, unless helped by the care committee, hope to provide her children with proper school uniform, pocket money, participation in school journeys, outings and collections, etc, nor indeed have any light or colour in her own life.[35]

Relationships between the School Care Service and the children's departments of the London boroughs (inherited from the LCC in 1965) were not good, so far as the Bedford researchers could ascertain. The staff of the children's departments were concerned to develop a highly professional family-based casework service and they felt that the maintenance of an education-centred service was likely to lead to a duplication of social service effort and to the confusion of those who were clients of both services. Moreover, they were critical of the role played by both organisers and voluntary workers in the School Care Service, describing it as a brake on the development of high standards of work.

Senior members of the care service, on the other hand, claimed that the children's departments, although unable through pressure of work to offer help to many families themselves, were often unwilling to communicate information which the School Care Service could use to the advantage of these families. The children's departments were also accused of the dismissal, without due consideration, of reports prepared by voluntary workers, simply on the grounds that they had been prepared by volunteers.

The Bedford Report did not advocate that the London boroughs' children's departments should take over the welfare services provided by the ILEA school care and school inquiry service. For one thing, it was thought that the work of the volunteers would improve with better selection, training and supervision. But also, it took the view that the children's departments 'have still to establish their own standards of work and improve their methods of collaborating with others in the health and welfare field.' Overall, it judged that there was a great deal to be said for maintaining an education-based social welfare service working in and with the school. 'It is in these institutions, after all,' it observed, 'that children spend so much of their waking time, and it is here that opportunities for the detection of early signs of distress or disturbance are likely to be greatest.' Any merger with the children's departments might increase the number of families who were failing to benefit from education welfare provision, by slipping through the close-knit net which the school care organisation had developed, 'partly as a result of the extensive use of a cadre of volunteers'.[36]

A review of school health care

Like the London School Board and the LCC before it, the ILEA was committed to prevention rather than cure – 'the idea of early identification and treatment as a means of preventing the development of more serious or irreversible defects'.[37] Prevention now took different forms, however, since the health picture of London had changed dramatically since school health care was first started in the late nineteenth century. At that time, the control of infectious disease and medical examinations were the main remit. But there had been enormous advances since then in medicine and the treatment of infectious diseases, notably the development of antibiotics; moreover, the NHS had made medical services available to the whole family, on the basis of need.

In the mid-1960s, the school health service employed school medical officers, school nurses, health educators, social workers and psychiatric social workers. All children attending school within London had a routine medical examination at the ages of 7 and 11. Care Committee workers still attended school medical examinations and helped to ensure that appointments were kept at hospitals and clinics .[38] However, medical staff were not always happy about the presence of the Care Committee volunteer. One of the school medical officers said that it was difficult to talk to a child or parent with a third person present and that sometimes there might be as many as five people in the room at a time. This gave the examination the atmosphere of an interviewing committee, he added, rather than a private consultation. In these circumstances, he added, 'it was not possible to get at the real problem, and, as a result, sometimes involved him in making home visits himself.'[39] The Bedford team shared this view:

> the invasion of the individual child's privacy ... in his examination before several people seems to us to be an unwelcome survival from an earlier time when little regard was paid to the feelings of the recipient of free medical services.[40]

No attempt was made to consult the children involved on what *they* thought about the presence of Care Committee workers at their medical examinations, which is a notable omission in the survey work. In this, as in every other aspect of the Bedford investigation, children were not consulted.

Overall, school medical staff believed that voluntary workers had a part to play in schools, but that this part should be limited to practical things like the organisation of holidays. One doctor said that he would hesitate to ask a volunteer to interview a mother with a problem and that this work should be dealt with by a trained social worker. Another indicated that it was difficult to identify the voluntary workers of poor quality because their reports were 'heavily edited' by the school care organisers. 'He hinted,' added the Report, 'that many unsatisfactory and anachronistic aspects of the School Care Service had survived because the voluntary workers themselves were often closely associated with or related to influential people in local and central government.'[41]

Child guidance facilities were the chief facility for dealing with maladjusted children in ordinary school. The types of service offered were child therapy or casework with the parent, which was provided by psychiatric social workers, educational psychologists and psychiatrists. Information about the child's home background was often provided by the School Care Service. Two-thirds of educational psychologists worked within the child guidance clinics and the remainder were based at County Hall. Educational psychologists were given a number of schools to cover, usually within a single division of the ILEA. The Bedford Report found that the ratio of educational psychologists to schoolchildren was approximately 1: 23,000, which it regarded as inadequate. However, it did not advocate increasing the numbers, on the grounds that this would 'lead to a greater utilization of the service and establishment of a new and lower threshold of need, thus leading to a demand for ever greater numbers'. The Bedford team recommended that this service should join the other services (voluntary Care Committee workers, school care organisers and school inquiry officers) in a new integrated school welfare service.[42]

The challenge of new immigration

The number of children deemed maladjusted had increased in recent years and so there was a growing demand for 'special' education provision.[43] One of the main reasons for this 'insatiable demand', suggested the Bedford Report, was 'an increased prevalence of maladjustment due to an influx of immigrant children who were more likely than native born children to be maladjusted.'[44] It was by no means a new phenomenon for London to be a multicultural city, but the immigrant cultures had changed character. In the 1950s, when there was near full employment in Britain, the British government and employers had encouraged immigration from the West Indies. There had been waves of immigration from India and Pakistan in the late 1950s and early 1960s; Poles and Italians also moved to London and the immigration of Greek and Turkish Cypriots to London quadrupled in 1960–1. Racism had become a serious problem and London's first race riot occurred in Notting Hill in late 1958, when white mobs attacked the homes of blacks.[45] The 1961 census showed that the number of people in Britain who had been born abroad had increased by about 40 per cent since 1951. From 1960 to 1962, total net immigration amounted to 388,000 people.[46]

By 1967, immigrants accounted for 28 per cent of the educationally subnormal places, although they only represented 15 per cent of the pupils in the ordinary schools. The ILEA recognised that although the children in special schools corresponded to official definitions of what was deemed to be educationally subnormal, the reasons for their failure to learn might be different from those of children born and raised in London. Extra funding was made available to teachers and schools with immigrant students, in line with suggestions made by the Plowden Report of 1967. This demographic change created new challenges for the School Care Service, but the Bedford team paid scant attention in its report to the requirements – in relation to language and customs, for example – of a society that was becoming increasingly multicultural.[47]

At the local level, however, some care workers made efforts to respond to the needs of immigrant pupils. Miss Maltby, Divisional School Care Organiser for the borough of Islington, stated in the *North London Press* that in her division, the Care Service had managed to recruit Greek- and Urdu-speaking helpers, although volunteers who spoke Turkish were still needed.[48]

Plans to merge the services

The ILEA set up a working party in 1968 to consider the conclusions of the Bedford Report. This was chaired by Mr W. Braide, Senior Assistant Education Officer, and its membership included the Education Officer, representatives of the Divisional Officers, and outside agencies like the Child Care and Probation Services. The Braide Report accepted the chief recommendation of the Bedford Report, which was the creation in London of a unified Education Welfare Service, incorporating the School Care Service and the School Inquiry Service. However, it rejected the idea of incorporating into the EWS the welfare and social services of the Medical Adviser's Department. The Braide Report proposed that the new EWS should be a professionally qualified social work service, through the recruitment of trained staff and the appointment of a Chief Education Welfare adviser with appropriate qualifications and experience.

The recommendations of the Bedford and Braide reports were consistent for the most part with the conclusions of key government inquiries – the Newsom Report (1963), the Plowden Report on children and primary schools (1967) and the Seebohm Report (1968). The Newsom Report had urged the need for liaison between schools and social services. The Plowden Report, stressing the importance of links between home and school for the effective education of children, had recognised the value and importance to this work of the Education Welfare Service (as delivered outside London). The Seebohm Committee picked up the School Social Work theme, highlighting 'the prime importance of the role of the teacher ... who sees the child daily in class and is thus the first to become aware that all is not well.' Although the Seebohm Committee's terms of reference did not involve the social and welfare services in education, its Report *did* suggest that welfare services within education should become part of family social services within local authority social service departments. It therefore rejected the idea that social work with schoolchildren should be provided by education authorities. However, this was not accepted by the government and for the most part was not accepted by local education authorities, including the ILEA. The recommendations resulting from the Seebohm Report (apart from those relating to education welfare) were embodied in the Local Government Social Services Act of 1970, as well as in the Children and Young Persons Act of 1969; this changed the role and responsibilities of Juvenile Courts in dealing with young people, including those attending school.

On 18 June 1969 the Education Committee of the ILEA accepted the recommendations of the Braide Working Party. As a next step, Miss I.O.D. Harrison was appointed to the post of Chief Education Welfare Adviser (soon to be designated 'Principal Education Welfare Officer').[49] The merger of the care service and the attendance service had been proposed twice before: in 1933 and in 1948–50. At both these times, the Care Service – led by the formidable Miss Morton and later by Miss Cram – had been powerful enough to resist integration and to protect its status as an autonomous and key service in the care of children. But voluntary service was no longer fashionable and few women in the 1960s had the time and the resources to do this kind of work; increasingly, middle-class women expected – and needed – to earn an income. Moreover, the volunteers of the Care Service had lost ground to professional social workers, who were seeking to colonise the territory of social welfare in education. Some of these were the very kind of women who would formerly have been Care Committee volunteers, although now they were trained and working for pay. And although Miss Wimble, the Principal Care Organiser, was as committed to the service as her predecessors, neither she nor her Care Committees carried much weight in the education department of the ILEA.

Notes

1. ILEA, School Care Committee Service, Report by the Education Officer, 1 December 1966, Patrick Ivin Private Collection.
2. Roy Porter: *London: A social history*, pp. 446.
3. John McIntosh, Fred Naylor and Laurence Norcross: *The ILEA after the Abolition of the Greater London Council*, p.2.
4. Stuart Maclure: *A History of Education in London 1870–1990*, p.146.
5. Bedford Report, p. C.95.
6. M. Penelope Hall: *The Social Services of Modern England*, pp. 205–6.
7. Bedford Report, p. B. 49.
8. Ibid., p. B. 45.
9. Ibid., p. B.49.
10. Ibid., pp. B.52 and B.57.
11. ILEA Education Officer's Department, General Instructions for the Guidance of School Inquiry Officers, 1966, Patrick Ivin Private Collection.
12. Quoted in a letter from F.W. Styles, President of the Children's Welfare Officers' Guild, to the Education Officer, 7 February 1966, Bedford Report, B.7.
13. *Islington Gazette* 1967.
14. Bedford Report, F. 43.
15. Frank Coombes and Dave Beer: *The Long Walk from the Dark*, p.18.
16. C.R. Heather to Secretary, GLC Staff Association, 1 December 1965, Patrick Ivin Private Collection.
17. R.T. Timson to Mr Miss, 20 December 1967, Patrick Ivin Private Collection.
18. The Open University Educational Studies: A Third Level Course E353 Society, Education and the State, p. 71.
19. Interview with Muriel Digny by DW, 13 July 1999.
20. 'ILEA Voluntary Care' by Alice Fay, *Guardian*, 26 October 1962.
21. ILEA, School Care Committee Service, Report by the Education Officer, 1 December 1966.
22. Miss Maltby interview in the *North London Press*, 14 July 1967.
23. Patrick Ivin to ASW and CM, July 2000.
24. Bedford Report, p. C. 90.
25. Peggy Jay to ASW, 2 November 2000.
26. Peter Ackroyd: *London: A biography*, p. 754.
27. Ibid., p. 762.
28. Ken Coates and Richard Silburn: *Poverty: the forgotten Englishmen*, pp. 17–20.

29. Report of the Schools Subcommittee to the ILEA, 19 January 1967, quoted in *Mary Morris: Voluntary Workers in the Welfare State*, p. 104.
30. Adeline Wimble: 'The School Care Committee', pp. 166–7.
31. Ibid., p. 166.
32. Bedford Report, p. A. 4.
33. Queen's Head Street School Secondary Modern and Popham Road Junior and Infants School Care Committee minutes 1960 and 1963, LMA, LCC EO/WEL/2/36.
34. ILEA, School Care Committee Service, Report by the Education Officer, 1 December 1966, Patrick Ivin Private Collection.
35. Ibid.
36. Bedford Report, pp. C. 94–7.
37. Ibid., pp. 1–2.
38. Ibid., p. F. 24 – F. 25.
39. Ibid., p. F. 18.
40. Ibid., p. C. 95.
41. Ibid., pp. F. 17–18.
42. Ibid., pp. E. 19 and E. 29.
43. Ibid., pp. F. 25 and F. 26.
44. Report to Education Committee by Medical Adviser and Education Officer, 18 May 1965, Education provision for Maladjusted Children, quoted in the Bedford Report, p. F. 28.
45. Roy Porter: *London: A social history*, p. 432.
46. A. Marwick: *The Sixties Cultural Revolution in Britain, France, Italy, and the United States, c.1958–c.1974*, p. 230.
47. Stuart Maclure: *A History of Education in London 1870-1990*, p. 167.
48. *North London Press*, 14 July 1967.
49. From the advertisement for the post of Chief Education Welfare Adviser, *Daily Telegraph*, 6 February 1970.

Chapter 8

MERGING THE SERVICES

'Together, we have more hope of helping.'[1]

ON 1 OCTOBER 1970, the new Education Welfare Service (EWS) of London was formally created, combining the School Care Service and the School Inquiry Service. To mark its start, a blue booklet was sent by the ILEA to every school 'describing the new service and its role and function for teachers and other relevant staff.'[2] At a superficial level, the integration of the School Inquiry Service and the School Care Service was a straightforward matter, underpinned by a shared commitment to help children take full advantage of their education. But at another, deeper, level, it was a complex and uneasy affair. For one thing, the balance of welfare and attendance was unclear. For another, the unification of the services involved radical change in structure and administration. The Care Committees that had been pioneered by Margaret Frere at the turn of the nineteenth century were abolished and the volunteers were absorbed into the new EWS.

At County Hall, the new service was directed by a Principal Education Welfare Officer (PEWO), whose post had been specifically created on the recommendation of the Braide Report (and had been designated initially as Chief Education Welfare Adviser). The PEWO was assisted by a Deputy and two Assistant Principal Education Welfare Officers. This tier of administration worked directly under the Assistant Education Officer, Joan Ridding, and later under various chief officers at the second tier level of the ILEA. The post of Education Officer was held by W.F. Houghton until 1971, Dr Eric Briault until 1977, Peter Newsam until 1982, William H. Stubbs until 1988, then David Mallen until 1990.

At the district level, the service operated under the management of the Divisional Officers (DOs), who were the local administrative representatives of the Education Officer. The Divisional Education Welfare Officers (DEWOs) were responsible for the day-to-day running of the service. They were supported by the following staff:

Deputy Divisional Education Welfare Officer (DDEWOs)
Assistant Divisional Education Welfare Officers (ADEWOs)
Senior Education Welfare Officers (SEWOs)
Education Welfare Officers (EWOs)
School Care Workers (SCWs)
Children's (Moral Welfare) Workers
Executive and clerical staff

The new EWOs were mostly the former inquiry officers, who now worked in teams under the immediate supervision and guidance of SEWOs; as before their overall management at the local level was provided by the DO. The volunteers became known as SCWs: their status as members of a Care Committee was replaced by a kind of honorary position in the structure of the EWS. They lost their Care Organisers and like the EWOs, worked under the aegis of their DO.

The duties of the EWO

The primary work of EWOs was in the area of attendance, but they also had to carry out duties relating to welfare benefits, transport, the employment of children and of school-leavers, special schooling, home tuition, census work and the placement of children.[3] But their role was not clearly defined and it varied between the ILEA divisions. What *was* common was the social class of the children they aimed to help. Their 'clients' were students at state schools: like the inquiry officers before them, they rarely followed up children attending private schools, 'fearing to upset either the school or the child'.[4] As before, they had to deal with the particular difficulties of inner-city London.[5] In 1974, the chairman of the ILEA subcommittee stated that 'two out of five children play truant in some schools during their last year'.[6]

The slip system was abolished. Instead, teachers marking registers had to inform the Head of any absence not covered by an acceptable explanation and amounting to more than one day in a week. In this way, observed Houghton, both teachers and education welfare workers would be relieved of a great deal of routine work for the majority of children attending school on a regular basis, leaving more time to follow up children with bad attendance.[7] The EWO then visited the child's home to investigate the matter. Other visits were made in an attempt to gain parental support in dealing with a problem affecting a child's progress at school or – now that the Care Committees were

Plate 18 *The cover of a leaflet on* Non-attendance at School, *which was produced by the ILEA in 1976.*

no longer in existence – to assess the need for some form of welfare provision such as free meals. In some children these needs overlapped, which had been one of the key reasons for combining the Inquiry Service and the Care Service.[8] Some schools needed the assistance of the Education Welfare Officer more than others, but overall it was estimated that an average EWO might have 30 active cases at one time.[9]

Education Welfare Officers who had formerly been inquiry officers experienced a rise in their overall workload after 1970, now that they were taking on many of the welfare aspects of school social work that had previously been carried out by volunteers. The workload of the EWS grew still further in 1972 with the raising of the school-leaving age (ROSLA) to 16. Not only did the number of children who ought to be at school grow larger, but also it was harder to persuade adolescents in their mid-teens of the value of going to school at all:

> In the third and fourth year I used to have days off here and there. Then in the fifth year I just never went at all – I refused to go to lessons. Some girls can go back to sitting at desks again after six weeks holiday, but I couldn't stand it, specially since I had a teacher who was twenty-two, and my boy friend is twenty-one. Ridiculous.[10]

The ILEA planned for ROSLA with care. 'We feel it is fair to say,' commented the EWOs' Guild, 'that the Authority have been making extensive arrangements for ROSLA and members can feel assured that these will continue.'[11] Even so, the tasks of the EWO increased, in relation both to school attendance and to the employment of school-leavers.

In preparation for the abolition of corporal punishment in schools in 1981, 78 new EWO posts were created; it was agreed that this would be an effective means of supporting disruptive pupils. The abolition of physical punishment had been expected ever since the Newsom Report of 1963 had argued against the continuation of the practice. The beating of children at school was phased out in two stages. In the first stage, it was abolished in ILEA primary schools in 1973. The next stage, affecting secondary schools, took another eight years. Britain was one of the remaining minority of western European countries officially to ban corporal punishment in schools. It was finally banned in all schools in 1981. The Education Officer of the ILEA, P.A. Newsam, sent the following circular to all heads of schools:

> From 1 February 1981 corporal punishment may not be administered in county primary, county, voluntary controlled and voluntary special agreement secondary schools and special schools ... A breach of ... this regulation shall be regarded as a serious offence. ... If any teacher contravenes ... this regulation the head teacher shall record the facts at the time in the school record book and shall also report the facts immediately to the Education Officer.[12]

There was a deliberate shift in the pattern of recruiting EWOs towards the end of the 1970s. New staff were sought from a wide range of different backgrounds, as opposed to the traditional ex-servicemen. Women, mainly young graduates, now made up between one-quarter and one-third of the service.[13] This change in recruitment was a slow process: an ILEA document in 1981 noted that 'men still outnumber women and the tradition of the man's experience of disciplinary work being viewed as the most relevant qualification for the job dies hard.'[14]

The ILEA set about in various ways to improve school attendance. A joint ILEA/Inner London Social Services working party was set up in 1974 to investigate the reasons for absence and to consider ways to prevent non-attendance.[15] In 1981, the ILEA Research and Statistics Branch conducted a survey of attendance in three ILEA comprehensive schools. Table 8.1 shows that the majority of pupils (68 per cent) who were absent from school spent the time at home, many helping their mother with chores.[16] Women EWOs may have been less tolerant than their male counterparts of girls staying at home in this way. One former truant remembered the impact of a visit from a woman EWO:

> It all began when I started secondary school ... The second week I pretended to my mum I was sick and she let me stay at home for the Thursday and Friday. When I got back [to school] it felt really funny walking in there and I felt like I didn't belong ... I stayed that day but the rest of the week I acted sick again and my mum let me stay off, looking after my two twin sisters who were three and my brother who was four.

Half-way through the second week, however, 'the education welfare officer, Miss [A], came round and wanted to know why I was off school.' The girl was surprised to see her: 'My mum said I was ill but I don't think Miss [A] was even half convinced that was the truth. She said my parents would go to court if I didn't go to school.'[17] This visit was swiftly followed by a return to school.

There was a slight overall improvement in attendance figures in London schools after the creation of the EWS. The Education Welfare Officers' Guild was triumphant:

> First things first. We have taken many beatings from a number of different quarters during the first five years as a service: it is nice for once therefore, not to sit and receive it but rather to hit back. *The E.W.S. in 1975 has had better school attendance figures for the I.L.E.A. than in 1969 when the School Inquiry Service was in operation*! (emphasis added)[18]

It is difficult to measure the contribution of the EWS to levels of attendance, since a range of variables were involved. What *is* clear, though, is that the

Table 8.1 *Pupils' whereabouts during absence from school in a sample of three ILEA comprehensive schools, 1981*

Places where pupils stated missed lesson time was spent	% of pupils *
Empty classrooms	18
Cloakrooms or toilets	18
Playground	4
Shops	21
Cafes	7
Going home or at school	71

Places where pupils stated the time when absent from schools was spent (for any reason except treatment or vacation)	% of pupils *
At home	36
At home with mother or helping with chores	68
At home with friends and/or siblings but not parents	14
At home with parents and friends	5
At a friend's house	20
Around the flats	9
Around the streets	14
Around the shops	25
Around the park	14
'Getting into trouble'	18
Meeting friends	9
Visiting places of interest	2
Other	25

Note: * Percentages total more than 100% as the majority of pupils gave more than one answer to these questions.

Source: Taken from ILEA Research and Statistics Report, 'Perspectives on attendance' RS 749/80

Plate 19 *A visit by school children in 1974 to the Lewisham Way Careers Office, which was set up by the Education Office of the ILEA. LMA, 74, 9232*

EWOs' Guild felt confident about the value of the service they offered, but were unsure that everyone else felt the same.

The policy of compulsory schooling was questioned by a number of social critics in the 1970s, who expressed doubt about the value of education in western society. This doubt was fanned by the publication of *Deschooling*

Society by Ivan Illich in 1971. 'In schools,' wrote Illich, 'we are taught that valuable learning is the result of attendance; that the value of learning increases with the amount of input; and, finally, that this value can be measured and documented by grades and certificates.' He argued against this, saying that the existence of a school simply produced its own demands for more schooling, independent of the needs of either learners or the education process itself.[19] This kind of view informed the development of educational practice at William Tyndale Junior School in Islington, where disagreements between teachers over pedagogy and political ideology between 1973 and 1975 brought teaching to a standstill.

Social workers and Education Welfare Officers often had different standpoints on compulsory education during this period. Some social workers claimed that school repressed individuals, while they in turn were criticised by the EWS for being too lenient towards truants and making excuses for an individual child or family. The President of NACEWO (National Association of Chief Education Welfare Officers) spoke out in support of compulsory schooling, from the point of view of an EWO:

> Personally I think the prospect of being an education welfare officer without the belief in compulsory education is an empty prospect. This is because there would still remain social handicaps to educational attainment. Voluntary education would only widen the division between those who value education and those who do not. As you may know most of our enquiries may start off as absentee enquiries but they rarely stay that way. It is our continuing responsibility – and we have to make sure that the child gets education suitable to his age, aptitude and ability. Now this may be at school or otherwise, but we have to be sure that he is receiving it and, hopefully, benefiting from it.[20]

Failure to attend school was described in different ways at this time. The term 'school phobic' was often applied to middle-class children and young children in primary school. 'Non-attender' was used for those children who had a justifiable reason to be absent, such as illness, and it was applied to girls more than to boys. The label of 'truant' was largely reserved for working-class boys and was seen to be linked with deviance and delinquency. However, numbers of boys – and girls, too – stayed away from school simply because they found it boring; they were perfectly happy to work hard at activities *outside* school. One 15-year-old London girl was quoted in a 1974 study as saying: 'I'd rather work than go to school every day. I don't mind work, I like it. I work in a hairdressers' every weekend. I help my family out. When my mum was ill, all the washing was done, and the housework, and the dinner was on the table.'[21]

140

A rapid drop in the number of volunteers

The volunteers of the former Care Service continued the work they had been doing for over 60 years. They now worked with a Code of Practice drawn up between Senior EWS staff and themselves; three times a year, the Central Committee of School Care Workers met at County Hall.[22] A report by the ILEA Schools Subcommittee was adamant that voluntary workers were a unique feature of schooling in London and should be retained. 'We consider that it is one of the service's most urgent tasks,' it stated, 'to ensure that the contribution of voluntary workers is used in the best way to provide more extensive help to schools and families and complement that provided by the education welfare staff.' [23] In the spring of 1971, the *Islington Gazette* – as well as other local papers in London – ran an article about the new Education Welfare Service and the need for more voluntary School Care Workers. When one applicant wrote to Miss Maltby, the Divisional Education Welfare Officer in Islington, to enquire about the work, she replied that the service was flexible in its recruitment – that age was no criterion for helping with school care work and that it depended on the individual.[24]

But despite views like these, the disappearance of Care Committees and the new structure of the EWS made school care workers apprehensive and uncertain. One woman who was a volunteer at the time of the merger explained that:

> Some of the people who had been doing it a long time didn't like it very much, they didn't like the idea of being attached to a team and I think they felt they wouldn't be so much in charge of their own school. I think some of them were quite elderly and didn't really want to tackle changing circumstances.[25]

A reduction in the number of compulsory medical examinations of children at school also had an impact on the role of some volunteers. This reduction was brought about by the reorganisation of the NHS, which meant that in 1974 responsibility for the School Health Service passed to the area health authorities (although the school health and psychiatric social workers remained with the GLC/ILEA Medical Department). A volunteer commented that: 'A lot of school care workers who had been doing it for years, [for whom] the medical was the chief reason for their existence, they were rather upset about it. One or two people I had to pacify.'[26]

In 1973 a Joint Working Party of EWOs and SCWs, chaired by Mrs E. Redstone, was set up to examine the functions of the School Care worker, 'with special reference to the EWO/SCW relationship'. Its findings included a high level of dissatisfaction by SCWs and a feeling that although the relationship between them and EWOs had been envisaged as a complementary one, the functions of each had never been clearly defined. The report gave the results of a postal questionnaire sent to SCWs and EWOs (a different questionnaire in each case), which suggested that relationships between the two groups were strained. Several SCWs said they were frustrated by their inability to get things done and one gave several instances of delayed trust fund and maintenance grants, as well as hold-ups on child guidance referrals.[27]

There was a drastic fall in the number of volunteers after 1970. A recruitment drive was launched by the ILEA in spring 1971, led by Canon Harvey Hinds, the Chairman of the Schools Subcommittee, but this produced very few new volunteers. The number of SCWs dropped from 2,350 in 1969[28] to 705 in 1973 and thereafter the number continued to fall. By 1980, there were only 340 active SCWs, deployed unevenly through the ten divisions. 'The volunteers were like old soldiers,' said a former SCW, 'they just faded away.'[29]

A growing emphasis on a social work approach

'The Education Welfare Service', stated a recruiting leaflet, 'is working towards becoming a fully professional Social Work Service.'[30] It was seen as crucial for workers in the service to be professionally trained as social workers and although unqualified mature applicants with relevant experience were considered, they had to be prepared to study for appropriate qualifications. In 1973 the ILEA commissioned a 'Social Work Consultant', Margaret Robinson, who was a lecturer in social studies at Goldsmiths College, to review the work of the professional staff and to provide guidelines on the professional functions appropriate to each grade. Her terms of reference included an assessment of the organisation and workloads of the staff. Her report, which called for better training and greater status to be given to Education Welfare Officers, confirmed the policy of the ILEA – as earlier set out by the Braide Report – to move towards a fully professional social work service. This approach was welcomed by the EWOs' Guild, which identified a link between improved attendance figures between 1969 and 1975 and the transition from the School Inquiry Service to the EWS. 'It is significant,' stated the Guild, 'that during this same period the Education Welfare Service has set itself to become a professional Education Social Work Service: we'll say no more!'[31]

The understanding of education welfare as a social work service was shared in many areas outside London and by central government. The Local Government Training Board Working Party, chaired by Sir Lincoln Ralphs, the Education Officer of Norfolk, produced a report in August 1974 which argued the need for official recognition of the Education Welfare Service as a professional service – in particular, as a professional *social work* service. In

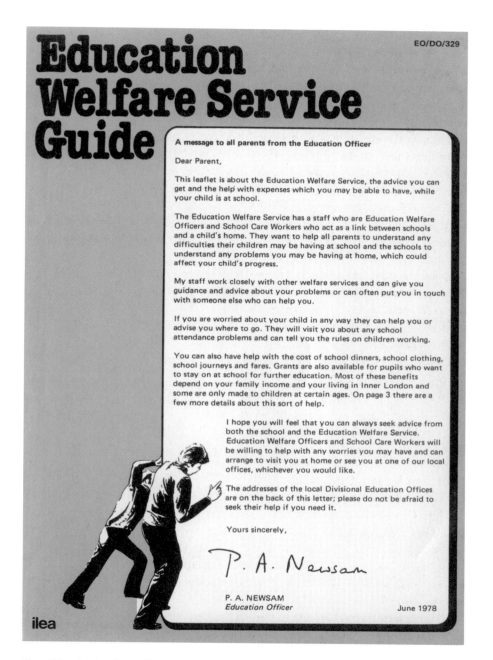

Education Welfare Service Guide

EO/DO/329

A message to all parents from the Education Officer

Dear Parent,

This leaflet is about the Education Welfare Service, the advice you can get and the help with expenses which you may be able to have, while your child is at school.

The Education Welfare Service has a staff who are Education Welfare Officers and School Care Workers who act as a link between schools and a child's home. They want to help all parents to understand any difficulties their children may be having at school and the schools to understand any problems you may be having at home, which could affect your child's progress.

My staff work closely with other welfare services and can give you guidance and advice about your problems or can often put you in touch with someone else who can help you.

If you are worried about your child in any way they can help you or advise you where to go. They will visit you about any school attendance problems and can tell you the rules on children working.

You can also have help with the cost of school dinners, school clothing, school journeys and fares. Grants are also available for pupils who want to stay on at school for further education. Most of these benefits depend on your family income and your living in Inner London and some are only made to children at certain ages. On page 3 there are a few more details about this sort of help.

I hope you will feel that you can always seek advice from both the school and the Education Welfare Service. Education Welfare Officers and School Care Workers will be willing to help with any worries you may have and can arrange to visit you at home or see you at one of our local offices, whichever you would like.

The addresses of the local Divisional Education Offices are on the back of this letter; please do not be afraid to seek their help if you need it.

Yours sincerely,

P. A. Newsam

P. A. NEWSAM
Education Officer

June 1978

ilea

Plate 20 *A leaflet about the Education Welfare Service distributed to parents by the ILEA in 1978.*

January 1979, a government circular to local authorities, 'The Education Welfare Service', emphasised the need for social work in education and for schools to strengthen their links with pupils' families. The circular commented that 'future developments seem likely to lead to Education Welfare Officers being given a wider role and greater responsibility'; it recommended that 'authorities ought to ensure that EWOs have appropriate professional training' and that the appropriate course would lead 'to the certificate of qualification in social work'.[32] The EWS was also described as a social service by the national Society of Education Officers in its 1980 report, 'The Education Welfare Service, its Role and Training'.[33]

The move towards social work was sealed with the introduction of the Certificate of Qualification in Social Work (CQSW) in 1972. Few EWOs in London were professionally trained and only 5 per cent held a professional qualification in social work. In contrast, 30 per cent of the staff in a London borough social services department had a professional qualification in social work; in a 'well staffed' borough, this figure rose to 80 per cent. An additional factor was that within the Education Welfare Service, the majority of employees were aged either over 40 or below 26, whereas in other social work agencies the majority of staff were between the ages of 28 and 45.[34] The Robinson Report warned:

> The younger ones are beginning to see themselves as birds of passage and the older ones as a stop gap to see themselves through to retirement. This will be most unfortunate if allowed to develop further as there are in the Education Welfare Service many social workers who are particularly interested (and becoming experienced) in education social work as a specialism within social work.[35]

The ILEA offered Education Welfare Officers the opportunity to be seconded to CQSW courses, but there were only 12 places available per year. In comparison with other professionals working with children, such as teachers and social workers, who operated within a structure providing finance for appropriate training courses and academic support services, EWOs were neglected. The EWOs' Guild was frustrated at the delays with which accepted policies were implemented. 'It has now been over a year,' it complained, since the publication of the Robinson Report, 'and months since its acceptance as ILEA policy. It is now being implemented in patchwork quilt fashion – an unfortunate situation to say the least when the argument for an ILEA is to provide a necessary uniform Education Service for inner London.'[36]

An important backdrop to these developments was the Seebohm Report of 1968, which led to the unification in April 1971 of each local authority's

Children's Department, Welfare Department and Public and Mental Health Social Workers into a Social Services Department (SSD). The Seebohm Report had also recommended that local authorities transfer some of the functions of their education welfare service to social services departments, but it was agreed that each local authority should decide on an individual basis whether their newly formed social services department would incorporate the education welfare service. The British Association of Social Workers supported such a step, but Education Welfare Officers and their official bodies were against it. They believed that it would be better to stay in the education sector, while improving their liaison with other services. A handful of authorities *did* transfer their EWS, though several then returned to the education sector; by 1979, all education departments except Cheshire, Somerset and Coventry contained a fully operational education welfare section.[37] In London, the picture was especially complex, because social services were the responsibility of the inner London borough councils, while the EWS was the responsibility of the ILEA. The seeds of future industrial problems were also sown. In 1970, EWOs had parity of pay with social workers, but this was eroded in the 1970s and led to disputes over pay and the deployment of the service.

The number of professionals employed in social services departments – social workers, teachers, child guidance services, psychologists, probation officers, police, youth services and various voluntary agencies – had dramatically increased by the 1970s. However, none of them had the natural access to a child in need as the EWO – 'the only social workers constantly in touch with families and the community';[38] the very fact of non-attendance raised questions about a child's welfare. These issues seemed especially important after the death in 1973 of Maria Colwell, a child in care in East Sussex who was murdered by her stepfather. The tragedy shocked the nation and also triggered a lack of confidence in the routes of communication between the EWO and the social worker:

> In the 'welfare link' between the school and social services the role of the education welfare officer is of considerable importance in many cases, as it was with Maria ... it is clear and somewhat disturbing that, in Maria's case, the division between education welfare services and the social services department made it more difficult for the education welfare officer's concern about Maria to reach the proper person (the social worker) with sufficient urgency and promptness.[39]

A report of the enquiry into Maria Colwell's death argued for co-ordination and for co-operation between all helping agencies.[40] Such co-operation was regarded as fundamental to the working of London's EWS: a key reason for the merger of the School Care and School Inquiry Service had been the need for a multi-disciplinary approach to children's needs. So far as the EWOs' Guild was concerned, better attendance levels would result from a high degree of liaison between the education welfare service, social services departments, juvenile bureaux and schools.[41] However, this was not always achieved. A 1984 report by the Inspectorate of Schools (HMI) on education welfare services in eight LEAs in England and Wales observed that although channels of communication were improving between these and other services, they remained problematic. 'There were some good examples of interchange of information between EWOs and social workers,' observed the report, adding that 'These usually occur where the services share the same premises or where the EWO makes a point of calling in the local SSD office. Good professional relationships have been established between EWOs and schools in many instances.'[42] The importance of communication between children's services was demonstrated in the following case study:

> E developed school phobia following his father's admission to hospital. He expressed alarm about his father's critical condition but it transpired that his chief anxiety was for his mother. The EWO who had made the original investigation referred the case to the child guidance clinic and after many visits by the psychiatric social worker and the EWO working as a team, E was persuaded to attend a day special school. To achieve and then maintain this entailed one member of the team escorting the boy to school every day for a number of weeks. He now attends regularly with consent.[43]

In her study of *Social Work and the School* (1973), Karen Lyons (who had worked for the EWS in the 1970s) argued that welfare work with school-aged children should be of a preventive nature to help break the cycles of deprivation with problem families. Education Welfare Officers were engaged in various types of preventive work. 'First Aid' support, for example, was largely financial, where the officer arranged for a child to be provided with school meals, clothing and maintenance grants; he or she also helped a family to obtain benefits from other agencies during times of hardship, including the Department of Health and Social Security. Means-testing became the norm, as it had been in the first half of the twentieth century. Meanwhile, services that had been provided free following the Second World War were dramatically reduced or cut. Free milk to children attending secondary school was abolished in 1968 and availability was limited further in 1971 – to children under 7 years of age and those in special schools or with a medical requirement. Margaret Thatcher, who was then Minister for Education, became widely known as 'Maggie Thatcher Milk Snatcher'.[44]

Poverty and deprivation were increasingly in evidence in London, especially after the election of Margaret Thatcher's Conservative government in 1979. Mrs Thatcher chiselled away at local authority expenditure during the 1980s and the Rate Support Grant was cut. The ILEA, the GLC and 14 London boroughs were rate- or poll-tax-capped and £7,900 million of Treasury support was lost to London boroughs in the 1980s.[45] In 1983, two in every five ILEA schoolchildren were eligible for free school meals; in 1984, the population of ILEA schoolchildren receiving free school meals (34 per cent) was double that for England as a whole (17 per cent,).[46] In 1985, five of the 12 boroughs covered by the ILEA were among the ten most deprived local authorities in the country. In 1986, more than one-quarter of ILEA schoolchildren came from one parent families and therefore from a lower income group than two parent family schoolchildren. DHSS calculations found that in inner London, 28 per cent of families were looked after by a single parent, compared to the national average of 14 per cent. In terms of population density, inner London was found to be 26 times more in need than the country as a whole, double that of Birmingham or Manchester and one and a half times that of Liverpool.[47]

New services for young people

Starting in the 1960s, each Educational Division of the ILEA had employed a welfare worker called a Children's Worker, who was concerned with the welfare of schoolchildren who were sexually vulnerable. London was then the centre of the 'Swinging Sixties', which had started in the bistros of the King's Road in Chelsea; the new 'hippy' culture was open about sexual matters and questioned traditional values like marriage. By the mid-1960s, 40 per cent of the general population of London were under 25, which meant that the fashions of young people were much in evidence.[48]

One former ILEA Children's Worker recalls that her work 'lay within the scope of Education Welfare, but was specialized.'[49] Schoolgirl pregnancies consumed the greater part of the Children's Workers' time. Despite the 1968 Abortion Act, which liberalised the grounds upon which women could have an abortion, and from 1975 the free provision of birth control on the NHS to anyone, regardless of marital status, more young women were falling pregnant while still at school; one important cause was the increase in the school-leaving age. Sometimes a headteacher would allow the girl to stay on until her pregnancy became obvious. Arrangements were then made for home tutoring or for the girl to spend the rest of her pregnancy in a special establishment which provided full-time schooling and antenatal care; mother and baby homes were run by the Salvation Army, the Church of England and some other organisations. After the birth some schoolgirls took their baby to their parents' home; in other cases, arrangements were made for fostering or adoption. The fathers of the babies were termed 'Putative Fathers'. More often than not, according to a former Children's Worker, they absented themselves and could not be found, especially 'in cases of under-age girls, against whom, legally, an offence had been committed'. In the case of older girls, it was sometimes possible to interview the fathers. Their reactions 'varied, from sheepish acknowledgment to unrealistic enthusiasm'. Occasionally, a responsible young man wanted to help, but it was then necessary to ensure that the mother and her family wished to continue the association.[50]

The following case history illustrates the scope of the responsibilities of a Children's Worker:

> EW [her initials have been changed], aged 14, was a school-reported pregnancy. As in many other cases, the parents were unaware and informed by the Children's Worker, who made a home visit after interviewing E– in school. E– was very frightened of her parents' reaction, with good reason as during the first half hour of the visit attempts were made to punish E– by hitting and abusing her. The presence of the Children's Worker had a restraining effect however, and when the first shock and anger had passed off, it was possible to talk calmly. ... E–'s father was the most difficult to reassure and remained angry and resentful for a long time.

E– was already five months' pregnant. Her mother was a good deal less punitive than her husband and was able to persuade E–'s father of the advantages of a Mother and Baby Home with tuition. The Children's Worker arranged this and E– went to the Home which was out of London. E–'s mother visited regularly and so did the Children's Worker. E– decided that the baby should be fostered, with a view to adoption. But when the baby – a boy – was born, her father underwent a change of heart and announced that he was not going to allow the baby to be adopted. The Children's Worker was concerned about this sudden change of mind and wanted to make sure that E–, 'who was intelligent and mature for her age,' was given the chance to sort out her own feelings. She finally resolved to keep her baby, relying on the support of her family:

> Mrs W– had gone out to work, but said she was willing to stay at home and care for the baby. ... Family income would be reduced, but Mr W– said he could earn more by doing overtime. The question of the Putative Father arose, but E– steadfastly refused to divulge his name and said that, in any case, 'he was out of work and gone away'.

After an interval, E– returned to school, leaving at 16. The Children's Worker kept in touch with this family for two years. The little boy, as he grew, knew his 'Mum' and his 'Gran' and an initially difficult situation settled well. The Children's Worker did hear some years later of E–'s marriage, but had no news of her son.[51]

Another special service for young people was the Young People's Advisory Service (YPS). It had been set up in 1957 on the initiative of voluntary care committee workers attached to a North Kensington secondary school, who felt there was a need to prepare children about to leave school at 15 for the adjustment to adult life. They did not feel that they themselves had either the training or the time to do this properly, so they enlisted an experienced social worker to take on the responsibility, in a paid capacity. This became known as the 'Avondale Project', which in 1961 was extended by the LCC to some other schools. In 1964, the service was taken over fully by the LCC and formalised as the Young People's Advisory Service; in 1965, it was established as one of ILEA's services for young people. The social workers, who were all women, were known as Young People's Advisers (YPAs) and were employed on a part-time basis.

The work of the YPS became more important after the abolition of care committees in 1970, which meant that pastoral care became the responsibility of hard-pressed teachers and the EWS. The raising of the school age to 16 in 1972 created particular difficulties in the case of 15-year-olds who were disenchanted with school and resented having to stay on. Adolescents at school were vulnerable to a range of stresses in this period – youth unemployment, a growing drug culture and higher rates of family breakdown. Teachers and EWOs identified the children who needed individual attention and referred them to the YPA associated with their school. Under the supervision of the DEWO, she offered individual counselling and encouraged children to make use of other services supporting young people, such as the Careers Service, the Youth Service and Colleges of Further Education. The YPA provided a kind of help that was not offered by any other service:

J– (15) the eldest in a single parent family was uncooperative, sullen and prone to sudden fits of temper. She was often absent and lacked any sense of motivation in her work. It emerged in counselling that she was frightened of her violent feelings and lack of control. She was also in a state of grief and confusion since a miscarriage she had had over a year ago, still mourned the lost baby and longed for another. She described coming to counselling as being able to 'turn on the tap that had blocked up', gave vent to her feelings and subsequently related more appropriately to her family and teachers.[52]

Close links were encouraged between the YPA and the EWO working with her school. One YPA, working at a school in east London, commented in 1982 that her school's EWO:

> knows who I am seeing and why. We meet at least fortnightly, often with the school careers officer and I find this very helpful. During the past year the Senior Education Welfare Officer to whom I am responsible, has brought me into the EWO team by encouraging workers to come for special consultations and asking me to talk to team members.[53]

In her annual report for 1983, she described the process of co-operation between herself, the EWO and the teaching staff:

> [The] 4th Year Head talked to me about Y– who looks so lost and neglected. Her mother has left home, her father works shifts and Y– is often left alone. How can we introduce more stability into her life? Y– will see me and the school EWO will visit.

In another case, recalls this YPA, the EWO 'will visit a Turkish family I already know. The parents are divorced and the mother has an undiagnosed illness, causing partial paralysis. A– (14) takes a lot of responsibility and falls behind at school.' The year head and tutor joined the discussion and they discussed their respective roles. 'Together,' commented the YPA, 'we have more hope of helping.'[54]

There were only two YPAs left in the ILEA by 1986. By the late 1980s, the service had virtually disappeared; among the reasons for this was the developing view that EWOs should and would provide social work care to children, making YPAs redundant. For about two decades, the YPS had filled the vacuum left by the disappearance of the After-Care service, which had been provided by the Care Committees to prepare pupils for their entry to the workforce. In the YPS, however, the emphasis was more on helping pupils to bridge the emotional gap between school and adulthood, than on the practical difficulties of finding and starting a job.

One YPA commented on her work with ethnic minorities in her annual report for 1982. 'Though work in this area has advanced since last year,' she wrote, 'I still have a definite need to extend my skills. It is a delicate balance, understanding the dilemmas of, for example, girls from an Asian background and yet not reinforcing rebellious attitudes which could precipitate rejection by their own cultures.' She had informal discussions with the headmistress of her school and they arranged a series of talks for teaching and other staff by members of the various ethnic groups represented in the school.[55]

The education policy of the late 1960s and the 1970s had aimed to integrate children of ethnic minorities into British society. The ILEA published a guidebook for teachers on the services it provided: after a list of classes for the ESN (Educationally Subnormal) and Maladjusted was a list of Special Centres, some for overseas children with language difficulties and some for older children who had recently come to London with little or no education.[56] But in the 1980s, the strategy was changed, in response to increased racial tensions and riots in the south London area of Brixton and elsewhere. The view now taken was that 'no child should be expected to cast off the language and culture of home as he crosses the school threshold.'[57] The ILEA consulted the views of parents of ethnic minority pupils on the best ways to develop an anti-racist policy.

A total of 161 different languages were spoken by ILEA schoolchildren by 1984. About one in five (nearly 57,000 schoolchildren) spoke a language other than English at home.[58] This created particular challenges for home visits by EWOs who did not speak the family's language and had to find other ways of communicating. Respect for the culture and traditions of their clients was essential to this process. Many people at the time assumed that immigrants – and especially West Indians – were unreliable in terms of school attendance. But in fact, as a 1980 paper by Peter Mortimore for the ILEA pointed out, pupils with a West Indian background 'had much higher levels of attendance than the indigenous groups or the pupils with parents from other different ethnic groups.'[59]

The balance of attendance and welfare work

The future direction of the EWS – in particular, the weighting of attendance and of welfare – was seen as a serious political issue. In 1984, the Secretary of State for Education, Sir Keith Joseph, told a conference in Sheffield that, 'The Government is committed to looking afresh at the educational welfare service. School attendance is their main task and should be their highest priority.' This had already been clearly stated in the Conservative Party Manifesto: 'We shall switch the emphasis in the education welfare service back to school attendance so as to reduce truancy.'[60]

Outside party politics, though, there was a growing consensus that the service should be social-work oriented; emphasis was placed on the support and help required by children at school rather than on the statutory need to ensure regular attendance. Absence from school was seen as a possible sign of emotional distress and the issue of attendance was seen as integrally related to the emotional and social well-being of the child. In January 1979, in response to repeated requests for clear government guidance on the role of the education welfare services, the DES, DHSS and Welsh Office issued a joint draft circular on the service. It observed that through the 1970s there had been an increasing awareness of the value of social work in education and of the need for schools to strengthen their links with pupils' families. Its chief recommendation was the further development and training of the service, building on the Ralphs Report of 1973. 'The essence of the service,' it argued, 'lies in its responsibility for helping to ensure that schoolchildren receive the full benefits of the education system.'[61] Ideas about school-based social work, the role of social service departments in schools, inter-service co-operation and training and development were also discussed. However, even though the draft circular mentioned the value of inter-agency work, the DES and DHSS and Welsh Office could not agreed on the final wording and withdrew it.

There was a growing consensus that the EWS needed to have school-attached EWOs and specialist field workers, in a more coherent and co-ordinated hierarchy. The chief requirement was that the EWS should be designated a *social work* service and a *professional* service. This was the main recommendation of an ILEA study by Dr Paul Corrigan, which in 1984 produced a report entitled, 'Educational Opportunity and London's Children: the role of a social work service'.[62] He also advocated a new management structure, so that the overall hierarchy would be reduced and increased resources would be made available at the levels of school, fieldwork and first-line management.

Corrigan's recommendations were supported by a spate of other reports which followed soon after. In March 1984, the ILEA received a report on improving secondary schools from the Committee on the Curriculum and Organisation of Secondary Schools, chaired by David Hargreaves.[63] The Committee recommended that all secondary schools should have school-attached EWOs, as the best model for secondary school support. In January 1985, the ILEA received a major report on primary education from the Committee on Primary Education, which made a similar recommendation to the Hargreaves Report, but for primary schools.[64]

Finally, the ILEA received a report in 1985 from a committee chaired by John Fish, entitled 'Education Opportunities for All?', which reviewed the provision to be made for special educational needs.[65] This report took a closer look at the three children's social work services provided by the ILEA – the education welfare service, the school health social work service and the psychiatric social work service. It criticised the fact that, in relation to special educational needs, these services worked 'independently in their own territories'. Again, this implied compartmentalisation and possible duplication. The report recommended to the ILEA that it consider steps to develop a unified social work service within the Education Officers' Department in which the special skills of the three services would be retained, but would be co-ordinated in their delivery to schools and clinics on a divisional basis. This echoed the earlier recommendation of the Bedford Report in 1966, which had been rejected at the time of the merger of the School Inquiry and School Care services.

The end of the GLC and changes for the ILEA

All these discussions about the future of education welfare care in London took place against the imminent demise of the GLC. In the national election campaign of 1983, the Conservative Party made a pledge to abolish the Labour-controlled GLC – and it was duly scrapped on 1 April 1986. The ILEA was granted a reprieve and was turned into a directly elected *ad hoc* authority. For the first time since the existence of the School Board for London (1870–1904), a single purpose local education authority for the capital was elected by the people of London. The problems it faced were massive: for on practically every indicator of deprivation and need, London was badly affected by social problems, aggravated by the economic recession and high unemployment. In 1986 *Faith in the City*, a report sponsored by the Archbishop of Canterbury, argued that it was the poor who had borne the brunt of the recession, adding that some council estates had 'a quite different social and economic system, operating almost entirely at subsistence level, dependent entirely on the public sector ... the degeneration of many such areas has now gone so far that they are in effect "separate territories" outside the mainstream of our social and economic life.'[66] The decade that saw the emergence of 'yuppies', writes Peter Ackroyd, also witnessed 'the revival of street-beggars and vagrants sleeping "rough" upon the streets or within doorways; Lincoln's Inn Fields was occupied once more by the homeless ... while areas like Waterloo Bridge and the Embankment became the setting for what were known as "cardboard cities".'[67] Continual demographic change added to the pressure on the ILEA in its efforts to deliver a high quality of education: the percentage of pupils whose home language was other than English increased from 14 to 25 per cent between 1981 and 1991.[68] Under the Conservative hand of Mrs Thatcher, the ILEA had been rate-capped in 1985, which meant that unlike other local education authorities, it did not have powers to raise rates to spend on education in inner London. On top of these material difficulties was the troubling suspicion – which was soon to be justified – that the ILEA was to be short-lived.

The EWS becomes a social work service

A directorate of the ILEA was formed to manage the Education Welfare Service. Its chief task was to implement the recommendations that the service should be recognised as a professional – and multi-disciplinary – social work service in education. Don Naik was appointed as Director, with three deputies: Ermine Lee-Kin (divisions 1–5), Patrick Ivin (divisions 6–10, staffing and finance) and Paul Corrigan (with responsibility for research, development and training). On 1 October 1987, the service was renamed the Education Social Work Service (ESWS),[69] 17 years to the day after the Education Welfare Service had been formed in 1970. This change of name signalled the commitment of the service to social work care, making the recommendations of Corrigan's 1984 Report into a reality.

The structure of the service changed, as shown in Figure 8.1. Divisional Education Social Work Managers were responsible for the maintenance of an attendance policy and the provision of social work support to children and families. Education Social Workers (ESWs), who were the same former EWOs but with a new name, were now attached to primary school groups and in secondary schools, while maintaining contact with the community-based Divisional Offices. The officers had direct links with teachers and offered them guidance and support in identifying children under stress. The service was designed to bring senior practitioners into the field, who had the experience and skill to work 'face to face' with children and families.[70] Their field of work included special needs, nursery education, child employment, travellers and homeless families. This work had to be sensitive to children's environments and also to the impact of national developments in the education sector. The introduction of the National Curriculum and attainment tests, for example, led to competition between schools that created extra stresses for schoolchildren.

An Equality Statement for the ESWS was published in 1987.[71] It stated that the service aimed 'to ensure that racism, sexism or any form of institutional discrimination and bias does not occur'[72] and stressed the need for the co-ordination of services. Areas given priority were special educational needs, support to the juvenile justice system and child protection. A new co-ordinated team to deal with child employment was set up, as well as a specialist service for homeless families in north London and for travellers.

The diversity of the ESWS was further increased when it was joined by the school health social work service in 1988. This restored the role in school health that had been such an important feature of the Care Service until 1970. However, the psychiatric social work service, which provided specialist input to child guidance units and offered a service to pupils with behavioural difficulties, did not join the ESWS. Its staff and the medical advisers of the ILEA were opposed to the idea, because they regarded themselves as medical professionals rather than education workers.

Figure 8.1 *Education Social Work Service structure 1987–90*

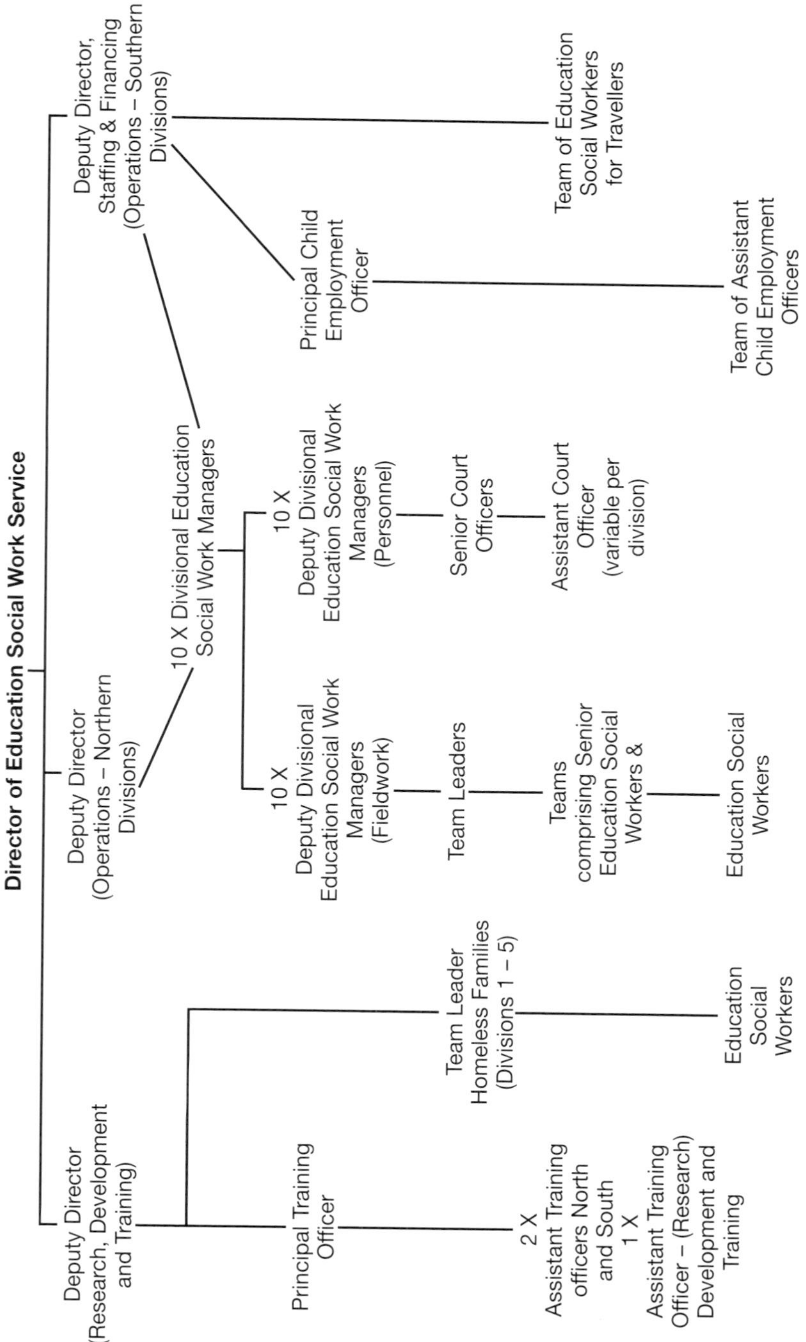

Director of Education Social Work Service

Deputy Director, Staffing & Financing (Operations – Southern Divisions)

Deputy Director (Operations – Northern Divisions)

Deputy Director (Research, Development and Training)

Principal Child Employment Officer

Team of Education Social Workers for Travellers

Team of Assistant Child Employment Officers

10 X Divisional Education Social Work Managers

10 X Deputy Divisional Education Social Work Managers (Personnel)

Senior Court Officers

Assistant Court Officer (variable per division)

10 X Deputy Divisional Education Social Work Managers (Fieldwork)

Team Leaders

Teams comprising Senior Education Social Workers &

Education Social Workers

Principal Training Officer

Team Leader Homeless Families (Divisions 1 – 5)

2 X Assistant Training officers North and South

1 X Assistant Training Officer – (Research) Development and Training

Education Social Workers

Source: ILEA Circular 374a/CIRC/BC10.

The abolition of the ILEA

In the run-up to the 1987 general election, the Conservatives made a promise in their manifesto to let inner London boroughs opt out of the ILEA and become the local education authorities for their areas. In April 1990, they abolished outright the single education authority for London. 'The government have consistently maintained,' stated Kenneth Baker, the Secretary of State for Education and Science, that:

> a single education authority for inner London could be justified only if that authority gave the children and students of inner London a good education service at an acceptable cost. ILEA has patently not done that. Its spending is profligate. Its service is poor.[75]

There was a determined campaign by supportive Londoners to save the ILEA and 'Save the ILEA' stickers appeared in car windows all over the capital. But it was a hopeless attempt, because the Conservative government was determined to destroy the Labour-controlled ILEA. 'When the break-up came', comments Stuart Maclure in his history of London's education, 'the motivation was political, not educational or administrative.'[76]

Responsibility for the ILEA's services was split between the 12 borough councils and the Corporation of the City of London. Each of them formed their own local education authority, which operated on the same basis as every other LEA, inside or outside London. In this way, the uniqueness of London's single educational authority became a thing of the past. The political position of each borough was reflected in its approach to the function and the remit of their education welfare service. Camden sought to use this new responsibility in an enabling way, so that it had 'a role in such policy issues as suspension and expulsion of pupils, equal educational opportunities and special needs'.[77] It announced a wish to establish:

> a positive supportive function concerning all families with children at school. It supplements the work of the schools in educating their children in the widest sense, so that children are helped to attain the highest educational standards of which they are capable and also to live and enjoy life as fully as possible in work and in leisure.[73]

Wandsworth and Westminster, on the other hand, were more concerned with the issue of attendance: 'to many workers they seemed to want a reversion to the role of school board men and kidcatchers.'[74] Some of the new LEAs planned to call the service the Education Welfare Service once more, while others toyed with the idea of including 'attendance' in the name. Still others aimed to continue the role of the ILEA's ESWS.

The debate continued as the boroughs decided how to transfer or recruit people to their new service. The run up to the transfer was extremely stressful for the staff of the ESWS, who needed to ascertain from the boroughs whether they had guaranteed employment and if so, on what grade and conditions. An appraisal scheme was set up to help staff evaluate their skills and assist them in making choices about the future of their careers. The service lost many experienced members of staff, including qualified social workers and senior managers who opted for redundancy or found jobs elsewhere. The exodus was greatest in boroughs which were slowest to say what they wanted and how many staff they would need. 'By this time,' wrote Ermyne Lee-kin, the director of ILEA social work services, 'everyone concerned was aware that the service would be budgeted and reined in by the Department of Education and Science.'[78] Hardly any volunteers remained: most had already left the service, while a few had qualified to become ESWOs.

Notes

1. Fourth Annual Report, Young People's Adviser, Haggerston School, August 1983, Personal Papers.
2. Patrick Ivin to ASW and CM, July 2000.
3. Robinson Report, p. 70, appendix 6.
4. The Open University Educational Studies: A Third Level Course E353 Society, Education and the State, p. 73.
5. Janet Clark: 'Education Welfare Officers', p. 75.
6. *Daily Telegraph*, 2 April 1974.
7. ILEA, 'Education Welfare Service. Guidance on Procedure for the Information of Schools', 2/70, Patrick Ivin Private Collection.
8. DES, *The Education Welfare Service. An HMI enquiry in eight LEAs*, p. 14.
9. Ibid., p. 14.
10. Anna Sproule: 'Local Authority Experiment: London', p. 103.
11. ILEA Education Officers' Guild *Main Mail*, August 1973.
12. ILEA circular, 'Corporal Punishment', April 1980, Patrick Ivin Private Collection.
13. DES, *The Education Welfare Service. An HMI enquiry in eight LEAs*, p.18.
14. The Open University Educational Studies: A Third Level Course E353 Society, Education and the State, p. 68.
15. ILEA leaflet, 'Non-attendance at School', 1976, Patrick Ivin Private Collection.
16. ILEA Research and Statistics Branch, 'Perspectives on Attendance', 1981.
17. Anon.: *Jackie's Story*, p. 29.
18. ILEA Education Officers' Guild *Main Mail*, Fifth Anniversary, 1975.
19. Carlen, Gleeson and Wardhaugh: *Truancy. The politics of compulsory schooling*, p. 29.
20. K. MacMillan: *Education Welfare*, p. 103.
21. Quoted in Anna Sproule: 'Local Authority Experiment: London', p. 103.
22. Education Working Party, Document 1/80,p. 7, Patrick Ivin Private Collection.
23. ILEA Education Committee, 15 March 1972, Report by the Schools Subcommittee, p. 1.
24. Patrick Ivin to ASW and CM, July 2000.
25. Interview with Muriel Digney, 13 July 1999.
26. Ibid.
27. Report of the [EWS] Joint Working Party, 'No Room for Complacency', 1 October 1973, Patrick Ivin Private Collection.

28. Mary Morris: *Voluntary Workers in the Welfare State*, p. 102.
29. Muriel Digney to DW, 13 July 1999.
30. ILEA, 'Education Welfare Service. Information for applicants for Education Welfare Officer and Senior Posts', March 1979.
31. ILEA Education Officers' Guild *Main Mail*, Fifth Anniversary, 1975.
32. DES/DHSS Draft Circular to LAs, 'The Education Welfare Service', January 1979, Appendix 4, para. 14, p. 7 and paras 20/21, p. 9.
33. Society of Education Officers, 'The Education Welfare Service, its Role and Training', 4 April 1980.
34. Robinson Report, p. 38.
35. Ibid., p. 27.
36. ILEA Education Officers' Guild *Main Mail*, September 1974.
37. Society of Education Officers, 'The Education Welfare Service, A reply to the ADSS paper, "Social Work Services for Children in School"', January 1979.
38. DES, *The Education Welfare Service. An HMI enquiry in eight LEAs*, p.4.
39. Colwell Enquiry 1974, para 184, quoted in M. Craft, J. Raynor and L. Cohen: *Linking Home and School. A new review*, p. 231.
40. Frank Coombes and Dave Beer: *The Long Walk from the Dark*, p. 26.
41. ILEA leaflet, 'Non-attendance at School', 1976, Patrick Ivin Private Collection.
42. DES, *The Education Welfare Service. An HMI enquiry in eight LEAs*, pp. 9–10.
43. K. MacMillan: *Education Welfare*, p. 74.
44. *The Times* 1973.
45. Roy Porter: *London: A social history*, p. 455.
46. DES Survey, October 1984.
47. ILEA, 'Welcome to the ILEA', June 1986.
48. Peter Ackroyd: *London. The biography*, p. 755.
49. Estella O. West to ASW, 24 March 2000.
50. Ibid.
51. Ibid.
52. Case study in Eighth Annual Report, Young People's Adviser, 1986–7, [school in east London], Private Collection.
53. Third Annual Report, Young People's Adviser, August 1982, [school in east London], Private Collection.
54. Fourth Annual Report, Young People's Adviser, August 1983, [school in east London], Private Collection.
55. Third Annual Report, Young People's Adviser, August 1982, [school in east London], Private Collection.
56. ILEA, 'Children Who Show Problems. Guide to teachers on the services provided and where to apply for help for children who show problems', Patrick Ivin Private Collection.
57. Bullock Report, 'A Language for Life', in Roy Lowe, p. 121.
58. ILEA, 'Welcome to the ILEA', June 1986.
59. Peter Mortimore, ILEA, Research and Statistics Branch, 'Non-attendance at School: Some research findings', October 1980, p. 7.
60. 'The last straw?' in *Social Work Today*, 14 May 1984.
61. DES, DHSS, WO: Joint Circular of Guidance – The Education Welfare Service, January 1969, Patrick Ivin Private Collection.
62. Corrigan Report, 1984.
63. ILEA, Improving Secondary Schools – Report of the Committee on the Curriculum and Organisation of Secondary Schools. Chair Dr David Hargreaves, March 1984.
64. ILEA, Improving Primary Schools – Report of the Committee on Primary Education, January 1985.
65. ILEA, Educational Opportunities for All? – Review of provision to meet Special Educational Needs. Chair John Fish, 1985.

66. Quoted in Peter Ackroyd: *London. The biography*, p. 766.
67. Peter Ackroyd: *London. The biography*, p. 767.
68. Stuart Maclure: *A History of Education in London 1870–1990*, p. 195.
69. ILEA circular 374a/CIRC/BC.10 'Change of Name of ILEA Educational Welfare Service', October 1987.
70. Ibid.
71. ILEA, Education Welfare Service, 'Equality Statement – Review and Forward Plans', 1987.
72. ILEA circular 374a/CIRC/BC.10 'Change of Name of ILEA Educational Welfare Service', October 1987.
73. Education Development Plan, London Borough of Camden, February 1989.
74. Ermyne Lee-kin: 'Breaking Up is Hard to Do', *Community Care*, 31 May 1990, p.viii.
75. Kenneth Baker MP, Secretary of State for Education and Science, quoted in, 'Education in Inner London', published by the Conservative Education Authority, Surrey.
76. Stuart Maclure: *A History of Education in London 1870–1990*, p. 237.
77. Draft Proposals for Education, London Borough of Camden, October 1988.
78. Ibid., p.viii.

Chapter 9

CONCLUSION

'A Cinderella type of service, waiting for a Prince Charming of some kind to fit a slipper.'[1]

THE OVERWHELMING LESSON to be drawn from the previous chapters of this book is that many children in London have needed help of various kinds to make productive and happy use of their schooling. This help has been provided by the education welfare services of London in various forms since the Education Act of 1870. It has been delivered in the interface between home and school, providing a supportive bridge between these two very different worlds inhabited by children. However, it has been achieved with differing degrees of success. Large numbers of individual children have been given invaluable assistance, but many opportunities have been lost and many hopes proved to be false. Here lies the value of history: for understanding the background to current policy and practice offers a better chance of developing an appropriate strategy for the future. 'Our lives in the present and future,' argue Aldrich, Crook and Watson in their history of the Department of Education and Employment, 'are governed to a great extent by what has happened in the past.' Each human situation, they add,

> is unique and we cannot predict the future with certainty. Nevertheless, the record of human experience that is usually referred to as 'history' provides a rich store of data which we neglect at our peril. Our understanding of the present and journeys into the future will benefit from possession of accurate maps of the past.[2]

The needs of children

Children have always been at the centre of attendance and welfare care, in the sense that without them and their needs, there is no reason for the services in the first place. But despite this obvious fact, the story of the education welfare services of London is one in which children seem to have played insignificant roles. At no point up to 1990 were they consulted on their feelings or expectations about the provision of education welfare care; or if they were, there is no evidence of such consultation in any of the records that are available. When the Bedford Committee conducted a large scale investigation into the ILEA's social welfare services in 1965–6, no attempt was made to discover the experiences and views of the children involved. A mass of data was collected, but only from official records and from the adults working in the services. If anything, children seem to have become *less* visible over the years in reports and discussions of the education welfare services. At the most literal level of visibility, the photographs of children that filled the annual reports of the LCC, especially in the 1920s and 1930s, have disappeared. There are no longer any pictures of children in the flurry of reports produced in the last decades of the twentieth century – just pages and pages of typescript, tables and endnotes.

One underlying cause is that the services have always been targeted at the (so-called) 'lower-class' children of society. From the start, attendance services were set up to get working-class children into elementary school, while the Care Committees were created to give food to the children of the poor. Even after the Education Act of 1944, the children of better-off families were still largely untouched by the hand of the education welfare services. The services have been riddled by problems of social class (making the history of education welfare care a peculiarly English story) – although nobody likes to say so. The class question has been complicated further by the different social status of the workers in this area of care: the early attendance officers were largely working-class; the volunteers and the care organisers were educated middle-class or upper-class; and the post-1970 EWOs and ESWOs have been professional workers on low pay. Because of their higher social class, the workers of the Care Service, both paid and volunteer, had more prestige and status than attendance officers – even though they were women and the attendance officers were nearly always men. Largely because of this difference in social class, the two groups worked separately from each other right up to 1970, despite their shared aim to help children at school. These class-related dimensions of the history of the education welfare care need to be unpicked and examined, as a first step to giving a voice to the children and as a way of interrogating the low rank of education welfare in the hierarchy of social services.

At first, the education welfare services were a direct response to the evident needs of children – to their hunger, their need for warm clothes and boots, and to their legal right to go to school. But the social work strand seems to have evolved in a way that met the needs of the people working in the service, rather than the children themselves. This was most apparent in the middle of the century, when the creation of the welfare state after the Second World War removed the need for some of the practical duties of London's School Care Service. In order to survive, the Care Service shifted its concerns away from material and practical difficulties, to problems of behaviour – away from children *with* problems, to children who were seen to *be* problems. The overwhelming concern was now *The Problem of 'The Problem Family'*, which was the title of a key social work text published in 1957 by A.F. Philp, a unit leader in the Liverpool Family Service Unit, and Noel Timms, a psychiatric social worker. No doubt this development was at least partially related to the growing interest in child psychology. At the start of the century, ill health and inadequate living conditions were identified as a primary influence on the welfare of the child; but increasingly from the 1930s, this 'medical' model was displaced by a 'psychological' model, which located the source of children's problems in their behaviour and personality.

The changing direction of the Care Service was also the result of a wish to survive. After the war, many organisations had to adapt to a new reality or simply disappear. The National Birthday Trust Fund, for example, a voluntary organisation that had been set up in 1928 to improve maternity care, had to find a new cause in the 1950s, when responsibility for maternity care was taken over by the NHS (and, in any case, the previously high rate of maternal death had dropped dramatically). It then shifted its focus away from mothers, to a new concern with babies and with social scientific research.[3]

In the selection of children for free dinners, London's School Care Service may have made mistakes – but although these mistakes would have been serious, they would not have been especially damaging. In the handling of children's psychological health, on the other hand, it was treading on more dangerous ground. It seems possible that the Care Service may have diagnosed and 'treated' a pathology of behavioural problems where this was inappropriate. This risk would been especially great in the case of volunteers who had received little or no social work training. The Care Service was repeatedly congratulated in the 1950s on its ability to adapt to the new reality of Britain, but this may have been more of a success for the service itself than for some of the children it was created to serve.

The push for the survival of the Care Service was driven by the growing professional status of the employed care organisers, who supervised the volunteers. No doubt they did the best they could for the children under their care, but they also used the service to establish a niche for themselves as qualified social workers. In his history of professional society in England since 1880, Harold Perkin has commented that most social services have been organised around professional skills rather than client needs. He quotes a Fabian critic as saying that a citizen reading the 1968 Seebohm Report, for example, 'might indeed conclude that it had more to do with the work satisfaction and career structure of the professional social worker than it had to do with his own needs or rights in the modern welfare state'; each additional social worker, added Perkin with the use of another quote, 'revealed the need for two more'.[4]

An additional factor in the case of school care organisers was that they belonged to one of the first generations of women becoming professional workers. For them, this was a valuable means of marking out the boundaries of female professional territory. The growth of the social work profession contributed to – and was promoted by – the attrition of volunteers after the creation of the EWS in 1970. This attrition was instrumental in the future development of the service: it moved from a situation where a partnership between the voluntary sector and the state was fundamental to the success of its work, to one where the voluntary sector had become irrelevant. One irony of this development was that many of the paid social workers came from a background not dissimilar to that of some earlier Care Committee volunteers.

The value of the volunteer

In carrying out the research for this book it was no surprise to find that attendance officers were very often resented and feared by families and children. What *was* surprising, however, was that many families were more comfortable with a visit from a volunteer, than from a professional social worker. The consensus in western society appears to be that a trained professional is better than a volunteer. It has been assumed, for example, that a working-class family would resent the social class of the volunteer, which was likely to be higher than its own. It has also been assumed that such a volunteer would find it almost impossible to avoid condescension: a 1962 book on the work of the psychiatric social worker observed that:

> for the most part the philanthropists [that is, volunteers] were confident in the sufficiency of their own beneficence and supremely untroubled by any uneasiness concerning the respective positions of donor and recipient. Their claim to assurance is epitomized in the following advice to a friendly visitor at the turn of the century: 'a chat about your holiday in Scotland or Rome or Clacton-on-Sea, a description of the last play you saw, ball you went to, book you read, or even your brother's or uncle's latest fishing story, may

carry you a great way into the affection of some tired housewife resting after Monday's washing.'[5]

Advice like this (taken from *Hints for Visitors*, 1910) was certainly given and no doubt it was often followed. But this was only part of the story: and too much emphasis on this part alone misses out a great deal else.

On the one hand, it is true that Care Service volunteers were perfectly willing (and allowed by their organisers) to advise mothers on the best ways to bring up their children, even though they had no direct experience of the working-class mother's struggle from day to day, trying to make ends meet to feed and clothe a hungry family. Baroness Serota, who was herself a Care Committee volunteer in the 1940s and then co-opted to the Education Committee of the LCC, remembers that 'many middle-class volunteers did not know how to boil an egg,' because they had servants to do their domestic work. But she also remembers that 'families were more accepting of voluntary workers than the professionals.'[6] Mothers and fathers often resented the hand of professionals and feared their power as agents of the state, who could even arrange for their children to be taken away: social workers, observes Harold Perkin, 'have to a large extent taken control of the lives and fate of large and vulnerable sections of the public.'[7] Volunteers, on the other hand, were seen as largely harmless. Adeline Wimble, the Principal Care Organiser in the 1960s, commented that 'the voluntary worker is regarded as a "friend of the family" and is not considered as one of "them".'[8] And while the difference in social class established a social divide, the fact that the volunteer was carrying out her work without pay was a testament to her genuine concern. She could be a real advocate on behalf of children, in their relationship with their school and the state. A key theme in the story of London's education welfare services is this bridge they supplied between school and home.

The 'bridging' aspect of education welfare work has been regarded as the great strength of the Education Welfare Officer (EWO), whose remit today includes both school attendance and welfare help. He or she is seen as 'vital to any attendance initiative',[9] because EWOs are likely to visit the family home and 'are detached from the school and yet familiar with its staff, structures and procedures'.[10] Repeated attention was drawn in the late twentieth century to the importance of the relationship between home and school (such as Home–School Agreements). EWOs are often the first line of defence, observes Ken Reid in *Truancy and School Absenteeism* (1985), since they are the first people to visit a child's home; on occasion, their commitment to the child can bring them into conflict with the wishes of the social services, schools and parents.[11] But like the social worker and the former school attendance officer, the EWO represents the state, so may not be trusted as a disinterested friend in the same way as the volunteer.

Balancing the needs of attendance and welfare

Should the EWS be a social work service or simply a service focused on attendance? What about the other problems and issues that obstruct learning and achievement? Who deals with these? These are urgent questions. A major obstacle is that the fusion of the attendance and welfare services in London in 1970 was not a natural development, but one that emerged largely out of external pressures. One of these was the shrinking pool of volunteers available for welfare work, in conjunction with the economic constraints of London local government. The new EWS followed the model of education welfare care outside the metropolis, in which School Board Men were chiefly responsible for attendance, but were also given welfare duties. But the vast and diverse metropolis of London has a very different set of needs from the rest of Britain.

Once the services had been merged, there were increasing calls for education welfare to become a social work service, with a primary emphasis on social work care. This culminated finally in the official renaming of the service in 1987 as the Education Social Work Service. However, its aims disappeared in the collapse of the service in 1990, as a result of the dismantling of the ILEA. Thereafter, the services provided by many of the individual local education authorities in London paid diminishing attention to social work care and became more focused on attendance, under pressure from central government. The EWOs of today are more like the School Board Men of earlier times – but there is no additional School Care Service to absorb and care for the welfare needs of London's children.

What is clear from the history of London's education welfare services is that a centralised operation on the previous scale is unlikely to re-emerge. But whatever the models are for the future, it will be necessary to establish an appropriate balance between attendance and welfare care, to ensure true inclusion and higher levels of attainment. While attendance is a prerequisite to achievement, there is always a danger that the most serious non-attendance is seen as a cause in itself and the deeper issues are not tackled or are ignored. There is a need to re-establish the role of the education welfare officer and to be much clearer about the role and intervention of non-educational agencies in general, in the achievement and well-being of pupils and their families.

Education welfare care in London has been described as 'a Cinderella type of service, waiting for a Prince Charming of some kind to fit a slipper'[12] – to help it to develop its full potential. But in order to achieve this very important aim, it will be necessary to avoid the mistakes of the past and to develop a coherent and planned strategy for the future. Most importantly, it will be necessary to put the needs of children at the centre of all its concerns.

Notes

1. Miss Mary Maclean to ASW and DW, 21 April 1999.
2. Aldrich, Crook and Watson: *Education and Employment*, pp. 18–19.
3. See A. Susan Williams, *Women and Childbirth in Twentieth Century Britain*, especially chapter 8.
4. Harold Perkin: *The Rise of Professional Society*, pp. 348–9.
5. Noel Timms: *Psychiatric Social Work in Great Britain*, p. 5.
6. Beatrice Serota to ASW, DW and RA, 15 June 1999.
7. Harold Perkin: *The Rise of Professional Society*, pp. 349.
8. Adeline Wimble: 'The School Care Committee', p. 159.
9. In Eric Blyth and Judith Milner (eds): *Improving School Attendance*, p. 145.
10. Eric Blyth and Judith Milner (eds): *Improving School Attendance*, p. 168.
11. Ken Reid: *Truancy and School Absenteeism*, p. 40.
12. Miss Mary Maclean to ASW and DW, 21 April 1999.

APPENDIX

After 1990: Education welfare services in the inner-London boroughs

THE LAST FIGURES for attendance in inner-London schools were published by the ILEA in 1989[1]. They showed that overall attendance in primary schools in 1988 was 91.2 per cent, which (with 1987) was the lowest figure for ten years; for secondary schools it was 83.7 per cent, the second lowest for ten years (it had been 83.3 per cent in 1987). These figures were global ILEA school totals and were not locally or institutionally disaggregated. At the end of the 1980s, the borough councils were busy preparing their Education Development Plans for the Secretary of State and consulting the public about their initial plans for taking over from the ILEA. Setting up the new local education authorities (LEAs) was a formidable task for the inner London boroughs, especially because of the shortage of time available.

Initially few people mentioned the fate of the ILEA Education Social Work Services. Some boroughs planned to name the service 'Education Welfare Service', while others toyed with the idea of including 'attendance' in the title. Still others said they would aim to continue the role of the ILEA service, keep a joint ILEA borough social services model for some special schools and employ some psychiatric social workers in the new LEA. This debate continued as the boroughs decided how to transfer or recruit people to their new service, as well as appoint Principal Education Social Workers or Principal Education Welfare Officers. At this time some staff left, either to take redundancy (from the age of 40 in the ILEA) or new jobs.

Early on, one or two boroughs stated that they recognised the importance of the role that could be played by the service in equality of opportunity and access to learning and achievement. In its draft proposals for running education in October 1988, Camden LEA described the service as follows:

> The service is the LEA's principal agency for ensuring compliance with the statutory requirements set out. ... Its focus has always been on children and their families in relation to schools and the wider community. It has a role in such policy issues as suspension and expulsion of pupils, equal educational opportunities and special educational needs.[2]

When Camden LEA published its Education Development Plan in February 1989, it had clear views about the priorities of its Education Social Work:

> The Education Social Work Service has a positive supportive function concerning all families with children at school. It supplements the work of the schools in educating their children in the widest sense, so that children are helped to attain the highest educational standards of which they are capable and also to live and enjoy life as fully as possible in work and in leisure.[3]

As the new LEAs began to operate, it became clear that less overall resources would be available to the new LEAs. Moreover, with the introduction of local management of schools in inner London in 1992, a debate about *centrally-based* resources vis-à-vis *school-based* resources was soon underway. Some of the new LEAs responded by seeking service level agreements and defining more tightly the role and resource distribution of the service. Schools that had received a full-time Education Social Worker and others that had received weekly visits might now receive less frequent visits and have a different route for referral. The targeting of need was beginning, with some LEAs basing resource distribution on the previous record of referrals and on attendance rates.

As time went on, further reductions in the overall LEA budgets were reflected in the size and scope of the education welfare and social work services in inner London. LEAs continued to undergo restructuring, which was reflected in the special educational needs and student services provision in the boroughs (including the education welfare service). The government had introduced targeted grants, as a part of specialist grants later called a Standards Fund, which allowed LEAs to bid for resources in the field of attendance and disaffection (latterly called 'social inclusion'). Some LEAs used these imaginatively to supplement and develop some specialist EWO/ESW posts.

A report from the Office of Her Majesty's Chief Inspector of Schools[4] looked at 12 LEAs (7 fully and 5 by one Inspector) between 1992 and 1994. Only one inner-London LEA was visited and fully inspected and the individual LEAs were not identified by name. However, some important issues were identified, such as communication between the service, schools, the parent LEA and other agencies. All services saw attendance as their central function and the Inspectors felt that the tension between the duty to secure attendance and the social work role was not fully explained or articulated by the services, the LEA or its partners and the schools. This was very important for the relatively new inner-London LEAs, as the ILEA between 1986 and 1990 had been preparing for a fully-fledged education social work service, with specialist roles and a career structure. Some of the new borough LEAs were seen to be ambivalent about the role of the education welfare or social work service, or to be too simplistic in their identification of attendance as the chief role of the service.

The Ofsted report concluded that the service needed to learn how to forge different types of relationships with (what were now) largely self-governing institutions. It called for the service to become more responsive to the needs of these institutions and to work more in partnership with the schools and the LEA. Among those who worried about the borough's stewardship of the service were those who shared the Ofsted perception that possibly some staff could not face change and were in any case unclear about what they were supposed to be doing. The issues of family support and school-based work were again raised.

As the 1990s continued, LEAs were called ever more to account and were open to Ofsted and Audit Commission inspection and scrutiny. LEAs were asked to produce Education Development Plans and Behaviour Support Plans, including work on attendance, pupil support and social inclusion. Some LEAs in inner London concluded during these exercises that their education welfare or social work service was not sufficiently focused on attendance. In the meantime, some schools were unhappy about access to support for the most challenging and disaffected pupils and were anxious to receive this support from the ESWS/EWS. Ironically, some schools wanted the EWO/ESW to be more of an all-round support to pupils, even as their LEA was narrowing their role and reducing their availability.

Some inner-London LEAs received highly critical reports on their efficiency; attendance and support to schools were picked out as problem areas. In the inspection report of Southwark education authority, the tensions between school wishes and available resources were highlighted. This LEA's Education Welfare and Attendance Service (EWAS) was seen as effective in employing strategies to ensure that the statutory duties for attendance were met. However, the report took the view that the schools did not always fully understand or endorse the LEA's methodology for resourcing the schools. The report concluded:

> The service maintains quite rightly that it does not have the staffing to
> respond in ways schools would prefer. ... Improving pupil attendance is a

priority in the LEA's Educational Development Plan and should provide a timely opportunity to redefine how best the LEA should support schools to raise attendance rates.[5]

Schools were beginning to wonder if education welfare care might be better deployed as a school-based service. Whereas the ILEA had introduced school-attached ESWs, this was from a sound resource base and primary and early years preventive work was well funded and catered for. The boroughs did not have – or did not choose to deploy – these resources and some schools, particularly some secondary schools, were wondering whether the EWO might be more effective based in the school, working as part of the school pastoral team; this seemed all the more likely as they now had experience of local management of schools.

In 1999 the Department for Education and Employment (DfEE) produced guidance on the role of the LEA in pupil support.[6] The DfEE argued that ESWs/EWOs should work closely with schools and families to resolve attendance issues. It suggested shared policies and operational practices between the EWS and schools, with clearly defined roles for school staff and ESWS/EWS staff. Additionally, the expectations of the quality of the service should be explicit and proper systems put in place for referral, regular review, monitoring and evaluation. Service level agreements, added the report, should be drawn up between LEAs and schools to achieve this.

As a result of Ofsted/Audit Commission inspection, one or two inner-London LEAs are out-sourcing the various services – including education welfare – to other organisations. Two inner-London LEAs are taking part in a pilot scheme, whereby the secondary school ESWs or EWOs are being devolved to groups of those schools. At the time of writing (mid-2001), 16 LEAs nationally are involved in this trial, which will be evaluated.

The Crime and Disorder Act of 1998 will also affect the work of the service in a number of ways. Section 8 of the Act allows for Parenting Orders to be made by the courts in any proceedings where a person has been convicted of an offence under Section 443 (failure to comply with a school attendance order) or Section 444 (failure to secure regular attendance at school of a registered pupil) of the Education Act of 1996. It has been suggested that such orders are desirable in the interests of preventing the commission of further offences under the Education Acts. They may be used in addition to any fine imposed for non-attendance.

The police have been given a new power under the 1998 Crime and Disorder Act, which will allow them to take truanting pupils found in public places back to school or to another place designated by the LEA. This power is designed to be used as part of a range of initiatives, to be discussed and agreed between the LEA and local schools.

All these developments will have an impact on the operation of the service, the standards of quality and the training needed for the efficient execution of the role. A number of other new ways of working may also emerge for the inner-London area over the next few years, with the development of the Connexions youth support service. In November 2000, the DfEE and the DfEE Connexions Service National Unit held a national conference on the EWS and the proposed new service.[7] EWOs now working with the Connexions clientele are part of the core Connexions team, in the role of Connexions Personal Advisers (PAs), supporting young people on an individual basis and working with other PAs, whose background may be in careers and youth work. Planning advice on Connexions from central government including a section on the importance of involving young people:

> Young people can make a uniquely valuable contribution to improving quality in the acting roles of monitor, inspector and evaluator, according to the guidance issued by the Government. This really does give an opportunity to plan a bottom-up rather than top-down service.[8]

The exact mechanics of the relationship of education welfare services to the new Connexions Service are yet to be defined exactly, but a role similar to that defined for Learning Mentors is expected. It is planned to involve schools and the pupils themselves in designing the most relevant and best model.

In October 2000, the Secretary of State for Education and Employment and the Home Secretary announced a national crackdown on truancy and promised more help and more funding for schools for this work. Schools that succeeded in cutting truancy in challenging circumstances were promised the chance to win a 'Truancy Buster' award of up to £10,000, from early 2001.

If new resources are put into Sure Start and early years work and also into secondary schools, which are to be welcomed, the support and preventive work in primary schools also needs to be effective. One of the early consequences of putting 50 per cent of the education welfare resources into secondary schools in the pilot projects in England has been to highlight the lack of EWO resources for primary schools in some areas. The Government has announced a new £450 million Children's Fund to help tackle child poverty and social inclusion. The fund will include initiatives for preventive work for 5–13-year-olds and their families. Interestingly, voluntary organisations will administer these local projects.

Other influences on the development of the EWS include the enhanced priority given to children in need and to children looked after by the local authority. Schools themselves face challenges, with LEAs, to reduce truancy and permanent exclusions and to raise achievement amongst disaffected young people. They also face the clawing-back of some dedicated resources in the 'truancy trigger' and exclusion targets. Recent guidance on Connexions has also intimated that an indicative resource for EWS input to secondary schools would be 50 per cent of the LEA EWS budget. This will have further implications for early year and primary preventive work. The role of the ESW/EWO is constantly open to redefinition and refinement, although the social issues do not change very much.

National developments will have a major impact on how inner-London LEAs shape their future services. One key issue will be the scale of need and the resources devoted to this work. Additionally, questions must be asked about where and how the need can best be met – at school or at LEA level, by the institution or in partnership with the LEA? Will access to other services for schools improve? Will pupils' needs be met at early years and primary level, as well as at secondary level? Training, supervision and development, as well as common standards of service, will continue to be important matters – as will the need to prosecute parents and to seek Education Supervision Orders under the 1989 Children Act. Questions must be asked, too, about methods of measuring service delivery and whether this should be done at school level or whether LEAs should be accountable for the overall service delivery. Above all, there is a need to re-establish the role of the Education Welfare Social Worker and to be much clearer generally about the role and intervention of agencies that are not strictly educational but support true inclusion and higher levels of attainment.

Notes

1. Education Statistics 1988–89, ILEA 1989.
2. Draft Proposals for Education, London Borough of Camden, October 1988.
3. Education Development Plan, London Borough of Camden, February 1989.
4. The Challenge for Education Welfare, Office for Standards in Education, 17/95/NS 1995.
5. Support to Improve Attendance section, Inspection of Southwark LEA, November 1998, Office of Her Majesty's Chief Inspector of Schools in conjunction with the Audit Commission.
6. Social Inclusion: the LEA role in pupil support, DfEE Publications, July 1999.
7. 'EWS and Connexions Conference Report', DfEE, November 2000.
8. 'Connexions Service – Planning Guidance', DfEE Publications, 2000.

CHRONOLOGY

1833	Factory Act. Children under 9 prohibited from working in mines and factories
1844	Ragged School Union
1862	Revised School Code
1870	Elementary Education Act (Forster). Created school boards
1875	Factory Act widening scope of 1833 Act
1876	Education Act (Sandon). School age fixed at 10. Employment of children in school hours prohibited
1880	Education Act (Mundella)
1884	The National Association of Board Officers formed (at first School Board Officers' Mutual Association)
1884	Children's Country Holiday Fund set up
1888	Local Government Act. Set up County and County Borough Councils
1889	London County Council (LCC) established
1890	Revised Code changed – increased emphasis on school attendance
1891	Education Act. All fees abolished in schools except where higher than 10 shillings
1893	Elementary Education Act. School-leaving age raised to 11 from 1894
1899	Board of Education established
1899	School-leaving age raised to 12
1900	Elementary Education Act. Empowered Boards to compel school attendance to 14, but with many exceptions
1899–1902	Boer War

1902	Education Act. Abolished school boards and passed education to County and County Boroughs
1903	Education (London) Act, transferring school responsibilities to LCC
1903	Employment of Children Act
1904	Medical Officers of Health set up nationally
1905	LCC sets up School Medical Service
1906	Education (Provision of Meals) Act
1907	Education (Administrative Provisions) Act. Medical inspections in schools
1907–9	LCC formalises care committees into School Care Service
1908	Children's Act. Allowed for removal of neglected children from their homes
1911	Unemployment and Insurance Act. Unemployment and health insurance for several million wage-earners, though not their dependants
1914	London School Care Service divided between Education Department and Public Health Department
1914–18	First World War
1918	Education Act (Fisher). Compulsory school attendance to 14 Child labour prohibited in factories and mines
1918	Maternity and Child Welfare Act
1919	Ministry of Health formed
1922	Section 8(1) of the Education Act 1918 brought into force, ending all exemptions from school attendance up to age of 14
1925	Nearly 6,000 Care Committee volunteers
1926	Hadow Report. Recommended post primary education from 11 to 18 or 19, secondary education and the 11 plus exam. No reference to school attendance
1929	Crash of New York Stock Exchange – Depression
1933	Proposal to merge London School Care Service and Inquiry Service, but not developed
1933	3 million unemployed
1933	Children and Young Persons Act. Prevention of Cruelty to Children, of children begging, children in bars
1936	Education Act
1937	854 School Care Committees, almost 5,000 voluntary workers
1938	Children and Young Persons Act
1939	National Association changes name to Education Welfare Officers' National Association (EWONA)

1939	A Care Committee in every London school
1939–45	Second World War: evacuation of children
1942	Beveridge Report
1944	Education Act (Butler). Restructured education into 3 groups: primary, secondary, further education
1946	NHS Act. Start of Family Allowances
1946	Report on the Care of Children Committee (Curtis Report) 1946
1947	School-leaving age raised to 15
1948	Proposal to merge London School Care Service and Inquiry Service
1948	Start of NHS
1948	Local authority Children's Committees and Departments set up. LCC sets up Children's Departments
1950	Merger plan dropped
1960	The Committee on Children and Young Persons (Ingleby Committee)
1960	Report on the employment of Children in the Theatre, Films and Ballet (Bateson Committee)
1962	Education Act
1963	Newsom Report
1963	Local Government Act
1963	Certificate in Education Welfare introduced
1965	Child Poverty Action Group set up
1965	LCC split up: creation of GLC Inner London Education Authority (ILEA)
1967	Bedford Report
1967	Plowden Report
1968	Seebohm Report
1969	Braide Report, agreeing with most recommendations of Bedford Report
1970	Merger of School Care Service, School Inquiry Service and the Welfare Benefits section to form EWS
1970	British Association of Social Workers formed. EWONA remains independent
1971	Abolition of free school milk
1971	Local Social Services Act becomes law. Social Services Departments set up, with comprehensive social work powers
1971	National Working Party of the Local Government Training Board (under Ralphs) on the Training of Education Welfare Officers
1971	Ralphs Report
1972	School-leaving age raised to 16

1973	Robinson Report – concept of ILEA education social work service
1973	EWONA Conference instructs National Council to prepare a case for parity of salary with other social workers
1974	ILEA loses School Health Service to area health authorities
1975	National agreement bringing education social workers' pay into line with mainstream social workers
1976	Education Act
1976	ILEA Education Welfare Officers' Guild joins EWONA
1977	Title of EWONA changed to the National Association of Social Workers in Education. NASWE starts new policies and approaches
1981	Physical punishment abolished in all schools
1982	Unemployment passes 3 million
1986	End of GLC; ILEA becomes a directly elected authority
1987–8	EWS merges with School Health Social Work Service to form ESWS
1988	Education Reform Act
1989	Children Act
1990	ILEA abolished. ESWS devolved to individual London boroughs

ARCHIVE SOURCES

Institute of Education Library
Archives and Special Collections
20 Bedford Way
London WC1H 0AL

London Metropolitan Archives
Centre
40 Northampton Road
London EC1R OHB

Modern Records Centre
University of Warwick
Coventry CV4 7AL

Private Collections:
   Patrick Ivin
   Others (various and anonymous)

Public Record Office
Ruskin Avenue
Kew TW9 4DU

Wellcome Library for the History
and Understanding of Medicine
Wellcome Trust
183 Euston Road
London NW1 2BE

PERIODICAL PUBLICATIONS

Community Care
Economic Review
Education
Education Social Worker
EWO
Fortnightly Review
Hansard
History Workshop Journal
ILEA Contact
ILEA News
Illustrated London News
Islington Gazette
The Listener
London County Council Education
   Bulletin

LCC Gazette
Main Mail (ILEA Education Welfare
   Officers Guild)
Manchester Guardian
New Society
Public Administration
School Attendance Gazette
School Child
Social History of Medicine
Social Work Today
Telegraph
The Times
The Times Educational Supplement
   (TES)
Twentieth Century British History

BIBLIOGRAPHY

Ackroyd, P. (2000), *London. The Biography*. London, Chatto and Windus.

Aldrich, R., Crook, D. and Watson, D. (2000), *Education and Employment: the DfEE and its place in history*. Bedford Way Papers no. 11. London, Institute of Education.

Anon. (1984), *Jackie's Story*. London, Centerprise Trust.

Anon. (1901), *The Pupil's Own Register of School Attendance*. No publishing details.

Ballard, P.B. (n.d. [1910]), *Margaret McMillan – An Appreciation*. No publications details given.

Barry, J. and Jones, C. (eds) (1991), *Medicine and Charity Before the Welfare State*. London, Routledge.

[Bedford Report] (1967) 'The Social Welfare Services of the Inner London Education Authority, 1965–66', Report of an inquiry by the Social Research Unit, Bedford College. London, ILEA.

Behlmer, George, K. (1998), *Friends of the Family: The English home and its guardians, 1850–1940*. Stanford, CA, Stanford University Press.

Black, C. (1907), *Sweated Industry and the Minimum Wage*. London, Duckworth.

Blyth, E. and Milner, J. (eds) (1999), *Improving School Attendance*. London, Routledge.

Booth, C. (1902) [though parts were published in 1889 and 1891], *Life and Labour of the People in London*. First Series: Poverty, 1. East, Central and South London. London, Macmillan.

Bourne, R. and MacArthur, B. (n.d.), *The Struggle for Education 1870–1970*. London, Schoolmaster Publishing Company.

Bowlby, J. (1951), *Maternal Care and Mental Health*. Geneva, World Health Organization.

[Braide Report] ILEA Working Party (1969), Report on the Conclusions of the Bedford Report.

Bryant, M. (1986), *The London Experience of Secondary Education*. London, The Athlone Press.

Burnett, J. (ed.) (1982*), Destiny Obscure. Autobiographies of childhood, education and family from the 1820s to the 1920s*. London, Allen Lane.

Cantlie, J. (1885), *Degeneracy among Londoners*. London, Field and Tuer.

Carlen, P., Gleeson, D. and Wardhaugh, J. (1992), *Truancy. The politics of compulsory schooling*. Buckingham, Open University Press.

Central Health Services Council, Standing Medical Advisory Committee (1967), *Report of the Sub-Committee, Child Welfare Centres*. HMSO.

Chamberlain, M. (1989), *Growing Up in Lambeth*. London, Virago.

Chaplin, C. (1964), *My Autobiography*. London, The Bodley Head.

Clark, J. (1976), *Education Welfare Officers. A study of the work of Education Welfare Officers and consideration of the future development of the service*, published by Mrs J. Clark, Herts.

Coates, K. and Silburn, R. (1970), *Poverty: The forgotten Englishman*. Harmondsworth, Penguin.

Coombes, F. and Beer, D. (1984), *The Long Walk from the Dark: School Board Man to Education Social Worker. A short history of the National Association of Social Workers in Education and its predecessors*. Birmingham, NASWE.

Copelman, D.M. (1996), *London's Women Teachers: Gender, class and feminism, 1870–1930*. London, Routledge.

Corrigan, P. (1979), *Schooling the Smash Street Kids*. London, Macmillan.

[Corrigan Report] ILEA (1984), 'Educational Opportunity and London's Children: the role of a social work service'.

Cosens, M. (1940), *Evacuation: A social revolution*. London, Charity Organization Society. Reprinted from *Social Work*, January 1940.

Council for Educational Advance (1970), 'Who Cares? A discussion of counselling and pastoral care in schools'. Report of a one-day national conference organized by the Council of Educational Advance on 19 March 1970, attended by representatives of educational organizations, LEAs, Colleges and Universities. London.

Craft, M., Raynor, J. and Cohen, L. (1980), *Linking Home and School. A new review*, 3rd edn. London, Harper and Row.

Cressell, W.D'A. (1948), *Margaret McMillan. A Memoir*. London, Hutchinson.

Cunningham, H. (1991), *The Children of the Poor. Representations of childhood since the seventeenth century*. Oxford, Blackwell.

Currie, M.R. (1998), 'Social Policy and Public Health Measures in Bedfordshire within the National Context 1904–38', University of Luton PhD.

Davies, J. (1975), 'Results from the DES Survey on Absences from School (January 1975) for ILEA schools only'. RED 626/75.

Davin, A. (1996), *Growing Up Poor. Home, school and street in London 1870–1914*. London, Rivers Oram Press.

Dawson, A. (1967), 'The Education Welfare Officer' in M. Craft, J. Raynor and L. Cohen (eds), *Linking Home and School*. London, Longman.

Delaney, S. (1956), *A Taste of Honey*. London, Methuen.

Dent, H. C. (1944), *Education in Transition. A Sociological Study of the Impact of War on English Education*. London, Kegan Paul, Trench, Trubner and Co.

Dent, H.C. (1944; twelfth edn 1968), *The Education Act 1944. Provisions, regulations, circulars, later Acts*. London, University of London Press.

Department for Education and Employment, Youth Justice Board, Home Office (1999), 'Tackling Truancy Together'.

Department for Education and Employment (1999), 'Social Inclusion: the LEA Role in Pupil Support', July.

Department of Education and Science (1984), *The Education Welfare Service. An HMI enquiry in eight LEAs*. London, HMSO.

DES, DHSS, WO (January 1979), 'Joint Circular of Guidance – The Education Welfare Service'.

Derrick, C.O.L. (1991), 'The Role of the Education Welfare Service: implications for change'. University of London Institute of Education, MA.

Devereux, W. (1982), *Adult Education in Inner London 1870–1980*. London, Shepheard-Walwyn in collaboration with ILEA.

Drake, B. (1933), *Starvation in the Midst of Plenty. A new plan for the state feeding of school children*. Fabian Tract no. 240. London, The Fabian Society.

Eliot, G. (1871–2), *Middlemarch*. Rpt. 1994, Harmondsworth, Penguin.

Elliot, Rev. W.H.H. (1912), 'Children's Care Committees' in J.H. Whitehouse (ed.), *Problems of Boy Life*. London, P.S. King.

Finlayson, G. (1990), 'A Moving Frontier: Voluntarism and the state in British social welfare 1911–1949', in *Twentieth Century British History* 1(2).

Frere, M. (1909), *Children's Care Committees: how to work them in public elementary schools*. London, P.S. King.

Gardner, P. (1984), *The Lost Elementary Schools of Victorian England*. Kent, Croom Helm.

Gibbon, Sir I.G. and Bell, R.W. (1939), *A History of the L.C.C., 1889–1939*. London, Macmillan.

Gosden, P.H.J.H. (1976), *Education in the Second World War*. London, Methuen.

Gowdridge, C., Williams, A.S. and Wynn, M. (1997), *Mother Courage: Letters from mothers in poverty at the end of the century*. Harmondsworth Penguin.

Gowing, R. (ed.) (1878), *The School Board and School Attendance Committee Directory*. London, Grant.

Green, F. (1980), 'On becoming a truant – the social administrative process in non-attendance'. Unpublished MA thesis, Cranfield Institute of Technology.

Greenwood, W. (1933), *Love on the Dole*. London, Penguin.

[Hadow Report] (1926), Board of Education, *The Education of the Adolescent*. London, HMSO.

Hall, M.P. (1952), *The Social Services of Modern England*. London, Routledge and Kegan Paul.

Hammond, J.L. and B. (1923), *Lord Shaftesbury*. London, Constable.

Hannington, W. (1936), *Unemployed Struggles 1919–1936*. London, Lawrence and Wishart.

Harris, B. (1991), 'Government Charity in the Distressed Mining Areas of England and Wales 1928–30', in J. Barry and C. Jones (eds), *Medicine and Charity before the Welfare State*. London, Routledge.

— (1995), *The Health of the Schoolchild. A history of the School Medical Service in England and Wales*. Buckingham, Open University Press.

Heller, F. (2000), 'Creating a holding environment in an innercity school' in N. Barwick (ed.), *Clinical Counselling in Schools*. London, Routledge.

Hendrick, H. (1992), 'Child Labour, Medical Capital and the School Medical Service, c. 1890–1918' in R. Cooter (ed.), *In the Name of the Child. Health and Welfare 1880–1945*. London, Routledge.

— (1994), *Child Welfare. England 1872–1989*. London, Routledge.

— (1997), *Children, Childhood and English Society, 1880–1990*. Prepared for the Economic History Society, Cambridge University Press.

Hinton, J. (1998), 'Voluntarism and the Welfare/Warfare State.

Women's Voluntary Services in the 1940s', *Twentieth Century British History* 9(2).

Hird, F. (1898), *The Cry of the Children: An exposure of the industries in which British children are iniquitously employed*. London, J. Bowden.

Hollis, P. (1987), *Ladies Elect: Women in English local government, 1865–1914*. Oxford, Clarendon Press.

Holness, M. (1989), 'Days of Caring', in *ILEA News* 79, 10 April.

Horn, P. (1994), *Children's Work and Welfare, 1780–1880s*. London, Macmillan.

Hume, J.H. (1883), *The School Attendance Guide, A handbook for the use of the members and officers of local authorities engaged in the work of compulsory education*. London, Knight.

Humphries, S. (1981), *Hooligans or Rebels? An oral history of working-class childhood and youth 1889–1939*. Oxford, Basil Blackwell.

Hurt, J. (1979), *Elementary Schooling and the Working Classes, 1860–1918*. London, Routledge and Kegan Paul.

—(1985), 'Feeding the Hungry Schoolchild in the First Half of the Twentieth Century', in D.J Oddy and D.S. Miller (eds), *Diet and Health in Modern Britain*. London, Croom Helm.

ILEA (1966), 'General Instructions for the Guidance of School Inquiry Officers'.

— (1970), 'Education Welfare Service. guidance on procedure for the information of schools'.

— EWS(1973), 'No Room for Complacency. Report of the Joint Working Party', 1 October.

— (1981), 'Perspectives on Attendance', Research and Statistics Branch, Document RS 749/80.

— (1987), 'Change of Name of ILEA Education Welfare Service', October, Circular 87/207.

Illich, I. (1971), *Deschooling Society*. London, Calder and Boyers.

Iselin, H. (1912), 'The Story of a Children's Care Committee', in *The Economic Review*.XXII(1), January.

Jay, P. in association with E. Tucker (1990), *Loves and Labours. An Autobiography by Peggy Jay*. London, Weidenfeld and Nicolson.

Jenkins, D. (1966), *The Educated Society*. London, Faber and Faber.

Jennings, H. (1930), *The Private Citizen in Public Social Work*. London, George Allen and Unwin.

Johnson, D. (1980), *Secondary Schools and the Welfare Network*. London, George Allen and Unwin.

Jones, G. (1986), *Social Hygiene in Twentieth Century Britain*. London, Croom Helm.

Lawson, J. and Silver, H. (1973), *A Social History of Education in England*. London, Methuen.

LCC (1933) Education Officer and Public Health Branch, Report of Inter-departmental Committee on Children's Care Work.

— (1963) 'The Work of L.C.C. School Care Organisers and Social Workers (Health Services)'.

— General Purposes Subcommittee to the Education Committee (1958), 'Report on the Work of the Care Committees'.

Lecky, E. (1959), 'Children Then and Now. A survey of Care Committee work in Putney from 1907 to 1958'. Privately printed. LMA, ILEA S/SB/04/2.

Leff, V. (1959), *The School Health Service*. London, H.K. Lewis.

Link, R. (1982), 'Before the Bell Tolls', in *Social Work Today* 13(31), April.

Llewellyn Smith, Sir H.(1937), *The Borderland between Public and Voluntary Action in the Social Services*, Sidney Ball Lecture, 27 January 1937, Barnett House Papers no 20. London, Oxford University Press.

Lowe, R. (1997), *Schooling and Social Change 1964–1990*. London, Routledge.

Lyons, K.H. (1973), *Social Work and the School. A study of some aspects of the role of an Education Social Worker*. London, HMSO.

LSB (1906), Report of the Education Committee on Accommodation and Attendance in Elementary Schools. London School Board papers, held at London Metropolitan Archives.

Macadam, E. (1934a), 'The Relations between the Statutory and Voluntary Social Services', *Public Administration* 12(3), July.

— (1934b) *The New Philanthropy. A study in the relations between the statutory and voluntary social services*. London, Allen and Unwin.

M'Gonigle, G.C.M. and Kirby, J. (1946), *Poverty and Public Health*. London, Gollancz.

McIntosh, J., Naylor, F. and Norcross, L. (1983), *The ILEA after the Abolition of the Greater London Council*, September. London, Centre for Policy Studies.

Maclure, S. (1990), *A History of Education in London 1870–1990*. Harmondsworth, Allen Lane.

MacMillan, K. (1977), *Education Welfare: Strategy and Structure*. London, Longman.

McMillan, Margaret (n.d. [1910]). *The School Clinic To-day*. Independent Labour Party (ILP).

— (1911), *The Child and the State*. Manchester, the National Labour Press.

— (1917), *The Camp School.* London, George Allen and Unwin.

— (1919), *The Nursery School.* London, J.M. Dent.

Mansbridge, A. (1932), *Margaret McMillan – Prophet and Pioneer. Her Life and Work*. London, J.M. Dent.

Marwick, A. (1998), *The Sixties Cultural Revolution in Britain, France, Italy, and the United States, c. 1958–1974*. Oxford, OUP.

Mildner, L. and House, B. (1976), *The Gates*. London, Centerprise Trust.

Morris, M. (1969), *Voluntary Workers in the Welfare State*. London, Routledge.

Mortimore, P. (1980), 'Non-Attendance at School: Some research findings', ILEA Research and Statistics Branch, October, RS 760/80.

Newman, G. (1939), *The Building of a Nation's Health*. London, Macmillan.

[Newsom Report] (1963), Central Advisory Council for Education (England) *Half our future*. London, HMSO.

Nicholson, J.H. (1925), *School Care Committees*. London, P.S. King.

O'Neill, G. (1999), *My East End. Memories of life in Cockney London*. London, Viking.

Orr, J.B. and Lubbock, D. (1940), *Feeding the People in War-Time*. London, Macmillan.

Parry, N. and McNair, D. (eds) (1983), *The Fitness of the Nation – physical health and education in the nineteenth and twentieth centuries*. Leicester, The History of Education Society.

Parton, N. (1991), *Governing the Family. Child care, child protection and the state*. London, Macmillan.

Paterson, A. (1911), *Across the Bridges. Or life by the south London river-side*. London, Edward Arnold.

Pedley, F.H. (ed.) (1967), *Education and Social Work*. Oxford, Pergamon Press.

Pember Reeves, M. (1913; rpt. 1988), *Round About a Pound a Week*. London, Virago.

Pennybacker, S.D. (1995), *A Vision for London 1889–1914: labour, everyday life and the LCC experiment*. London, Routledge.

Pepler, D. (1914), *The Care Committee. The child and the parent*. London, Constable.

Perkin, H. (1989), *The Rise of Professional Society: England since 1880*. London, Routledge.

Philp, A.F. and Timms, N. (1957), *The Problem of 'The Problem Family'. A critical review of the literature concerning the 'problem family' and its treatment*. London, Family Service Unit.

[Plowden Report] (1967), Central Advisory Council for Education (England), *Children and their Primary Schools*. London, HMSO.

Porter, R. (1994; rpt. 2000), *London. A Social History*. Harmondsworth, Penguin.

Prochaska, F.K. (1980), *Women and Philanthropy in 19th Century England*. Oxford, Clarendon Press.

Pugh, M. (1994), *State and Society. British political and social history 1870–1992*. London, Edward Arnold.

[Ralphs Report] (1971), *Report of the Working Party on the Role and Training of Education Welfare Officers*, Local Government Training Board.

Rathbone, E. (1924; rpt. 1986), *The Disinherited Family*. Bristol, Falling Wall Press.

Reeder, D.A. (1977), 'Predicaments of City Children: Late Victorian and Edwardian perspectives on education and urban society', in D.A. Reeder (ed.), *Urban Education in the Nineteenth Century*, proceedings of the 1976 Annual Conference of the History of Education Society of Great Britain. London, Taylor and Francis.

Reeves, J. ([1913], *Recollections of a School Attendance Officer*. London, Arthur H. Stockwell.

Reid, K. (1985), *Truancy and School Absenteeism*. London, Hodder and Stoughton.

Ringshall, R., Miles, Dame M. and Kelsall, F. (1983), *The Urban School: buildings for education in London 1870–1980*. London,

GLC in association with the Architectural Press.

[Robinson/O and M Report] (1973), Report of the Social Work Consultant on the Professional Staff of the Educational Welfare Service, March. Education Welfare Service, ILEA.

Robinson, M. (1978), *Schools and Social Work*. London, Routledge and Kegan Paul.

Robinson, T. (1978), *In Worlds Apart: Professionals and their clients in the Welfare State*. London, Bedford Square Press.

Ross, E. (1993), *Love and Toil. Motherhood in outcast London 1870–1918*. Oxford, OUP.

Rubinstein, D. (1969), *School Attendance in London, 1870–1904: A social history*. New York, Augustus M. Kelley.

Runciman, J. (1885), *School Board Idylls*. London, Longmans and Co.

[Seebohm Report] Department of Social Services (1968), *Report of the Committee on Local Authority and Allied Personnel*. Cmnd 3703. London, HMSO.

Service, A. (1979), *London 1900*. Frogmore, St Albans and London, Granada Publishing.

Shairp, L.V. ([1910]), *Hints for Visitors*. Leeds, Richard Jackson.

Shipman, M. (1990), *In Search of Learning*. London, Blackwell.

Simon, B. (1991), *Education and the Social Order 1940–1990*. London, Lawrence and Wishart.

Sims, G.R. (1883), *How the Poor Live*. London, Chatto and Windus.

Skinner, A., Platts, H. and Hill, B. (1983), *Disaffection From School*. Leicester, National Youth Bureau.

Smart, C. (1992), *Regulating Womanhood. Historical essays on marriage, motherhood and sexuality*. London, Routledge.

Society of Education Officers (1979), 'The Education Welfare Service', a reply to the ADSS paper, 'Social Work Services for Children in School', January.

Sproule, A. (1974), 'Local Authority Experiment: London', in B. Turner (ed.), *Truancy*. London, Ward Lock Educational and the National Children's Bureau.

Stedman Jones, G. (1976), *Outcast London*. Harmondsworth, Penguin.

Steedman, C. (1986), *Landscape for a Good Woman. A story of two lives*. London, Virago.

—(1990), *Childhood, Culture and Class in Britain: Margaret McMillan, 1860–1931*. London, Virago.

—(1995), *Strange Dislocations. Childhood and the idea of human interiority 1780–1930*. London, Virago.

Stephens, W.B. (1998), *Education in Britain 1750–1914*. London, Macmillan.

Stevenson, E. (formerly Principal of the Rachel McMillan Training College) (1954), *Margaret McMillan. Prophet and pioneer*. Publication for Margaret McMillan Fellowship by University of London Press.

Stevenson, J. and Capes, J.H. (1939), *Handbook for School Attendance Officers*. London, Sir Isaac Pitman and Sons.

Stewart, J. (1993), 'Ramsay MacDonald, the Labour Party, and Child Welfare, 1900–1914', *Twentieth Century British History* 4(2), pp. 105–25.

Stocks, M. (1953), *The Philanthropist in a Changing World*. Liverpool, The University Press.

Thom, D. (1992), 'Wishes, Anxieties, Play, and Gestures: Child guidance in inter-war England', in R. Cooter (ed.), *In the Name of the Child. Health and welfare 1880–1945*. London, Routledge.

Thomas, J. and Williams, A.S. (1998), 'Women and Abortion in 1930s Britain: A survey and its data' in *Social History of Medicine* 11(2).

Thoms, D.W. (1980), *Policy Making in Education: Robert Blair and the London County Council*. University of Leeds Press.

Timms, N. (1964), *Psychiatric Social Work in Great Britain (1939–1962)*. London, Routledge.

Titmuss, R.M. (1950), *Problems of Social Policy*. London, HMSO.

— (1968), *Commitment to Welfare.* London, Allen and Unwin

Tours, H. ([1994]), *Children's Country Holidays Fund. The first 110 years.* London, CCHF.

Townsend, P. (1979; rpt. 1983), *Poverty in the United Kingdom.* Harmondsworth, Penguin.

Urwin, C. and Sharland, E. (1992), 'From Bodies to Minds in Childcare Literature: Advice to parents in inter-war Britain' in R. Cooter (ed.), *In the Name of the Child. Health and welfare 1880–1945.* London, Routledge.

Vincent, D. (1981), *Bread, Knowledge and Freedom. A study of nineteenth-century working class autobiography.* London, Europa Publications.

Webb, B. (1926), *My Apprenticeship.* London, Longmans, Green and Co.

Webster, C. (1982), 'Healthy or Hungry Thirties?', *History Workshop Journal*, 13, Spring.

— (1983), 'The Health of the School Child during the Depression', in History of Education Society, *The Fitness of the Nation. Physical and health education in the nineteenth and twentieth centuries*, Conference Papers, December 1982.

— (1997), 'Government Policy on School Meals and Welfare Foods 1939–1970', in David F. Smith (ed) *Nutrition in Britain.* London, Routledge.

Welshman, J. (1998), 'Evacuation and Social Policy during the Second World War: Myth and reality', in *Twentieth Century British History* 9(1).

'Where War is Blessed. The chronic poverty of London' (1916), in *The School Child and Juvenile Worker* VI(1), January.

Wilding, P. (1982), *Professional Power and Social Welfare.* London, Routledge and Kegan Paul.

Williams, A.S. (1997), *Women and Childbirth in the Twentieth Century.* Glos, Sutton.

— (2000), *Ladies of Influence. Women of the elite in interwar Britain.* Harmondsworth, Penguin.

Wimble, A.M., 'The School Care Committee', in M. Craft, J. Raynor and C. Cohen (1967), *Linking Home and School.* London, Longman.

Wooldridge, A. (1994), *Measuring the Mind: Education and psychology in England, c 1860–1990.* Cambridge, Cambridge University Press.

INDEX